PowerUp⁸

Discover the 8 critical capabilities to navigate an unpredictable world

ENDORSEMENTS

What an exceptional book from such a talented person. Debbie has captured a coherent approach to building the beliefs and habits to take on the challenges of the next decade. We are all aware that knowledge is not enough and Debbie provides a powerful roadmap to developing new skills through "doing". I wholeheartedly recommend that you buy this book and use it to build a more powerful you to take on our exciting future.

Mark Cotterrell, Chairman and CEO: MAC Consulting

PowerUp^8 is a greatly valuable source of inspiration; it provides energy and learning optimism to develop yourself beyond this book. The ability to 'manage change' in the current VUCA world requires new thinking, capability to learn and experimentation of oneself. Debbie provides the perfect guidance and tools to set yourself up for success in the years to come. A great gift to leaders who want to leave a legacy and positive impact on the people around them.

Kurt Droeshout, COO: Ismaeel Abudawood Trading Company, Kingdom of Saudi Arabia

Over the past 30 years, much has been said and written about all aspects of how to prepare for, and deal with, change in this fast-paced world. Despite this, too often people remain overwhelmed and isolated when their lives are disrupted by a relentlessly changing environment. Black Swan events such as the Global Financial Crisis and COVID-19 have shaken this interconnected world to its core and have compounded the challenge immeasurably. This comprehensive and well-designed work has "Got It". It is an invaluable companion for all who are constantly called upon to revise and reposition themselves, and their organisations, for success in an ever-changing environment. The 8Cs is presented in a practical and logical style and provides the reader with all the knowledge that is needed to understand change, adapt to it, then redesign and rebuild with confidence.

Leigh Mann, Managing Director: Buckman Asia-Pacific (Retired)

Ever wondered why it is so difficult to change our behaviour and habits and make new (and better ones) stick? The good news is our brains are adaptable and we can actually change how we think, feel and act! The book tells you HOW! Written in a lucid and 'easy to read' manner, Debbie's book cuts through complexity to lay out the 'Commandment of 8Cs'. It's a must-read for all age groups and personality types. By the end of the book, you will realise that you have the 'Power of Choice' and will thank yourself for choosing the right book!

Shailesh Tiwari, Chief General Manager:
Indian Oil Corporation Ltd. (A Fortune 500 Company)

PowerUp⁸ is a must read for any leader and/or people practitioner who wants to challenge what they thought they knew about building sustainable cultures managing talent and ensuring organisations are 'future-fit' in a world of constant disruption. Debbie's pragmatic approach in each chapter, demonstrates the richness of her know-how which she so generously shares, thus enabling more people to confidently apply the principles within their own contexts.

Taryn Marcus, VP Human Resources, Transformation
and Platform Services: NTT Ltd.

I found this book really difficult to put down but consistently paused to scribble my own notes in the border or apply a specific concept directly to what I'm currently working on. Debbie does a great job of setting the context and exploring the tools to navigate it in a practical and adaptive manner. The core capabilities are outlined and explored in a systemic way that encourages the reader to deeply consider their value, impact and application. This book has shifted my thinking and I value when shift happens.

Themba Chakela, Principal Head, Human Resources:
Dimension Data MEA

The world looks different, our environment has changed, and the way we are having to work has been radically altered. Changes we anticipated – and many we didn't – are upon us… in order to survive, individuals and businesses are having to urgently change and adapt in a very short space of time. This disruptor book by Debbie Craig is a "must read" for anyone who wants to adapt and succeed in the fast-changing world of work! Its easy-to-read writing style with story characters to embellish learnings and self-development make for pleasurable reading. Highly recommended!

Chris Blair, CEO: 21st Century

PowerUp⁸ is the optimal book to read not only during this globally chaotic time, but also to keep you ready and geared towards the future. It is a comprehensive path with practical skills and solutions that would help any professional navigate through storms of uncertainties and a turbulent business environment. It discusses the speed of emerging technologies that are swiftly changing our world, and the progressive human skills needed to be a true professional regardless of your field or years of expertise. It gives you the tools to navigate through all potential business and personal developmental challenges. I found the 8Cs a great survival skill set, essential to strive and secure a prosperous future.

Bahaa Hussein, Managing Partner & ATD Master Training: SIMDUSTRY®, Middle East

PowerUp⁸ is an exquisite act of generosity, creativity, courage, collaboration, critical thinking, raising consciousness, navigating change, choosing to act and contribute. The content and design of this book could provide the material for an entire semester's class in an advanced graduate programme on 21st century, COVID era leadership and management. Each chapter persuasively excels in offering context, wisdom, stories, models and references in guiding readers to tangibly navigate paths through this tumultuous time in the history of the world, the evolution of human consciousness, the universal impact of the human presence. *PowerUp⁸* presents a refreshing, accessible, inspiring 'how to' playbook for individuals, teams and organisations to answer the current call for meeting extraordinary global needs.

Carol Ann Langford, Executive Coach: Korn Ferry, International & Founder, Langford Leadership, New York, USA

We have been catapulted into a new world disorder. This book will assist you to position yourself and your company perfectly for this new era. Whilst we all have certain elements of the wide spectrum of personality traits, we need to nurture our skills as Maze Navigators. Read on to find the other skills we need to hone in on. Well done Debbie on yet another fantastic book. I enjoyed the read.

Dr Mark Bussin, Chairperson: 21st Century

It was awesome to contribute a chapter to *PowerUp⁸*, but as I read through the whole book, I was blown away by how Debbie has integrated it into the broader framework she presents. The book is practical and useful with personal insights from Debbie that make it a very human book. As someone who has the privilege of knowing Debbie in person, I love the way she has integrated her personal journey and growth into content that is so useful for the rest of us. When you've finished this book, you will be left with one burning question: "When is Debbie releasing her next book?"

Ray De Villiers, Keynote Speaker & Consultant:
The Future of Money and Digital Disruption

Debbie's book is a vital resource for those of us grappling with how to deal with and capitalise on the challenges and opportunities of the global pandemic and the resulting acceleration of the fourth Industrial Revolution. The thoroughly researched and supported eight meta-capabilities framework, covered in detail in the book, provides the basis for development plans that will prepare leaders and their teams for the next exciting chapter in this increasingly unpredictable world.

Harry Steadman, Director: MAC Consulting

Debbie masterfully weaves together a multitude of wisdom using powerhouse change agents, scientific data, and her own vast personal experience to provide a crystal-clear path to catapult the reader into a quantum shift. Her eight meta-capabilities are brilliantly outlined, bringing you face-to-face with yourself, where you'll be inspired to make some tough decisions on who you want to be moving forward in your life and work. Then, Debbie coaches you on exactly how to do it. This is a must read for anyone seeking to make changes in their life.

Abby Havermann, Coach, Speaker & Author of the upcoming book Control
Freak. Colorado, USA

2020 showed us a whole new level of unpredictability. The option of waiting for things to "return to normal" is no longer valid. If we need the world out there to be a certain way before we can function, success and fulfilment will elude us. We need to find our power in the world behind our eyes. Debbie has done an outstanding job of showing us how to find our power in an unpredictable and uncertain world of work.

Joan Peters, Leadership & Team Coaching Specialist

Debbie has acted as "the guide" in the hero's journey by putting together a field guide/manual that navigates the reader through the science of what creates successful behaviours in this disrupted world. Then, most importantly, she has laid down a roadmap through her 8Cs framework to build out the skills required to be competitive and content in this modern world of work.

Matt Lambert, Managing Director: Summit Training & Director: Invictus Education Group

PowerUp^8 is a masterpiece for people to live their best lives. This is the only book anyone needs to read ... it's a combination of the best thinking, tools and strategies with ways of being, and all interwoven with beautiful, honest stories. Your book is challenging, brave, human and kind. I love it.

Jenny Wensing, Executive Coach and Neuro-linguistic Programming (NLP) Trainer

Debbie has done a fantastic job tackling some of the most needed truths around how we are responding to and working with technology today. Her synthesis of these truths, combined with a pooling of experience and research, provide practical application in today's crazy world. The eight core capabilities remain amazingly relevant in a world in lockdown – struggling to deal with complexity, ambiguity and the ever increasing integration of technology. A truly worthwhile read!

Deon Greyling, Senior Vice President, Middle East & Africa: BTS

During these exponential and challenging times, innovation, new models of doing things, and digital strategies are needed to rethink and improve our skills. Power Up 8 is full of useful concepts, practices and tools to help companies, teams, and individuals to enhance both their skills and results. Debbie's book masterfully challenges us masterfully to build our capabilities in critical thinking, assertiveness, tolerance, resilience, decisiveness, and vulnerability. Her book is also a great resource to train others on how to be brilliant communicators and collaborators. She speaks in a very honest way with empathy and respect for the audience. She reminds us that we are the creators of our own existence and when we change our energy, combining clear intentions and elevated emotions, we can change our lives. It has been a privilege and honor to have read this book that is an inspiration, joy, and expansion for all of us.

Margarita Sanchez Mora, NCS Trainer Consultant:
NSC by Dr. Joe Dispenza. Mexico.

This is another great book by Debbie offering lots of moments for great reflection. It challenges us on how we show up as influencers of change in the world, as collaborators and contributors. Changes around us can be overwhelming and almost paralyse us, this books helps us to look at this from a different lens. I most enjoy the emphasis on our agency to impact our experiences through our ability to choose our thinking and behaviour as we respond to the world around us.

Njabulo Mashigo, Human Resources, Africa, Middle East &
Eastern Europe: Heineken International

Copyright © KR Publishing and Debbie Craig

All reasonable steps have been taken to ensure that the contents of this book do not, directly or indirectly, infringe any existing copyright of any third person and, further, that all quotations or extracts taken from any other publication or work have been appropriately acknowledged and referenced. The publisher, editors and printers take no responsibility for any copyright infringement committed by an author of this work.

Copyright subsists in this work. No part of this work may be reproduced in any form or by any means without the written consent of the publisher or the author.

While the publisher, editors and printers have taken all reasonable steps to ensure the accuracy of the contents of this work, they take no responsibility for any loss or damage suffered by any person as a result of that person relying on the information contained in this work.

First published in 2020.

ISBN: 978-1-86922-874-3 (Printed)
eISBN: 978-1-86922-875-0 (PDF ebook)

Published by KR Publishing
P O Box 3954
Randburg
2125
Republic of South Africa

Tel: (011) 706-6009
Fax: (011) 706-1127
E-mail: orders@knowres.co.za
Website: www.kr.co.za

Printed and bound: HartWood Digital Printing, 243 Alexandra Avenue, Halfway House, Midrand
Typesetting, layout and design: Cia Joubert, cia@knowres.co.za
Cover design: Marlene De Lorme, marlene@knowres.co.za
Editing and Proofreading: Jennifer Renton, jenniferrenton@live.co.za
Project management: Cia Joubert, cia@knowres.co.za

PowerUp⁸

Discover the 8 critical capabilities to navigate an unpredictable world

by Debbie Craig

2020

TABLE OF CONTENTS

ACKNOWLEDGEMENTS   v
ABOUT THE AUTHOR   vii
ABOUT THE CONTRIBUTORS   x
ABOUT CATALYST CONSULTING   xi
FOREWORD by *John Gatherer*   xii
HOW THIS BOOK CAME ABOUT by *Armin F. Philipps*   xv
PROLOGUE: INVITATION TO AN ADVENTURE   xviii

Chapter 1: TOP DIGITAL TRENDS DRIVING CHANGE – by *Raymond De Villiers*   1

1. INTRODUCTION   1
2. FOURTH INDUSTRIAL REVOLUTION   2
3. DIGITAL NATIVES, IMMIGRANTS AND DINOSAURS   3
4. TOP TECHNOLOGY TRENDS   4
5. THE GOOD, THE BAD AND THE UGLY   12
6. WHAT DOES IT MEAN TO ME?   13
7. TIPS, TOOLS AND RESOURCES   14

Chapter 2: WHICH CORE CAPABILITIES DO I NEED?   17

1. ARE WE FUTURE FIT?   17
2. CHANGING FOCUS OF SKILLS   19
3. WHAT ARE THE EXPERTS SAYING?   20
4. THE POWER OF 8   22
5. TIPS, TOOLS AND RESOURCES   25

Chapter 3: THE POWER OF CHOICE   27

1. WHY IS CHANGING OUR BEHAVIOUR SO DIFFICULT?   27
2. HOW CAN WE CHANGE OUR BRAINS?   28
3. WHAT DO WE NEED TO KNOW ABOUT OUR BRAINS?   31
4. BRINGING BACK CHOICE   38
5. TIPS, TOOLS AND RESOURCES   50

Chapter 4: CURIOSITY — 53

1. CURIOSITY IS ACTUALLY A SECRET SUPER POWER — 53
2. DID CURIOSITY KILL THE CAT? — 55
3. HOW CURIOUS ARE WE? — 57
4. WHAT HAVE MY BELIEFS GOT TO DO WITH IT? — 62
5. DAILY HACKS AND HABITS FOR CURIOSITY — 64
6. TIPS, TOOLS AND RESOURCES — 69

Chapter 5: CREATIVITY — 71

1. CREATIVITY IS NOT A COMPETITIVE SPORT — 71
2. MOST ADULTS HAVE ONLY 2% CREATIVITY LEFT — 73
3. CREATIVITY CAN BE LEARNT — 75
4. AN ATTITUDE OF CREATIVITY — 78
5. BELIEVING I STILL HAVE IT — 83
6. DAILY HACKS AND HABITS FOR CREATIVITY — 84
7. TIPS, TOOLS AND RESOURCES — 92

Chapter 6: COURAGE — 95

1. THE COURAGE TO BE VULNERABLE — 95
2. ARE THE RISKS OF COURAGE WORTH THE REWARD? — 100
3. WHERE DOES FEAR COME FROM? — 103
4. WHO DO I WANT TO BE? — 104
5. WHAT DO I BELIEVE? — 108
6. DAILY HACKS AND HABITS FOR COURAGE — 109
7. TIPS, TOOLS AND RESOURCES — 114

Chapter 7: CHANGE NAVIGATOR — 117

1. HOLDING ON TO A WORTHWHILE VISION — 117
2. TO RESIST OR TO NAVIGATE? — 121
3. CHOOSING IN THE MOMENT — 122
4. WE ARE WHAT WE BELIEVE — 127
5. DAILY HACKS AND HABITS FOR NAVIGATING CHANGE — 128
6. TIPS, TOOLS AND RESOURCES — 140

Chapter 8: CONSCIOUSNESS   **143**

1. ARE YOU PAYING ATTENTION TO YOUR INTENTION?   143
2. OVERWHELMED OR FOCUSED?   147
3. WHERE IS YOUR TIME (AND LIFE) GOING?   148
4. TAKING THE ROAD LESS TRAVELLED   154
5. DAILY HACKS AND HABITS FOR CONSCIOUSNESS   156
6. TIPS, TOOLS AND RESOURCES   164

Chapter 9: CRITICAL THINKER   **167**

1. THE QUALITY OF OUR THINKING   167
2. THE IMPACT OF OUR THINKING   170
3. DEFAULT THINKER OR MEANING MAKER?   171
4. SEEING IS BELIEVING   176
5. DAILY HACKS AND HABITS FOR CRITICAL THINKING   178
6. TIPS, TOOLS AND RESOURCES   187

Chapter 10: COLLABORATOR   **189**

1. UNLEASHING VALUE ACROSS BOUNDARIES   189
2. DISASTERS AND DERAILERS   192
3. WHAT'S TRUST GOT TO DO WITH IT?   197
4. DOES IT COME NATURALLY?   200
5. RECALIBRATE TO COLLABORATE   204
6. DAILY HACKS AND HABITS FOR COLLABORATION   207
7. TIPS, TOOLS AND RESOURCES   213

Chapter 11: CONTRIBUTOR   **215**

1. "ME FIRST" Vs. "UBUNTU"   215
2. DOING GOOD IS ACTUALLY GOOD FOR YOU   218
3. CONSUMING OR CONTRIBUTING – WHAT'S YOUR BALANCE?   221
4. BE INSPIRED AND BELIEVE   226

5.	DAILY HACKS AND HABITS FOR CONTRIBUTORS	228
6.	TIPS, TOOLS AND RESOURCES	238

Chapter 12: CALL TO ACTION — 239

1.	RESILIENCE POTENTIAL SELF-ASSESSMENT	241
2.	RESILIENCE POTENTIAL ACTION PLAN	245
3.	RESILIENCE POTENTIAL COMMUNITY	245

Chapter 13: BUILDING THE 8Cs IN ORGANISATIONS — 247

1.	THE IMPERATIVE FOR BUILDING META-CAPABILITIES	247
2.	SHIFTING TALENT STRATEGIES	249
3.	BUILDING FOUNDATIONAL CAPABILITIES – WHAT NOT TO DO	251
4.	BUILDING FOUNDATIONAL CAPABILITIES – WHAT TO DO	252
5.	LEARNING JOURNEY EXAMPLES, OPTIONS AND TIPS	254

LIST OF REFERENCES	255
INDEX	269

ACKNOWLEDGEMENTS

Heartfelt thanks and mountains of gratitude and appreciation go to the following people for their support and contribution to this book:

Armin Philipps – for your significant contribution to the core idea of the book and the characters along the journey. I am truly grateful for the many hours exploring ideas, sharing knowledge and encouraging me to write this. This book wouldn't have come to light without our many conversations, the Singularity Learning Summit experience and your treasured friendship.

John Gatherer – for your continued support, generous contribution and inspiring example to my life and business. I am really blessed to have spent many years with you as my business partner, mentor and friend. Your perspective and feedback on the book has been invaluable.

Lita Currie – for your amazing creative genius in expressing the 8Cs in visual characters for the book and for your brave example of someone living the 8Cs and reaping the benefits.

Ray De Villiers – for your incredible chapter on Top Tech trends from your immense knowledge and experience in speaking and consulting on the future of work. I am truly privileged and grateful for your part in the book, and for sharing so generously of your time and self in our many conversations.

Catalyst Core Team – Kathy, Michele, Ndumi and Nomfundo, without whom this would not have been at all possible. Thank you for your dedication to carrying me and this book over the finish line, for the incredible effort to bring it to life and share it with the world AND for creating space for me in the business to pursue my passions of writing, designing, learning and innovating. You have all given me both LOVE and LIFE!

Knowledge Resources – thanks to Wilhelm, Cia and team for being fantastic partners, collaborators and publishers, and for all your ideas and assistance in making this book the best it can be.

Catalyst Clients – thanks to all of our many clients, many of whom have become dear friends, who have partnered with us in the spirit of experimenting and innovating to find the best ways of enabling potential and inspired results in the workplace...often in rapidly changing and complex environments.

Friends and Family – to all those very special family members and friends who support my dreams, generously share their time and wisdom with me, give me honest feedback and keep it real. I couldn't do any of this without you. In particular, thank you to my ever-supportive husband, Andrew, who gives me wings to explore my dreams and creates a safe haven to return to again and again.

Debbie – September 2020

ABOUT THE AUTHOR

DEBBIE CRAIG

Debbie is a passionate adventurer, traveller, mountain climber, dolphin swimmer, philosophical dreamer, dysfunctional over-achiever, compulsive seeker and sharer, difference maker, patriotic South African, author, facilitator, yoga nut, wine snob, dog lover, guardian mom, step mom, wife and friend. Debbie is the founder and MD of Catalyst Consulting and has been transforming organisations, teams and individuals for over 20 years, both locally and internationally in over 5 continents and 15 countries.

Debbie and her team are courageous, creative, collaborative Catalysts connecting people with purpose in the areas of talent, learning, change and HC transformation... with a key focus on systemic solutions and behavioural and mindset shifts. Debbie is a skilled strategist, design architect, team builder, powerful facilitator, change agent and executive coach. She holds a B.Com, PDM and MBA, and is a registered Master HR Professional through the SA Board for People Practices (SABPP). She is also a certified international NLP and NeuroChange Solutions consultant, game ranger and Reiki master. Debbie has published three books, *I am Talent*, *I am Alive* and *Accelerated Learning*, written numerous articles, appeared on radio talk shows, presented at conferences and given public talks. She is an engaging presenter with practical advice and information that is easy to apply.

Debbie has travelled to more than 60 countries, with many deep inward journeys and outward adventures, in pursuit of finding the keys to personal and organisational transformation. Debbie has hiked to Machu Pichu, Kilimanjaro and Everest Base Camp, walked the Spanish and Italian Caminos, and swam with dolphins in many places in the world. She has designed and facilitated over 70 deep personal transformation workshops and is a warm and down-to-earth facilitator, leader and life coach. Debbie's philosophy is to live, love, learn, laugh and let go AND be unique, be bold, be kind and be a change maker for a better world.

BOOKS BY DEBBIE CRAIG

I am Talent by Debbie Craig and John Gatherer

I am Talent is a user-friendly guide and toolkit to stimulate ideas and practical approaches to accelerate your personal and career development, and help you cope and flourish in today's competitive and dynamic global business environment. It will support you as you take stock of your inner strengths, personal attributes, skills and capabilities on your journey to building your brand and being the best that you can be. *I am Talent* is a highly sought-after learning programme with many thousands of people around the globe having benefitted from it − available as a 2-day workshop as well as an online course. Learn more about the Workshop and Online Learning at: https://catalystconsulting.co.za/wp-content/uploads/2019/06/Overview-I-am-Talent.pdf.

Accelerated Learning by Debbie Craig and Kerryn Kohl

Accelerated Learning focuses on the shift from traditional training to collaborative learning in the digital and socially networked age, using latest research in neuroscience. It outlines the key frameworks, processes and tools to adopt and implement accelerated learning in organisations to build and sustain an adaptive learning culture. It is packed with practical case studies and tools to fast track your relevance and impact in the learning world. Accelerated learning workshops have been run at leading business schools, corporates and for the public to build capability for designing the next generation of accelerating learning and learning culture. Learn more about the workshop at: https://catalystconsulting.co.za/wp-content/uploads/2019/06/Overview-Accelerated-Learning.pdf.

I Am Alive by Debbie Craig

I am Alive takes you on a deeper journey into the self – a journey of discovery, sense-making and a fuller understanding of "Who am I?" and "Why I do what I do". It is packed with practical advice and tools that anyone can use to grow and develop their self-mastery. The personal story that is written alongside the content gives it a very personal touch and makes the journey real. Alive is a highly sought-after personal transformational retreat process that many hundreds of people throughout South Africa and internationally have benefited from. Learn more about retreats at: https://catalystconsulting.co.za/wp-content/uploads/2019/06/ALIVE-Retreat-overview-2019-1.pdf.

ABOUT THE CONTRIBUTOR
RAYMOND DE VILLIERS

Ray works with organisations around the world to understand dynamics influencing the future world of work. He has a diverse background that he draws on to tell stories that simplify and make sense of some of the trends and dynamics around our changing world in the Fourth (and subsequent) Industrial Revolution. When not speaking he can be found on a surfboard or bicycle on the roads and beaches of Cape Town.

Ray can be contacted at raydevilliers.com, linkedin.com/in/raymond-de-villiers or facebook.com/RaymonddeVilliersFuturist.

ABOUT CATALYST CONSULTING

The 8Cs and accompanying resources and tools are brought to you by Catalyst Consulting. We are an organisation development consultancy with a 20+ year track record in transforming organisations, teams and individuals both locally and internationally. We are collaborative, courageous, creative Catalysts that connect people and organisations with purpose AND accelerate learning and change in a fast, friendly and fun way. We partner to co-create high performance, high engagement organisations and teams through developing leaders, building capacity and leveraging talent. We specialise in talent, leadership, learning, change, digital and HR transformation. We are proudly BEE level 2. See more at https://catalystconsulting.co.za

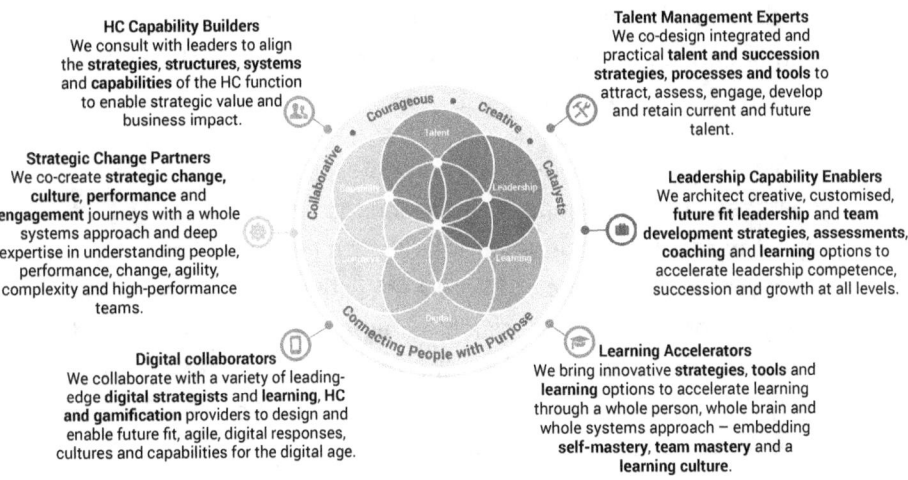

HC Capability Builders
We consult with leaders to align the **strategies, structures, systems** and **capabilities** of the HC function to enable strategic value and business impact.

Strategic Change Partners
We co-create **strategic change, culture, performance** and **engagement** journeys with a whole systems approach and deep expertise in understanding people, performance, change, agility, complexity and high-performance teams.

Digital collaborators
We collaborate with a variety of leading-edge **digital strategists** and **learning, HC and gamification** providers to design and enable future fit, agile, digital responses, cultures and capabilities for the digital age.

Talent Management Experts
We co-design integrated and practical **talent and succession** strategies, processes and tools to attract, assess, engage, develop and retain current and future talent.

Leadership Capability Enablers
We architect creative, customised, **future fit leadership** and **team development strategies, assessments, coaching** and **learning** options to accelerate leadership competence, succession and growth at all levels.

Learning Accelerators
We bring innovative **strategies, tools** and **learning** options to accelerate learning through a whole person, whole brain and whole systems approach – embedding **self-mastery, team mastery** and a **learning culture**.

FOREWORD by John Gatherer

Debbie Craig's new publication *Power-Up^8* is a masterpiece!

Not only is it an essential handbook and resource for anyone who is grappling to assert themselves in the turbulent and highly competitive global business environment, but it has huge relevance to our current reality – a world reeling in chaos as a result of the global COVID-19 pandemic. I believe that it is an extraordinarily significant and topical publication for managers and leaders to lead us into the next decade.

If the relatively new concept of disruption as a frame of reference was seen by some cynical people and dismissed as another change management label, the COVID-19 pandemic should have altered that viewpoint. Within a dramatically short timeframe, infections have swept across the world, representing the single biggest global challenge affecting society, business, markets, international travel, the health services and personal freedom since the Second World War.

Debbie sets out the backdrop and context to the book expertly, spearheaded by the rampant digital and technological trends that impact us, as we transition into the Fourth Industrial Revolution. Her coverage of the notion of "future fit", with its imperative for the changing focus of skillsets such as higher cognitive, social and emotional and technological is supported and reinforced by some highly respected and credible international research studies and findings from a range of acclaimed experts.

This leads into the core elements of this publication, which feature the eight meta-capabilities and their interesting paradoxes (continuums) which are examined and worked through in-depth. We first explored this thinking in our book *I am Talent*, which we co-authored in 2010 under the chapter called *Qualities for Success*. It highlighted the yin and yang of one's behaviours, mindset and habits – on one side of the continuum a meta-competency, whilst on the other extreme a derailing behaviour. Debbie has taken this thinking to new heights and her descriptions, storytelling, illustrations, hacks and habits for each of the eight meta-capabilities provides a meaningful guide for understanding and applying them to our own repertoire of skills. Each of the eight meta-capability chapters contains reader-friendly high level overviews, supported by a rich feast of relevant resources integrated with action learning tips, self-assessment tools and references to articles, publications and video links to explore further.

I have known and worked with Debbie over the last 20 years, initially as her client where we were involved together in rolling out a massive transformational leadership development intervention across a global mining organisation. Over the last 13 years I was her business partner in Catalyst Consulting where we forged an Organisation Development consulting business, specialising in strategic change, leadership development and talent management, working locally and internationally with a variety of clients from a range of business sectors.

Debbie is one of South Africa's significant thought leaders, and with her vast experience working across the fields of strategic management, leadership development, talent management, personal mastery and learning and development, Debbie is superbly qualified to write this new publication. Debbie is a walking example and role model of the eight meta-capabilities in this book – she eats, sleeps and breathes them!

When you read through her list of descriptors and attributes in her profile at the beginning of this book, the list might appear long and deep, but it is totally honest and without any exaggeration. That is who Debbie Craig is – and what she does.

Debbie is a successful business owner, change management strategist and executive coach, driven by a restless energy and curiosity to hone her craft and pass on her expertise and thinking to others. She has worked hard to find balance in her busy life, has a committed family focus and is an avid adventure traveller, but performs at her very best when facilitating her speciality workshops to management groups in different parts of the country and across the world.

One of Debbie's special qualities is her relentless enthusiasm for her work and she has an insatiable appetite for exploring new international trends, learning technologies and engagement techniques across the fields of personal leadership and organisational transformation.

Debbie has used her wisdom from her life's journey, her expertise as a workshop facilitator as well as feedback from her previous three books to powerful effect. She has written this book as a master-coach with a conversational style of writing, laying out opportunities for the reader to examine their current skills, habits and attitudes, and encouraging and coercing the reader to dive deeper to test and practice new skillsets, insights and perspectives in each of the chapters in the book.

The Resilience Potential self-assessment at the end of the book ties the themes and characteristics of all the meta-capabilities together brilliantly. The tool is a typical "call to action" learning tactic used by Debbie. She stimulates new thinking, skillsets and takeaways for the reader to be better equipped for their changing personal, business, customer and market circumstances.

Her single final question that she leaves the reader is, "What are you going to do about it?"

I wish Debbie and her team all the very best with the publication of this book.

John Gatherer
12 July 2020

HOW THIS BOOK CAME ABOUT –
Armin Philipps

When Debbie and I initially arrived at Singularity University (SU), San Francisco (USA) in November 2017, we found ourselves faced with an abundance of emotions simultaneously, namely surprise, challenge, excitement and complete awe. It was our first time in Silicon Valley and we were there for the first ever SU Global *Re(solve) Learning* Immersion. We joined 56 participants from over 20 countries to explore the current global challenges of education and learning with international experts from established businesses, start-ups, higher education, schools and strategic consulting. We had an intention to shift our thinking and to collaborate in bringing back and sharing learning in our local context. We left a week later, utterly inspired to make a real difference to many people in the learning arena.

We spent a number of months, in between our busy work schedules, developing our ideas with other like-minded change agents from our SU group and local network. We experimented with ideas around learning technologies to enable a common vision of learning access for anyone, anytime, anywhere. We co-designed some really cool frameworks and experiences to bring exponential thinking and perspectives to business and people leaders – including our interactive Future Design Possibilities immersion. We had fun piloting and sharing this, and our clients experienced the impact.

But we also got busy and distracted. We fell into the trap of staying in our comfort zones and waiting for our dreams and ideas to take off. We also doubted our early conviction of making an exponential 10X leap into the unknown and perhaps took the easier route of sticking to what our clients wanted – more traditional and tried and tested solutions – not yet ready to break the mould. Our early excitement faded, people went their separate ways and life went on. We had dreamed of making a significant difference, and yet hadn't yet created something concrete.

At a point in time we got together and asked ourselves some tough questions. Did the euphoria of our San Francisco experience and the associated inspiration simply wear off? Why weren't we able to maintain our momentum and take a lasting step in making a difference? What was holding us back? After some robust discussions around our intentions vs. actions, we realised that the only option was to change our own thinking and beliefs around what we could or could not create. We began putting our intent into action, committing priority time in our diaries, and sticking to it no matter what. And so, the idea and theme for this book emerged, and became the focus of our thinking, research and activities. This was a way that we could share our SU experiences and our life-long passion for learning, and help others to develop their capacity to become curious life-long learners.

This book is based on just that – learning and change! It is about becoming aware of your thinking and choices and how to shift limiting identities or beliefs to more empowering and productive beliefs, behaviours and habits. The book will help you assess where you find yourself with your thinking and your belief systems. You will be able to identify which behaviours support you and which are counterproductive to achieving your goals. Most importantly, this book will enable you to change these old thinking and mental models with practical behaviour change exercises.

This is a powerful tool and workbook you have in your hands. If you really desire to shift and transform your own formulated success journey and become the best version of yourself – be it in your career, or in your personal life – this is the tool to help you attain it. It also builds on previous books written by Debbie, such as *I am Talent* and *Accelerated Learning*, both of which I refer to often as inspired works and testimony to Debbie's commitment to personal transformation and learning.

I would like to thank Debbie for the interactions, shared inspiration and vision to achieve this final product. I sincerely hope this work will make an impression on you as much as it did for the two of us. Whilst we both started this dream together and formulated the themes and characters collaboratively, this book is a result of Debbie's efforts in pulling it all together and putting the proverbial "pen to paper". I am grateful to have been a part of this journey. I trust that this will encourage you, the reader, to continue to learn, integrate and develop yourself further, far beyond the reach of this book. The only constant we, as a global nation, are presently faced with, is change. Only when each of us truly embrace that, we will appreciate that standing still is not an option. I am certain this book will be the perfect companion on your continuous learning journey to be your best self and achieve the results you desire.

Yours in Learning!

Armin F. Philipps
Johannesburg, July 2020

PROLOGUE: INVITATION TO AN ADVENTURE

Moments of truth

Many years ago, I remember the shock of being informed that I was being retrenched. It was my first managerial job and I was so excited about the difference I was making and could make at this company. I thought I was so good at handling change until change was forced upon me. So many feelings, fears and questions flooded my overwhelmed mind. How was I going to pay the bills? What would my family and friends think of me? Would I find another job in an economic downturn? What about all the future plans I had made with my team? Did I do something wrong? Why didn't I see this coming so I could have been more prepared? So often curve balls of unexpected change take us by surprise and we spend weeks and months feeling bad, or angry or analysing what could have or should have been said or done differently. We then try to figure out how to adapt and move forward and create a new vision for the future.

During the first few weeks of the COVID-19 pandemic, as we sat locked up in our homes, similar thoughts and feelings played themselves out as we grappled with the biggest global event in recent history impacting the entire world. Our daily freedoms and activities were suddenly constrained, and our social behaviour and technological skills had to adapt in a matter of days as our lives and economic futures hung in the balance. After an initial flurry of anxious activity to learn how to Skype, Zoom, Team or Mural and try and keep a 'semblance of sanity', many of us slumped into an uneasy malaise, feeling uncertain, confused, tired, sad and unmotivated, whilst others were risking their lives to save lives and keep economies going. As the situation extended, and we realised that life was unlikely to return to "normal" in the near future – or ever – many of us started to wonder about our futures, our value as a person and our choices. Even armed with many positive thinking and "create your own happiness" techniques, it became harder and harder to ignore the news, the suffering and the underlying feelings and beliefs of our inadequacy and lack of control in our lives. For some it was a difficult time, for some a relief to step out of the rat race for a while, for some a time of great insight, learning and reinvention. It is through tough times like these, that we face a test of who we are and who we want to become. These are our **Moments of Truth** which force us to confront our identities, core beliefs, habits and choices about how we live our lives – both now and in the future.

There have been many times in my life where I have faced heart-sore moments or cross-roads and had some difficult choices to make. I have experienced a sense of "loss" so many times. I lost my home, family income and beloved Labrador in matric, when my dad had a brain tumour. I lost "friends" when I was promoted into leadership roles. I lost loved ones in divorce, betrayal and in death. I lost my faith and furniture during my ex-husband's sequestration. I lost job security and a stable income when I started my own business. I lost my health and income due to physical injuries more than once. I lost so many potential clients, projects or associates to competitors or market conditions over the years.

I have also gained so much. Looking back on these and many other moments of truth, I know that I would not be who I am today without them. In their own way, they have shaped my character, enhanced my wisdom and clarified my purpose. For every loss, there has been significant gain. New healthy, fulfilling relationships, new business opportunities and teams, profound life-long lessons, and new vision. I have managed to build a business over 20 years and have journeyed with many clients in over 20 countries through transformation, growth and change. I have consulted to and coached many thousands of leaders and teams, to achieve their almost impossible goals. I have written a number of books, travelled the world, overcome physical limitations and climbed some majestic mountains. I am also blessed with a rich life of friends and family and so much more awareness of my own strengths, weaknesses and blind spots than I had growing up as a bold, brash, optimistic young adult. And I continue to stretch and learn every day. There are always new challenges and old fears and insecurities lurking. There still too many frustrating moments when I lose my awareness, empathy and trust in divine synchronicity. AND there are so many amazing opportunities to go deeper, expand my potential, quieten my mind and open my heart. When we look back at the COVID-19 impact one day, I am sure we will remember the struggles AND notice the many benefits of this time and the possibility of a more connected, kinder, efficient, and healthier world.

I am sure each of you have had your own many "moments of truth" in your life so far.

These are the times we are driven to a deeper, wiser part of ourselves; to ask big life questions, make difficult, seemingly impossible, decisions and choose a path. It is so tempting to choose the familiar and comfortable route rather than the daunting, twisting path into the wilderness that is certain to be full of surprises, obstacles and challenges. We also instinctually know that, on the lesser travelled path, we are likely to meet parts of ourselves that have been hiding in the shadows, running the show or waiting for their time to shine.

A call to adventure – the hero's journey

Joseph Campbell[1], the originator of the Hero's Journey, would call these moments a **call to adventure**. In a typical Hero's Journey (see diagram), the "hero" gets called out of day-to-day life to an adventure, faces many challenges and choices, and in a decisive crisis (the abyss) wins a victory, and then comes home changed or transformed in a way that enriches others.

It is the moment that Neo was offered the red or blue pill in *The Matrix*,[2] or Alice's decision to follow the unusual rabbit down the rabbit hole in *Alice in Wonderland*,[3] or Katniss's choice to take her sister's place as a tribute in the *Hunger Games*.[4]

It is the many moments of persistence after failure and rejection that our heroes of today have overcome. Jack Ma[5] was rejected by Harvard University and Silicon Valley funders multiple times, faced many failures and now runs Alibaba, one of the biggest e-commerce companies on the planet. J.K. Rowling's first *Harry Potter* book was rejected 12 times before being accepted to become one of the best-selling book series in history.[6] Elon Musk's space rockets failed to launch or exploded many times (at massive cost) before he mastered the art of reusable space launch vehicles.

Following the Hero's Journey elements, these choices often **call for a separation**... from the predictable and the safe... and from our current activities and identities. These times call upon us to face obstacles and confront our darkest fears. We are forced to question, to doubt and to feel those uncomfortable emotions of loss – anger, sadness, grief and shame. We have to **shatter the**

illusion of what we believed in and deconstruct our worldviews and mindsets that have gotten us this far. It is a time to discover our **true purpose** and potential, as well as the gifts and talents we bring to the world. We can wait to be called or **disrupted** out of our comfort zones, or we can **disrupt ourselves** and choose to live a life of adventure and continuous growth that prepares us for any eventuality.

Of course, there is **temptation to return** to the comfort of our daily dose of busy-ness, entertainment and distraction to keep us numb. But the reality around us is too insistent to succumb without giving up a piece of our soul. So, we step out on the path, armed with little else but our wits, some skills and a few brave friends, and we start crafting a new narrative for who we are becoming. We push on through many **dark nights of the soul**, navigate our way through many trials, face many interesting characters, and find a new strength and identity on the other side.

Characters you will meet along the way

This book, if you dare, will take you on a journey along which you will meet many different characters. Some will be familiar and some relatively new. Some you will want to spend time with, and some will make you squirm. These characters are here to encourage you to mirror and explore parts of yourself that may or may not have seen the light and decide how much time you want to spend with each of them. You will come across the curious explorer, the possibility connector, the courageous adventurer, the maze navigator, the wise discerner, the meaning maker, the trust cultivator and the community builder. We will also invite you to get to know and embrace the safe spectator, the cautious dreamer, the anxious controller, the passive resistor, the distracted operator, the default thinker, the independent competitor, and the status consumer.[a]

---

a. Thanks to Lita Currie who created these amazing drawings to illustrate our characters. See https://www.3stickmen.com/

Book characters[b]

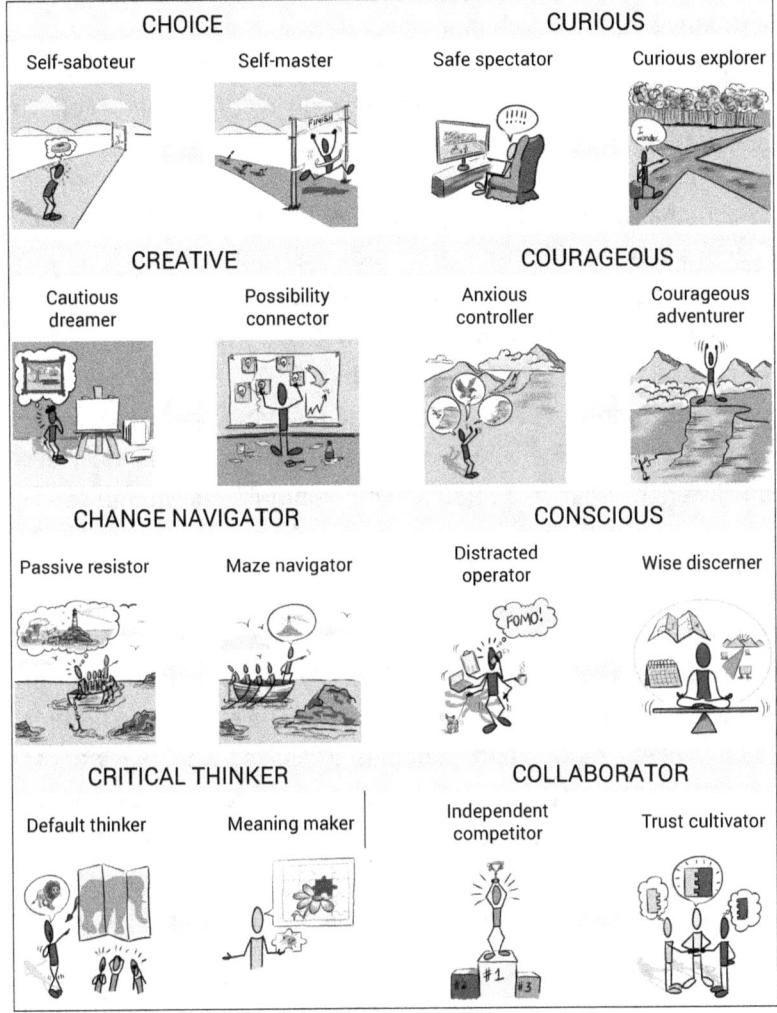

Each of these characters play a role in our lives and help us grow or keep us safe. They encourage us to stand up or stand out. They enable us to give and take. Take your time, investigate, imagine. How does it feel to be with a courageous adventurer versus an anxious controller for a while? What quality does each character bring to your life? What are the costs or benefits of being in their

---

b. Thanks to Lita Currie who created these amazing drawings to illustrate our characters. See https://www.3stickmen.com/

space? What do they enable you to do? How do they empower you with the thinking, beliefs, skills and habits to adapt, survive and thrive in an ever-changing world – at work or at home or the emerging space in-between. When are they useful and empowering or limiting and risky? Who do we call upon in our moment of choice or call to adventure?

Which characters will help you feel inspired rather than insecure, fearless instead of fretful, exhausted vs. energised? Which will help you shift from guilt to gratitude, from feeling isolated to invincible, or help create clarity from confusion? We live in a paradoxical world of light and dark, good and bad, black and white, yin and yang. The more we can acknowledge and embrace both our light and our shadow sides, the more we can explore, experience, learn and live rich, creative diverse and meaningful lives without fear.

Become your own hero

This book will explore these characters or identities through eight core capabilities and examine how they can differentiate and empower you to be your best self. You will be exposed to different ideas, beliefs, stories and examples to assess what will work for you. You will also gain many juicy daily hacks, habits and resources to build muscle in these areas. You can dip in and out of the different chapters depending on what you are most interested in. At any time you can complete a Resilience Potential Assessment (see Chapter 12) to see where you would like to focus more.

Bringing this book to life has been a journey of discovery and peeling away the layers of assumptions or buzz words to reveal the gold within. It is a life-long passion of mine to explore the mysteries of the universe and to live my best life. I have also spent two decades partnering with other brave visionary leaders to build cultures that unleash and grow talent. This past year has been a personal journey of attempting to live and breathe these Core Capabilities in the midst of running a business, reaching a big birthday milestone, navigating relationships, delivering on an international consulting contract, travelling extensively, embarking on a deep spiritual journey, being certified as a global NeuroChange consultant with Dr Joe Dispenza, and coping with COVID-19. I have had to dig deep, reflect, feel and choose. Mostly this journey and this book is about CHOICE – choosing who and what we choose to do and be and become. I hope that in sharing some of my learning and insights along the way, you find some magic for yourself.

This book is an **invitation** to enter an adventure... to become the **hero** of your own life and discover a world in which you can contribute and make a difference with your unique gifts and talents. It is an opportunity to unveil some inherent or learnt powers to navigate any journey of change and confront the illusions, "villains" or beliefs that may hold you back or thwart your dreams. It is an invitation to imagine possibilities of a future you, and a future world in which you can choose to live from your heart and not your ego, invite and connect with difference rather than isolate and judge. A world that believes in abundance rather than lack, flow rather than control, listening more than talking, and awareness and mindfulness rather than ignorance and noise. A reality in which you choose gratitude over greed and happiness over having.

Welcome to an adventure!!

TOP DIGITAL TRENDS DRIVING CHANGE

Raymond De Villiers

"Going from Paypal I thought: 'Well what are some of the other problems that are likely to most affect the future of humanity? Not from the perspective: 'What's the best way to make money?'"
−Elon Musk

1. INTRODUCTION

Change, and living in times of change, is not a new facet of the human condition. It is, in fact, the one consistent factor that has endured through all of human (and pre-human) existence. The changes we are experiencing today as we transition into the Fourth Industrial Revolution, driven by the rapid rise of digitisation, are just the most recent expressions of this persistent truth. Once we move through this, there will be the next epoch of change to be navigated… whatever that may be. We aren't just looking at the trends driving change today to merely survive and stumble through to whatever is next. Our task is to understand the dynamics of the present so that we can succeed today, AND position ourselves to thrive and flourish in the emerging world.

2. FOURTH INDUSTRIAL REVOLUTION

Klaus Schwab[1], the head of the World Economic Forum (WEF), coined the term *Fourth Industrial Revolution (4ID)* in 2015. The rise of digital technology and its pervasive distribution through almost every area of our lives made this not just a tweak to the internet age, but rather a complete revolution of our reality.

It is almost impossible to create a comprehensive list of the technologies and trends behind the 4ID because it is a part of almost everything in our world. The catch-all phrase used to describe the heart of the 4ID changes is "Cyber-Physical", which means that cyber technology is becoming seamlessly integrated into every element of our lives. At the 2015 WEF meeting in Davos, Eric Schmidt, then CEO of Google, was asked about the future of the internet. He said that, "the internet would cease to exist". He explained that the internet as a place to go to – "I'm going online" – would stop because the internet would be wherever we are.[2]

Some of the key technologies enabling this and driving the changes are:

Autonomous technology	Internet of Things	Big Data & Data Science	Distributed Legers/ Blockchain
Artificial Intelligence	Next Gen Mobile Connectivity	Sensor Technology	Robotics
Extended Reality	Quantum Computing	Fintech/Digital Money	

As we see workplaces adapt to this Industry 4.0 shift, many people are afraid of losing their jobs and adjusting to significant changes to the way we work. While these fears are understandable, we

---

1 Schwab, 2015.
2 CNBC, 2015.

need to get some perspective and realise that this is the fourth time society is navigating a significant shift in the human value proposition (hence "4" I.R.). We have adjusted successfully before and we will do so again. Automation, robotics, and other technologies are not the harbingers of human redundancy and doom. They are rather the next step in the continuous evolution in the way in which we humans add value to the workplace.

In the first Industrial Revolution when we harnessed the power of steam, the big strong individual who could successfully control four horses or oxen and plough a field in a few days was suddenly out of work. A skinny individual who could do nothing before, could now sit behind the wheel of a steam powered tractor and plough the same field in a day. We can imagine that the former strong individual faced a similar crisis to those people seeing their jobs automated today. Just as the "strongman" needed to adjust his view of his human value proposition, so too do we. Humans will always add value to the workplace, just not necessarily in the same way as the past 80 years.

3. DIGITAL NATIVES, IMMIGRANTS, AND DINOSAURS

Marc Prensky coined the term "Digital Natives" in a paper[3] he wrote about the different digital exposures and preferences of students and educators. Digital natives (the younger students) he says, have grown up in a world where digital was normal, and the absence of digital was abnormal. The presence of these technologies was so pervasive that this generation didn't need to learn how to use them; they had an instinctual ease and intuitive understanding of how to use them.

"Digital Immigrants", on the other hand (the older educators), had to learn how to use these technologies to do their jobs. Just like a person who learns a foreign language as an immigrant almost

---

[3] Prensky, 2001.

always speaks with an accent, so too do digital immigrants. Many in business leadership and positions of influence also fall into this immigrant group.

I believe there is a third group of people we need to consider in this digitally-driven social revolution – "Digital Dinosaurs". This generally older generation grew up in a pre-technological age. Many of them are largely technophobic – digital technology scares them a little. When they encounter new digital technology today, or hear about hacking, cybercrime, or phishing, they generally shy away from the perceived risks of getting it wrong and avoid engaging where they can!

Each of these groups typically (with some exceptions) navigate the new world with very different responses. Digital Natives get excited and intrigued. Digital Immigrants get a little confused and uncertain. Digital Dinosaurs are terrified and overwhelmed.

Where are you on the digital agility scale? Are you a dinosaur, an immigrant or a digital native that is showing us the way? Understanding your instinctive response to these digital dynamics is the first part of a healthy journey towards coming to terms with the shifts. Think through where your natural response puts you on the scale and then look one level lower. What could you do to move beyond your knee-jerk reaction and be one level more "natural"? For Digital Natives, what tempering elements could be useful for you to incorporate from the other demographics?

4. TOP TECHNOLOGY TRENDS

There are a significant number of technologies and trends driving change in our society, each with a deep field of specialist information behind them. Understanding some of the drivers of our future will enable you to be the architect of your future, and not just a victim or passenger in someone else's vision. This is a very brief overview of the technology trends. There is some great additional reading in the resources below.

4.1 Artificial Intelligence (A.I.)

Artificial Intelligence used to mean a computer that interacted as if it were human – essentially what we have seen in so many science fiction movies over the past 80 years. This type of A.I. is called Artificial General Intelligence but is still some way from being achieved. The Achilles heel of most current A.I. is that it can only function effectively within the very narrow band for which it was specifically developed. Artificial General Intelligence will only be realised when A.I. is able to function and respond effectively in much the same way as a human being does. In 2020 the level of Artificial General Intelligence development is producing results that underperform a two-year-old human child.

However, within the narrow bounds for which a specific A.I. is developed, it is increasingly true that A.I. outperforms humans. The A.I. cannot pivot and switch into something else like a human can, but from a task-driven and output-oriented perspective, A.I. is superior to humans. It is this specialised and targeted development and implementation of A.I. that is driving so much disruption in the world today. A.I. cannot replace human beings, but it can replace a specific task in a specific context. Lee Sedol, a master in the game of Go (a highly complex Eastern board game), recently retired from the game because an A.I. called AlphaGo had been developed that made it impossible for a human to ever be the best at the game again. AlphaGo is however so specific to that game that it wouldn't be able to figure out how to beat a five-year-old at Monopoly.[4]

There are many branches of A.I. development, such as Machine Learning, Neural Networks, Reinforcement Learning, Graduate Adversarial Networks, Algorithms, Digital Assistants and Chatbots, among others. Keeping up with developments in such a dynamic field is mind boggling. At a minimum it is important to notice how A.I. is becoming a more integrated part of every aspect of our lives.

---

[4] Wikipedia, 2020.

4.2 Autonomous Tech and Robotics

One of the main areas where A.I. is being applied is in Autonomous Technologies and Robotics, with the automotive industry leading the way. Robots can pick up and weld sheet metal with higher degrees of accuracy and efficiency than human beings were ever able to do. As long as A.I. stays in the background and just crunches data, it has limited value because the outputs of those processes still need a person to enact them. Yet autonomous technology and robotics are moving into this space and addressing what is called human agency — those things that only human beings were able to do before — more efficiently.

In the finance industry we are seeing A.I. beginning to conduct micro-transactions that buy and sell equities within a fraction of a second. These technologies work in smaller increments of time and take advantage of very small movements in price. The A.I. buys and sells the stock in a fraction of a second, initiating and concluding hundreds (or thousands) of transactions in the time it takes a human to initiate one.

As with so many of the other technologies and trends reviewed here, the statements just made are only true within the narrow field for which the specific technology was developed. Self-driving cars cannot be picked up and used for self-riding motorcycles as it is a completely different product and process for development. A human being can, however, drive a car, climb out of the car and ride a motorcycle (or skateboard, or bicycle) — or even go for a swim or a run. Autonomous technologies and robotics have none of this cross-functional flexibility yet. Within their area of development, they out-perform humans significantly, but move them only slightly adjacently and they function worse than a toddler.

4.3   Internet of Things

The phrase Internet of Things (IoT) was coined in 1999 by Kevin Ashton from MIT.[5] What he proposed, and we have seen it come to pass, is a world where computers and technology platforms speak directly to each other without the involvement of a human being.

The first IoT device was a Coke vending machine at Carnegie Mellon University. It was a distance away from the computer labs so Dave Nichols, a programmer, put sensors into the vending machine and wrote software that would let people know from their desks if the machine was stocked, and if the drinks were cold. The person restocking the machine didn't need to change any settings or inform anyone, and the programmers on the other end didn't need to reload or update software – everything happened automatically as one machine spoke to the other over the internet ... hence an internet of things.

Today our smart homes, connected workplaces, and ultimately smart cities are all based on the power and potential of the IoT. Your smart fridge notes that you are low on certain items and can automatically order them via the online portal of your local store. Delivery is arranged using Uber, Lyft or the store's own delivery scheme and delivered to your door without you even knowing you needed to restock. Extrapolate that to the city level and you have traffic lights actively managing traffic flows based on information received from CCTV cameras. Maintenance and other issues can be automatically triggered through image recognition technology that dispatches crews.

Autonomous technology like self-driving cars and delivery drones also rely on the IoT. An environment where cars and drones (and other connected devices) speak to each other creates an active local ecosystem that self corrects and adjusts dynamically to the inputs of all connected devices.

---
5   Ashton, 2009.

From a workplace perspective, we are seeing sensors in products that are shipped to end consumers. These sensors upload data on usage to the manufacturing organisation. The organisation collates this data and uses it to update and direct the smart machines on the production line. These machines then only produce the products needed for current or projected demand. Products are loaded onto trucks whose routes are determined by efficiency, demand and expected traffic. Routes are then continuously updated to adjust for shifting traffic patterns to reduce idling time. UPS, the global courier company, has developed a system called ORION (On-Road Integrated Optimization and Navigation) that dynamically updates route plans that lead to less engine idling at intersections and drop- off points. By 2016, ORION had saved 10 million gallons of fuel annually, reduced 100,000 metric tons in CO^2 emissions, and saved an estimated $300 million to $400 million in cost avoidance.[6]

4.4 Connectivity

Many of us remember the days of dial-up internet access when we had to unplug the phone in order to go onto the internet and then block our ears as the modem screeched and squawked to connect. Once we did get online, the length of time it took to load an internet page was excruciatingly slow.

Today, the roll-out of a different mobile frequency (5G) allows for significantly more data to be transmitted. Expanded data connectivity is a key enabler of the technologies shifting and changing our lives today. 5G is the terrestrial or land-based enabler of connectivity, but there are many places in the world where it is physically or economically unfeasible to roll out towers. We are seeing projects by the large internet companies to put sky-based connection infrastructure in place, the most advanced being the Starlink satellites being placed in low-earth orbit by SpaceX (which is part-owned by Google).

---

6   UPS, 2016.

Beyond the infrastructure element we have the platform that manages the actual allocation of website URLs or IP addresses. In 2020 we are currently functioning within the parameters of IPv6 (Internet Protocol version 6). IPv6 is so comprehensive that there are sufficient IP addresses available to give every atom on the planet its own address to connect to the internet. The total number of IP addresses available in IPv6 is 340 uncedillion. To put that into a number most of us understand it would be 340 billion billion billion billion (yes that is four billions – this isn't a typo).

With so much latitude available for connecting devices to the internet and each other, the amount of data that will be generated and processed is incomprehensible. 5G and high-speed fibre optic, and soon Quantum Computing, are critical because they are the pipes or conduits that allow this data to be transmitted. Like all pipelines, the bigger and more efficient the pipe, the more the items on each end of the pipeline are able to achieve.

I remember my first computer as a student had a 1 GB hard drive which I thought was HUGE. Today my mobile phone has hundreds of times that memory – let alone what I have in my laptop and desktop. Our experiences with internet bandwidth are similar. We now download files in minutes across fibre connections that are significantly larger than what a whole hard drive used to store.

4.5 Big Data and Data Science

We live in a world where everything is generating data in a continuous and perpetual manner. We are surrounded by a digital haze as we generate a consistent steam of data vapour. The healthcare industry is beginning to track the data we generate by just living, and it is estimated that the human body generates two terabytes of data each day just through brain activity and muscle performance.[7] Internet companies like Facebook, Google, Twitter and others track this information in relatively minute detail

---

7   Eastwood, 2016.

in order to direct intelligent and targeted advertisements at us. These companies are able to use the digital "bread crumbs" we leave all over the internet to develop profiles of all seven billion of us on the planet. On many levels, through this data, they may even know us better than we know ourselves. They are able to use this information to anticipate our needs and target us with products and info before we even knew we would be interested in it or need it.

If we cannot capture, store and make sense of all this data, then it is useless. The fields of big data and data science are rising to help us benefit from all this available data. They are focused on not only finding the right answers in the data, but on identifying the right questions. The answers we get from our data interrogation will always depend on the quality of the questions we ask. Data scientists who formulate these questions have a mind for mathematics, statistics and patterns, but not necessarily for communication. These unique insights often require translation for the average person on the street through data visualisation and sense-making, i.e. graphs and infographics.

In the connected IoT world there is a lot of transferring and processing of data between machines with little human intervention, i.e. it happens in a Black Box. Making sure we get the question right is almost more important than whatever the answer may be. Critical thinking skills and the ability to see beyond the obvious are key to being successful (and useful) human beings into the future.

4.6 Quantum Computing

This is where things get a little confusing and feel like they may be spinning off into the realm of science fiction. Quantum computing is, however, the future of technology because of the exponentially more powerful way it can process data.

The first true computer was called ENIAC and was developed in 1948. From ENIAC to our modern super computers we have essentially developed machines using the same logic and process, just squeezing more speed and efficiency out of them over time. Quantum computers make a giant leap ahead in processing power – as big as the car compared to the horse. Using two principles from Quantum Theory called Superposition and Entanglement, quantum computers are able to use the same amount of energy to process exponentially more complex data more quickly than modern computers. At the moment, super computers still outperform quantum computers, but this won't be true for too much longer.

Let's revisit the horse and car analogy. When automobiles first came onto the scene they were noisy, slow, unreliable, and expensive – all of the things a horse was better at. Very soon, though, cars began to outperform horses. Quantum computers and traditional computers are currently in the same tension. Quantum computers are error prone, environmentally sensitive, expensive, and need to be run by teams of specialist scientists and engineers – nothing like a normal computer. There is a point just on the other side of our horizons, however, where we will look back and be astounded that we ever thought the power of today's computers was anything special – just as we do when we think of a horse and carriage.

4.7 Fintech and the Digitisation of money

The final trend we need to consider for an integrated view of the technological factors driving change in our world is the way digitisation is changing money. When we moved from hunter-gatherers into towns and villages, we created coins and moved away from barter to facilitate transactions. The industrial era was bedded down when we moved from coins to paper. In 1948, ENIAC started the technological age. Two years later Diners Club came out with the first credit card and we moved from paper to plastic. These changes have become permanent – a new way of using money.

Today, with the rise of cryptocurrencies, digital wallets, mobile money and other digital financial services, we are seeing that money has changed again; it is being digitised. When money changes, the world changes. As with several trends reviewed in this chapter, these digital solutions are not yet mature and reliable, and have been prone to abuse. They are, however, milestones on the path toward the inevitable (and irreversible) change in the way our society functions. When you have time, go back and re-read this chapter but do it looking at each area as part of an integrated system drawing on the others too. How much more incredible does A.I. sound when fed by the perspectives of Big Data, which is processed by the power of Quantum Computing, and delivered seamlessly into our lives through the invisible Internet of Things?

> *"When you do Innovation in a Big Company, the immune system of that company will attack you."* Salim Ismail, Singularity University

5. THE GOOD, THE BAD AND THE UGLY

TechnoEthics or the Ethics of Technology is a new area that has developed to look at how these technologies influence our view of right and wrong, and good and bad. It also looks at the way the tech is being used in light of our current worldviews and ethics. Increasingly the question we need to ask is not "Can we do it?", but "Should we do it?" or "What happens if we do it?" Technology can do more and more of the things that have historically sat in the realm of human imagination, and our discussion needs to be about the consequences of technology, not only the possibility of it.

We are also starting to see that we are unconsciously introducing our own biases and cultural perspectives into the tech we are creating. In 2019, the Georgia Institute of Technology looked at eight operating systems used for the management of self-driving cars. They looked at the process the technologies used to identify pedestrians and other objects, and found that across all eight platforms there was, on average, a 7% greater chance of being hit by a self-driving car if you were a dark-skinned person than if you were white. The programmers who wrote the threat and safety protocols had unconsciously codified their social bias into the programming of the operating systems.

We also have the ever-present risk of militarisation of the technology. From hackers being recruited into cyber-warfare military divisions to putting explosive charges into autonomous technology. Boston Dynamics, a robotics company, has built some incredible machines that have applications in many fields. One of their robots was almost mothballed because they first deployed it to the U.S. military as a bomb defusing and disposal unit, but the initial prototypes were deemed too bulky and cumbersome. The same robot is now being considered for use in warehouses to move heavy and bulky items. Exoskeletons that a person straps on that augment strength and extend endurance have been developed for the military, but are now being brought into industry to enable workers to pick up and move items that weigh hundreds of kilograms. These same exosuits are being investigated to give mobility to paraplegic individuals.

The sad reality is that there is more money available in the world for war than almost any other industry, and many of these technologies are first being considered to enable us to kill each other more efficiently, with other applications being secondary.

6. WHAT DOES IT MEAN TO ME?

How much of the above tech trends you understand or explore or become an expert in will depend on your career ambitions, your sense of how fast the world is changing, and how ready or involved you think you need to be. No matter your role or chosen industry, being informed and asking the right questions can make the difference between being seen as just an employee or as "talent", and being watched, nurtured and developed. As an entrepreneur or gig economy contractor, it could mean the difference between making it or missing the trend and becoming irrelevant very rapidly. Being fascinated by tech trends and staying abreast of recent developments, start-ups and experiments can also make you a very interesting conversationalist. Sign up to a few future trend forums where you can receive ground-breaking news, i.e. Singularity University, World Economic Forum, leading consulting tech blogs or even the New York Times technology blog, Bits. Explore emerging technologies, build innovative solutions, learn and improve your technology skills, and find a job with IBM Digital Nation Africa. Be prepared, be ahead of the curve, be informed, be relevant and be resilient. We will explore more of the skills needed and how to do this in the rest of the book to help you not just survive but thrive and flourish in the emerging world.

> *"It's life Jim, but not as we know it"* Captain James T Kirk, Starship Enterprise

7. TIPS, TOOLS AND RESOURCES

If you are interested in exploring and learning more, here are some of our favourite tips, tools and resources on future trends. (See https://catalystconsulting.co.za/power-up8-resources/)

Websites & Blogs

PowerUp⁸ Resources: https://catalystconsulting.co.za/power-up8-resources/

Flipboard for additional information and extended reading: https://flipboard.com/@raymond3311/debbie-craig-intro-chapter-gmuqq562z

www.raydevilliers.com

https://www.raydevilliers.co.za/presentations

https://www.raydevilliers.co.za/videos

The Fourth Industrial Revolution What It Means and How to Respond: https://www.foreignaffairs.com/articles/2015-12-12/fourth-industrial-revolution

Google's Eric Schmidt: 'The Internet Will Disappear': https://www.youtube.com/watch?v=Tf49T45GNd0

Digital Natives, Digital Immigrants: https://www.marcprensky.com/writing/Prensky%20-%20Digital%20Natives,%20Digital%20Immigrants%20-%20Part1.pdf

'AlphaGo versus Lee Sedol': https://en.wikipedia.org/wiki/AlphaGo_versus_Lee_Sedol

That Internet of Things' thing: http://www.itrco.jp/libraries/RFIDjournal-That%20Internet%20of%20Things%20Thing.pdf

ORION: The algorithm proving that left isn't right: https://www.ups.com/us/en/services/knowledge-center/article.page?kid=aa3710c2

Patients key to making sense of medical data: https://mitsloan.mit.edu/ideas-made-to-matter/patients-key-to-making-sense-medical-data

Videos

What is the Fourth Industrial Revolution?: https://www.youtube.com/watch?v=kpW9JcWxKq0

World Economic Forum | Centre for the Fourth Industrial Revolution https://www.youtube.com/watch?v=EO2fi9acHWc

A Day Made of Glass: https://www.youtube.com/watch?v=6Cf7IL_eZ38

Top 20 predictions from Kurzweil – Future Technologies: https://www.youtube.com/watch?v=WhxhOLm1bjE

What is Digital Twin? How does it work? https://www.youtube.com/watch?v=iVS-AuSjpOQ

Demo: The magic of A.I. neural TTS and holograms at Microsoft Inspire 2019: https://www.youtube.com/watch?v=auJJrHgG9Mc

Boston Dynamics' Atlas Robot Can Do Parkour: https://www.youtube.com/watch?v=hSjKoEva5bg

How artificial intelligence will change your world in 2019, for better or worse: https://www.youtube.com/watch?v=XvzNuw5VjBU

Retail 2020 | 5 Technologies that will change the way you shop: https://www.youtube.com/watch?v=iRvaWHk3A8k

Google AI books a haircut and restaurant visit: https://www.youtube.com/watch?v=D5VN56jQMWM

Forums and Subscriptions

Singularity University Blog: https://su.org/blog/

World Economic Forum Reports: https://www.weforum.org/reports/

New York Times Technology Bits: https://www.nytimes.com/column/bits

McKinsey Insights – Future of Work: https://www.mckinsey.com/featured-insights/future-of-work

Deloitte Blogs: Future of Work: https://www2.deloitte.com/bd/en/pages/human-capital/topics/future-of-work-blogs.html

Skill building

https://developer.ibm.com/digitalnation/africa/

Chapter

WHICH CORE CAPABILITIES DO I NEED?

"The illiterate of the 21st century will not be those who cannot read and write, but those who cannot learn, unlearn, and relearn."
–Alvin Toffler

1. ARE WE FUTURE FIT?

Every day we are bombarded with another avalanche of change – change in our roles, who we report to, what systems we use, which products we sell and what our customers are demanding. We are flooded with information about new trends, new technologies, new jobs, redundant careers and new skills required. We join companies or communities, make friends, get betrayed, build relationships, fall ill and lose loved ones.

Every day there seems to be more and more urgent demands on our time, our energy and our ideas – to assist, rescue, firefight, support and resolve. We also have to deal with our geyser bursting, our neighbour's dog barking all night, a sick family member, study or work assignments, election politicking, crime and load-shedding when we get home at night. In recent times, we have had to deal with an unprecedented change in our lives and livelihoods as we faced the global pandemic of COVID-19, and had to adjust overnight to economic, social and physical lockdown, and the accompanying fears of an unknown, unseen virus and uncertain future. The global marketplace has never been more digitally connected and yet physically isolated through this experience.

Industries, places and brands we loved have come under threat and some even ceased to exist.

Are you ready for the evolution of technology touching every part of our lives? Are you feeling confident to adapt successfully to the shifting daily demands?

In a matter of weeks, my own consulting business had to shift from face-to-face facilitated sessions to shorter bi-weekly virtual sessions. Our tried and tested techniques and tools suddenly became less impactful and we had to create virtual approaches very rapidly. We had to establish new ways of working for effective teaming and still deliver. At the same time, we had to manage our own fears, learn on the fly, listen with compassion, and adapt when our clients or team were overwhelmed with scenario planning and crisis management.

The digital revolution is real. Political and economic evolution is inevitable. Social transformation to create a more inclusive, collaborative and sustainable way of life for all has just been given wings. These dramatic shifts in our world are resulting in many jobs and skills evolving, transitioning or becoming obsolete. Many jobs or skills of the future have not yet been invented, so it is imperative that we adopt and practice the mindsets and skills that will keep us informed, adaptable, relevant and future ready.

> We need to be like off-road race-car drivers, who, no matter what happens on the day, can adapt quickly to changing conditions and competitors, using the equipment and technology at our disposal and relying on our many hours of training and intuitive ability to respond to what we sense, feel and see (sometimes even around the next bend). We need to be energised by the challenge and not afraid to take chances and know when to brake or call the race off when the risk is too great. We need to know when to accelerate through the turn, keeping an eye on all available options. And when things don't work out as we

> expected or our equipment fails, we need to be ready to pause, fix, adjust and dive back into the race with the possibility of surviving and even winning another day.

2. CHANGING FOCUS OF SKILLS

The McKinsey Global Institute is tracking a range of jobs based on human skills and how they are likely to be affected by A.I. and automation. They place work skills into five categories: physical and manual; basic cognitive; higher cognitive; social and emotional; and technological. They say that physical or basic cognitive tasks that can be performed by relatively low skilled labour or require only low-level data input and processing are likely to be quickest to be replaced.[1] Examples of jobs that will require new skill sets to work side-by-side with technology (or in time be replaced by) are drivers, assembly line workers, nurses, electricians, crafts people, cashiers, customer service staff, typists and clerks.

While demand for skills in these areas might be decreasing, McKinsey predicts a significant increase in demand in the higher cognitive; social and emotional; and technological skill areas. Examples of these are:

> **Higher cognitive:** advanced literacy and writing, quantitative and statistical skills, critical thinking, and complex information processing, e.g. doctors, accountants, research analysts, writers, and editors.
>
> **Social and emotional (soft skills):** advanced communication and negotiation, empathy, the ability to learn continuously, to manage others and to be adaptable, e.g. business development, programming, emergency response and counselling.
>
> **Technological:** basic to advanced IT skills, data analysis, engineering, and research, e.g. software developers, engineers, robotics, and scientific experts.

---

[1] McKinsey Global Institute, 2018.

The World Economic Forum (WEF) says that by 2030 there will be huge demand for skills such as creativity (e.g., coming up with creative marketing strategies), critical thinking (e.g., solving complex systemic problems), complex information processing (e.g., analysing trends and impact on the company) and decision-making (e.g., sifting through masses of data to make decisions despite uncertainty).[2] In addition to these, resilience has increased in importance as our world and certainty has been rocked by recent events.

 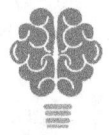  

Digital	Cognitive	Social	Resilience
Tech trends, digital savvy, eco-systems, remote work, tech & data concepts & processes, data analytics & visualisation, AI, security	Critical thinking, problem solving, creativity, innovation, scenario planning, complexity thinking, project management	Relationship skills, leading influencing, remote teaming, engagement collaboration, customer connection, conflict management	Self-awareness, confidence, growth mindset, adaptability, focus, effectiveness, stress & energy management, mental well-being

Are you, your team and your organisation ... **RELEVANT, RESILIENT AND READY** for the future?

Whilst various digital and analytical skills will be important, the skills that will be the most critical, regardless of your chosen technical field, will be those that enable continuous learning, adaptability and dealing with ambiguity. These skills are the focus of this book.

> *"We define our hiring and our education system on skills. There is no skill which is robot-proof, someone can build a tool to do it better faster cheaper."* –Dr Vivienne Ming

---

2   World Economic Forum, 2020.

3. WHAT ARE THE EXPERTS SAYING?

> **Project Oxygen: 10 behaviours of Google's best managers**
>
> 1. Is a good coach
> 2. Empowers team and does not micromanage
> 3. Creates an inclusive team environment, showing concern for success and well-being
> 4. Is productive and results-oriented
> 5. Is a good communicator – listens and shares information
> 6. Supports career development and discusses performance
> 7. Has a clear vision/strategy for the team
> 8. Has key technical skills to help advise the team
> 9. Collaborates across Google
> 10. Is a strong decision maker

One of the earlier studies that fascinated me was Google's Project Oxygen, which set out to test its hiring philosophy to identify the long-term predictors of success in Google's top employees. What they found was a surprise. It turns out that it wasn't the expected STEM skills (science, technology, engineering, maths) that were the best predictors of performance. Rather the most productive and successful employees shared a good balance of people skills AND thinking skills.[3]

This was confirmed in a World Economic Forum report on future skills.[4] (See box for 2022 trends.)

> **WEF future skills trending 2022**
>
> 1. Analytical thinking and innovation
> 2. Active learning and learning strategies
> 3. Creativity, originality and initiative
> 4. Technology design and programming
> 5. Critical thinking and analysis
> 6. Complex problem-solving
> 7. Leadership and social influence
> 8. Emotional intelligence
> 9. Reasoning, problem-solving and ideation
> 10. Systems analysis and evaluation

Another study that resonated with me is research by the Korn Ferry Institute, which revealed the ideal leader for tomorrow's disruptive business environment: The Self-Disruptive Leader.[5] This new model of a high-performing leader incorpo-

---

3   Strauss, 2017.
4   Harrel & Barbato, 2018.
5   Korn Ferry, 2019.

rates and builds on existing concepts of agile, digital, and inclusive leadership, but also highlights the importance of leaders who are experts in the creation of opportunity and the capitalisation of the flow of knowedge. In this model, the new source of competitive advantage is a leader who can connect resources and people adeptly to build an innovation ecosystem. This enables them to bring robust ideas to market at a rapid pace, and crucially, to adapt quickly to change by disrupting themselves again and again.

A COVID-relevant update of capabilities needed in a crisis were **Decisiveness** (making bold decisions in uncertainty), **Collaboration** (consortiums working together to innovate and prevent infection and fatalities), **Agility** (building new supply chains as existing ones were shut down), **Innovation** (switching to alternative channels, e.g. social media, to sell products and services) and **Empathy** (engaging and responding to staff needs in a crisis).[6]

In our own local South African context, Future Nations Schools founder, Sizwe Nxasana, at a SingularityU South Africa event, said that the predictors of success in South Africa that need to be built at school level are: the ability to deal with uncertainty including grit, a positive mindset and resilience; cognitive abilities and how to distinguish right from wrong; problem solving skills; the ability to understand and deal with complex systems; and the ability to assimilate important and useful information from a lot of noise from various external sources such as social media.[7]

For those of you interested in raising children to thrive in a very different world and contribute in a variety of roles, I highly recommend reading: "Becoming Brilliant: What science tells us about raising successful children."[8] Their findings show that the foundational skills for success are collaboration, communication, content, critical thinking, creative innovation, confidence and the ability to rapidly learn just about anything. They suggest that: "real success and

---

6   Korn Ferry, 2020.
7   Singularity University Summits, 2017.
8   Psychology Today, 2016.

brilliance come when we support happy, healthy, thinking, caring, and social children so that they become collaborative, creative, competent, and responsible citizens tomorrow."

There are many other sources of future skills and core capabilities listed in the resources section if you want to explore further from research and consulting firms such as the Institute for the Future, The Centre for Creative Leadership, Deloitte, EY, Korn Ferry and others.

4. THE POWER OF 8

After sifting through many of these studies, testing and debating with friends and colleagues, eight core capabilities emerged as the most useful and relevant for the future of work (and life) over and above the important skills of digital savvy and technical skills. The extent to which we can access these capabilities are centred around our ability to consciously choose our response in any situation – our ability to master our thoughts, feelings and actions.

The world needs people who are:

- intensely **curious** (about themselves, others and the world);
- uniquely **creative** (experimenting, learning and willing to fail);
- **courageously** committed (to their vision for self, team or cause);
- **consciously** choosing (where to focus attention and how to show up);
- **critical thinkers** (who can resolve dilemmas and make meaning out of noise);
- trust building **collaborators** (who combine perspectives and strengths into lasting relationships and value);
- **change** navigators (who navigate the maze of change for positive impact); and
- generous **contributors** (who build lasting healthy communities).

Identity Shifts

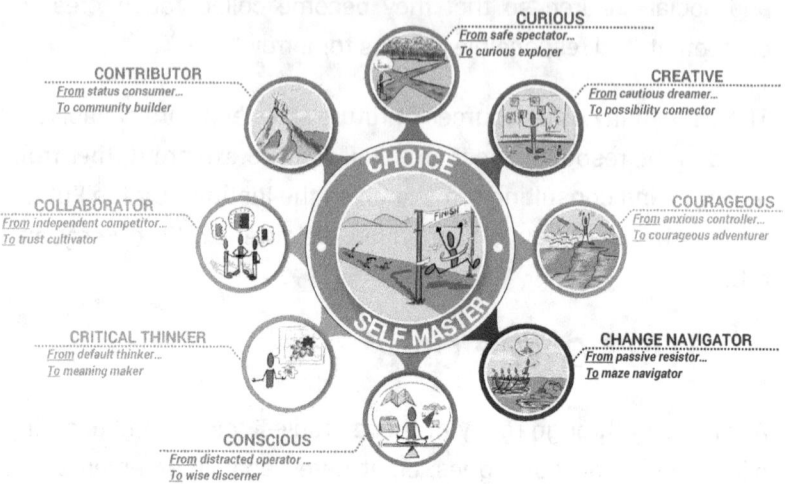

These abilities may not be new or surprising. They do, however, need some fresh thinking and insight into how we build the underlying identities, beliefs, habits and neural pathways to make them effortless. Despite knowing that these are critically important for success, we still don't seem able to create a lasting foundation of these in our families, teams, organisational cultures and communities as a whole. We still suffer from narrow, short-term thinking, defending the status quo, working in silos and competing with scarcity mindsets. Many people are also persistent victims of fear... fear of loss, of rejection, of betrayal, of failure. Fear and frustration pull our energy inward, making us doubt and feel insecure. It keeps us playing small and feeling alone. It prevents us from reaching out, opening up, experimenting, learning and sharing our thoughts, feelings and ideas.

So how do we move above and beyond our automatic, protective programming of survival to create a future of possibilities and adventures in which we can live and lead with courage and authenticity?

My ongoing interest in the Neuroscience of Change and the Neurochemistry of Stress has reinforced the importance of digging a bit deeper and shifting our perspective. We need to create opportunities to examine and rewrite our stories, to reimagine our identities and cultivate new thinking to dance through change with confidence and grace. We need to learn how to move powerfully between our light and shadow selves and harness our emotional energy for connecting and creating. We need to know when to charge forth boldly or retreat and recharge for another day. We need to have access to these eight capabilities and become wise enough to know in which moments to call on them. The intent is not to create an ideal identity, but rather to give you possibilities to explore what works best for you and takes you closer to your ultimate goals and dreams.

5. TIPS, TOOLS AND RESOURCES

If you are interested in exploring and learning more, here are some of our favourite tips, tools and resources on future capabilities. (See https://catalystconsulting.co.za/power-up8-resources/).

Blogs

Google project oxygen – the evolution 2018: https://rework.withgoogle.com/blog/the-evolution-of-project-oxygen/

WEF Future of Jobs 2018: http://www3.weforum.org/docs/WEF_Future_of_Jobs_2018.pdf

https://www.weforum.org/reports/the-future-of-jobs-report-2018

21 jobs of the future: a guide to getting – and staying – employed in th next 10 years; Cognizant; Centre for the Future of Work, 2019: https://www.cognizant.com/whitepapers/21-jobs-of-the-future-a-guide-to-getting-and-staying-employed-over-the-next-10-years-codex3049.pdf

How to select and develop individuals for successful agile teams: A practical guide; McKinsey & Company, 2018: https://www.mckinsey.com/business-functions/organization/our-insights/how-to-select-and-develop-individuals-for-successful-agile-teams-a-practical-guide

Leadership skills for an uncertain world – Centre for Creative Leadership , 2020: https://www.ccl.org/articles/leading-effectively-articles/leadership-skills-for-an-uncertain-world/

The Self-Disruptive leader; Korn Ferry, 2019: https://infokf.kornferry.com/rs/494-VUC-482/images/KF-Disruptive%20Leader%20Final-Digital.pdf

Seven essential elements of a lifelong-learning mind-set; By Jacqueline Brassey, Nick van Dam, and Katie Coates, McKinsey & Company, February 2019: https://www.mckinsey.com/business-functions/organization/our-insights/seven-essential-elements-of-a-lifelong-learning-mind-set?_lrsc=ad78db0c-8fd3-4dc6-b251-d7a909cb799b&cm_mmc=OSocial_Linkedin-_-Security_Security+Brand+and+Outcomes-_-WW_WW-_-Elevate&cm_mmca1=000034XK&cm_mmca2=10010257

Leadership in a crisis: Responding to the coronavirus outbreak and future challenges, March 2020: https://www.mckinsey.com/business-functions/organization/our-insights/leadership-in-a-crisis-responding-to-the-coronavirus-outbreak-and-future-challenges?cid=other-eml-alt-mip-mck&hlkid=37fc9d2ecd944a61a227b410ffa855ee&hctky=10140929&hdpid=16a43b5b-480b-4b3b-b8cf-bc20fcc11b08

Accelerating through the turn Preparing for a future beyond the crisis – Korn Ferry Apr 2020: https://www.kornferry.com/challenges/recovery

Videos

Self-disruptive leader: https://www.youtube.com/watch?v=kEVuU-1Um00

The Future of Education | Sizwe Nxasana | SingularityU South Africa: https://www.youtube.com/watch?v=obsZvO3YjHA

The Digital Skills Gap and the Future of Jobs 2020 – The Fundamental Growth Mindset: https://www.youtube.com/watch?v=Y9FOyoS3Fag

Digital transformation: are you ready for exponential change?: https://www.youtube.com/watch?v=ystdF6jN7hc

Digital Transformation: Future Scenarios 2030 | Deloitte: https://www.youtube.com/watch?v=M908RNjj0n8

Future of Skills: Jobs in 2030: https://www.youtube.com/watch?v=62WWcs9EY1w

Atlas of Emerging Jobs: http://atlas100.ru/en/

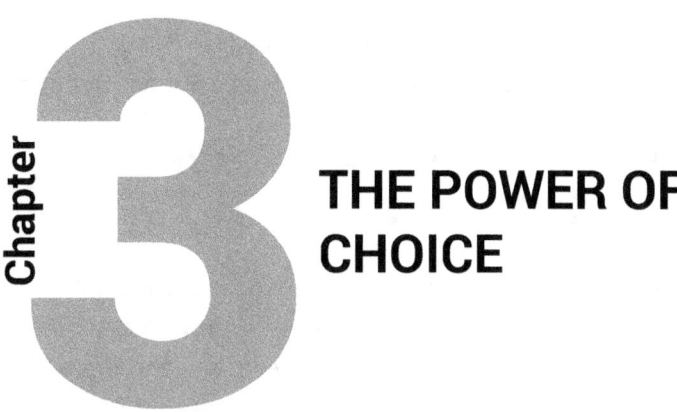

Chapter 3
THE POWER OF CHOICE

"We are the creative force of our life, and through our own choices rather than our conditions, if we carefully learn to do certain things, we can accomplish those goals." –Stephen Covey

1. WHY IS CHANGING OUR BEHAVIOUR SO DIFFICULT?

How many times have you set good intentions but not made much progress? Have you tried to be more organised, patient, and healthy? Have you wished you could speak up, listen more or make more time for your kids or special people? How often have you set goals to grow your skills, read that book or start that new project or career and kept postponing? Do you sometimes procrastinate, make excuses, or rationalise NOT DOING IT? I know I have. Even with all the tools I know and personal work I have done, I still get caught in the trap of wanting to learn and change, but not quite creating the important mindset and habit shifts to make it reality. Research shows that approximately 54% of people who resolve to change their ways fail to make the transformation last beyond six months, and the average person made the same life resolution 10 times over without success.[1] Most often it is my enthusiasm and optimism to explore interesting projects that derails me, as I forget to focus and commit to the few important things and then stick to them. I know that if I want to build these eight core capabilities

---
1 Lally, van Jaarsveld, Potts & Wardle, 2009.

to be future fit, relevant and resilient... I need to CHOOSE! So let's explore how the functioning of our brains can help us in this quest.

2. HOW CAN WE CHANGE OUR BRAINS?

The good news is that after many years of believing our brains and personality were pretty much fixed, we now have a much better understanding about how our brains work and the ingredients needed for learning and changing toward our goals. We now know that **OUR BRAINS**, including the way we think, process information, respond emotionally and make decisions, **CAN CHANGE**. Science has proven that our brains can be re-trained and re-organised to work more effectively. This is known as neuroplasticity. The Oxford English Dictionary defines it as follows:[2]

> *Neuroplasticity = "the ability of the brain to form and reorganize synaptic connections, especially in response to learning or experience."*

Neuroscience and how the brain functions is a mammoth subject with a multitude of researchers in different specialist fields discovering new insights every year. There are, however, several widely accepted assumptions and principles that can help us optimise our own potential today. I am going share with you my own high-level summary of what I have discovered, tested and practiced, and what works for me. I may over-simplify some very complex terms and topics to keep this practical and relevant. I encourage you to explore the many resources listed below for a deeper understanding.

First, a few key terms and principles which are useful to know when building future mindsets and habits are summarised below.

---

[2] Lexico, 2020.

Adaptability: Our brains are adaptable, can learn and grow, and are not fixed at any age. We can change how we think, feel and act, and change how we show up and our attitudes (neuroplasticity).

Attention: We can develop our brains through consistent, focused attention on the new thinking, feeling and doing habits we wish to create (where focus goes, energy flows[3]).

Repetition: We can build new habits through repetition or "stopping" old habits. A great analogy is noticing how a path in the bush becomes a road (or even a highway) with plenty of use or gets grown over when not used. (Hebbian Law = nerve cells that fire together, wire together[4]).

Imagination: We can change the structure of our brain by regularly imagining a future vision for ourselves AND feeling it as if it has already happened. Our brains can then more easily recognise opportunities to create that future. (Our brains do not know the difference between imagination and reality[5]!).

Stress: We have an inbuilt stress response (fight or flight) as a natural survival mechanism to protect us from potential threats. "We can trigger the stress response by thought alone"[6] when we imagine worse case scenarios. We can also minimise the impact of stress through our awareness and choosing more appropriate thoughts.

Brainwaves: Our brains operate at different frequencies depending on our mental activity levels, e.g. worrying, problem solving, learning, relaxing or sleeping. We can utilise different brainwave states to optimise our ability to imagine, create, learn, de-stress and rewire our brains.[7]

---

3   Team Tony, 2020.
4   Wikipedia, 2020.
5   Hamilton, 2014.
6   Dispenza, 2019.
7   Neurohealth, 2020.

Subconscious: The majority of our bodily functions, beliefs, memories, default thinking and behavioural patterns are stored in, or driven from, our subconscious minds.[8] We can access these patterns and programmes through certain brain wave states and other techniques to accelerate change.

Chemistry: Triggers in our environment and our thoughts initiate a cascade of chemicals[9] (feel good or stress hormones) which result in feelings. These in turn influence thoughts, causing a positive or negative thinking, feeling loop.[10] We can manage our mental and emotional state by developing the ability to self-regulate and pause and reflect before responding.

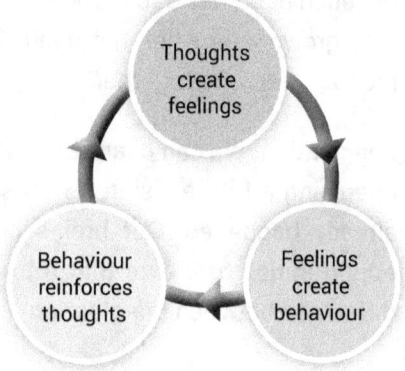

Coherence: Our heart is in regular communication with our brains and body. We can utilise the powerful nerve centre in our heart to activate coherence or "harmony" in our brain, nervous system and electromagnetic field around us.[11] Certain breathing techniques can counter the stress response and switch on our rest and renew response instead.

Meta-cognition: We have the ability to observe ourselves (our thoughts, feelings, actions), pause and choose more empowering responses to life.[12] We can learn to delay reacting emotionally to an external trigger (e.g. criticism) or internal trigger (e.g. craving) until we have more information, are calmer and can make better choices. This is emotional intelligence in action.

---

8   Brian Tracy International, 2020.
9   Harvard Health Publishing, 2020.
10 Dispenza, 2013.
11 HeartMath, 2020.
12 Brain Facts, 2012.

Let's explore a little about how the brain works, to help you make sense of these principles.

3. WHAT DO WE NEED TO KNOW ABOUT OUR BRAINS?

3.1 Purpose, structure and hardwiring

Our brains are an accumulated record of all our past memories, beliefs, experiences, emotional associations and even our genetic history. Our brains are made up of approximately 100 billion nerve cells, called **neurons**, which gather and transmit **electrochemical signals** throughout the body. The brain works like a giant computer, processing information that it receives from the senses and the body through the nervous system. For example, we see a friendly or angry face and we prepare ourselves automatically for engaging or avoiding. Neurons are like the gates and wires in a computer, facilitating the type and speed of messages to and from different parts of the computer.[13]

There are tiny gaps or **"synapses"** between the neurons, which store chemical messengers (neurotransmitters). These enable communication across the synapses to other neurons and so on to various parts of the nervous system. Over time, the neurons form paths and clusters in high traffic areas which become automated, i.e. without any conscious thought or intervention. For example, if you have once been bitten by a dog, you will automatically react with stress chemicals (cortisol) when seeing another dog and want to avoid it merely through association. If, on the other hand, you have had only positive experiences with dogs, you will automatically generate feel good chemicals (oxytocin) and want to reach out and connect with the dog you see.

---

13 Mayo Clinic, 2020.

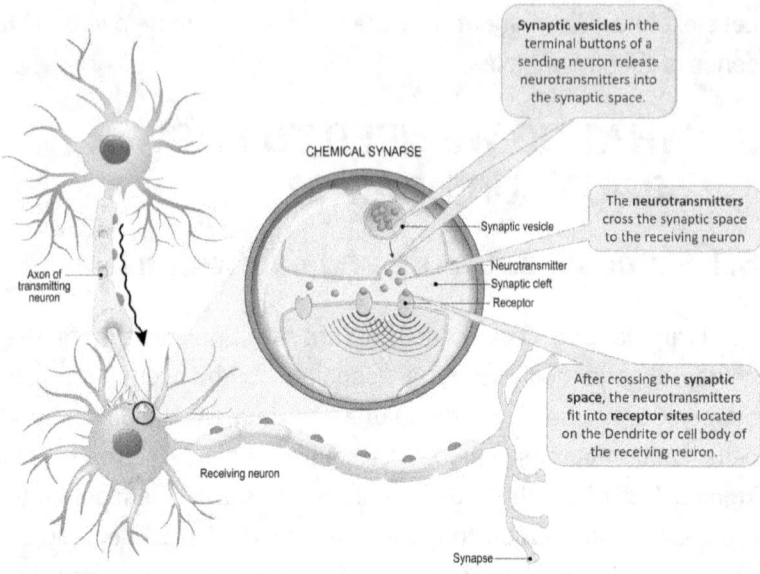

The few big things we need to know to optimise and accelerate our ability to learn and change are automated responses, the stress response, impact of our emotions, shifting our comfort zones and creating a new future.

The brain has a primary aim to conserve energy and will **automate** any regular processes that don't need conscious intervention. This includes not just breathing, heart-rate and digestion, but also patterns of thinking, feeling and responding to external or internal stimuli such as hunger, cold, anger, criticism, love etc. Hebbian Law has shown that "nerve cells that fire together, wire together".[14] This means that the more you repeat a thought, belief, feeling or habit, e.g. "I am not creative" or "I am courageous", the more this becomes automated and part of your default personality or attitude. It becomes **hard-wired** and difficult to change!

3.2 The stress vs. restore response

The autonomic nervous system, which consists of the brain, the spinal-cord and the peripheral nerves, connects the environment to

---
14 Dispenza, 2008.

the brain and body through the senses. It runs automatically at a subconscious level. It has two primary functions – to manage threats and emergencies, and to conserve and restore energy and resources.

The **sympathetic nervous system (SNS)** is activated when there is either quick action required (e.g. running a race, presenting at a meeting) or a perceived threat identified through the senses (e.g. physical danger or emotional pain). The limbic brain, or primal survival brain, reacts with a stress response of fight, flight or freeze, increasing breathing and heart rate, shutting down basic functions like digestion, and sending blood to the limbs to act or run. This utilises a lot of energy.

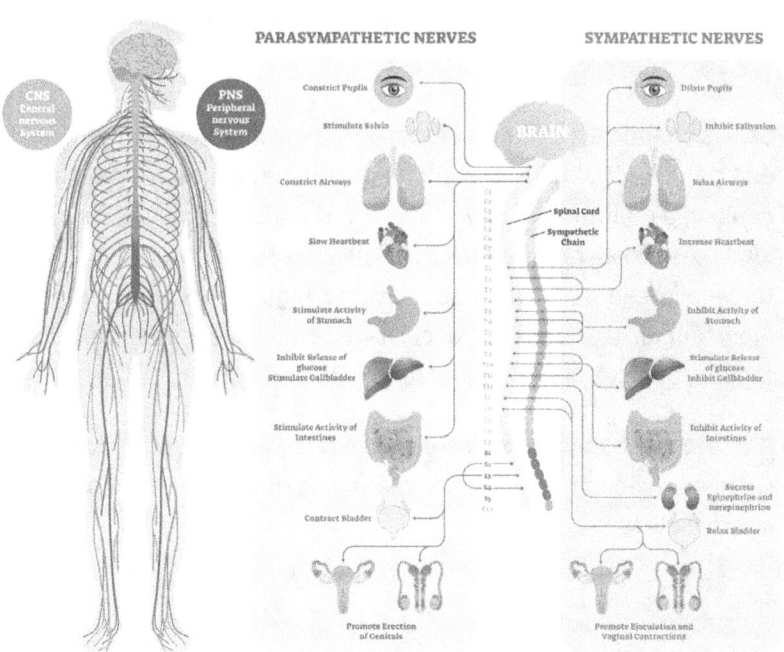

The **para-sympathetic nervous system (PNS)** is activated when there is harmony and no threat, which enables the body to relax, heal and restore. This happens automatically during restful sleep and generates energy for use during the day. Ideally, we are designed to move in and out of these states in a normal day.

However, due to our **stressful lifestyles** and anxious thoughts, we may spend most of our waking hours in the stress response, leading to a state of exhaustion and breakdown of health. After an initial shock of a physical threat (e.g. a near-miss traffic accident) or even an anxious thought of an imagined personal failure, the stress hormones adrenalin and cortisol are released into the body by the SNS and can remain in the body for about 20 minutes after the event.[15] The problem is, every time we then remember a shocking event or think about a future painful scenario, we reactivate the SNS, which releases more stress hormones, and we stay in a state of high alert. Our bodies were only designed for short-term stress (e.g. fleeing briefly from a predator and then relaxing again). We are not designed for constant stress.

> *"Our brains don't know the difference between an imaginary threat and a real one."* –Dawson Church

Stress chemicals, accumulated over time without time to rest, heal and renew fully, build up and cause inflammation in our systems causing a multitude of physical and mental symptoms. It can also lead to adrenal fatigue and burnout. Chronic high cortisol leads to widespread body damage including high blood pressure, high blood sugar, heart disease, accelerated aging, Alzheimer's disease, fatigue, obesity, diabetes, and many other effects.[16]

It is almost impossible to learn or create in this "survival" state. So, we need to become masters at managing our stress response and internal state.

---

15 Church, 2018.
16 Church, 2018.

Flight – Fight – Freeze mode (SNS)	Executive Decision mode (PNS)
Limbic system (emotional brain) – Reacts within 0.05 secs. Manage fears or threats (stress) for safety and survival.	Pre-frontal cortex (thinking brain) – slower to respond. Seat of concentration, motivation, working memory – evaluates, integrates, chooses.
Sympathetic nervous system (SNS) – amygdala, brain shut-down of non-essential neural paths, releases hormones (cortisol, adrenalin).	Parasympathetic nervous system (PNS) – vagus nerve, slows heart rate, releases hormones (oxytocin, vasopressin, dopamine).
Feel anxious, fearful, irritable, frustrated, out of control, distorted perceptions (threatened), judgemental, negative.	Feel positive emotions, optimism, well-being, compassion, energised, greater intuition, heightened learning state, social judgement, in flow.
Rapid heart rate, increased blood pressure, sweating and an increased respiratory rate.	Reduced heart rate, calm, deeper breathing, relaxed.
Perception of limited resources, withdrawn, closed, selfish, need for safety and low risk, holding on to the known.	Perception of possibility, open-minded, flexible, creative, ease of learning, better memory. Higher risk tolerance, more sharing and caring.
Reduced immune function and general metabolism.	Greater potential for long-term health.

3.3 Impact of emotions and addiction

Research in neurochemistry shows that thoughts produce chemicals which in turn allow our body to "feel" how we are thinking. For example, when we have happy, hopeful thoughts, our brain manufactures chemicals (e.g. dopamine) that make us feel joyful and optimistic. If, however, we have negative or angry thoughts, the brain produces chemicals (e.g. cortisol or ACTH) that make us feel angry, frustrated or even aggressive. These feelings then stimulate responses or behaviour. When we stay in a particular mode of thinking for a while, this can become our "mood" or "personality". Just like a drug that we use often, we can become addicted to these chemicals and emotions of stress. Notice how some people will subconsciously "seek out" experiences to get their "fix", i.e. pick a fight, do something to feel guilty or help someone in need. We are creatures of habit, and will often repeat patterns – in relationships, in jobs, in finances, in health, etc. – until we make different conscious choices.

3.4 Shifting our baseline or comfort zone

Our brain craves comfort and predictability, and are pattern recognizing machines. Our comfort zones and our ability to shift them determine our capacity for learning and change. Once we create a baseline of feeling a certain way, e.g. insecure or always disappointing others, our brains will create the thoughts to reinforce that experience. We will then FEEL insecure or bad about letting others down and get our chemical fix. This all reinforces the baseline and we struggle to consistently feel a different way even though we may want to feel more confident or happy. Shifting our comfort zones on a daily basis, e.g. to be more "comfortable with discomfort" and moving in stretch or learning zone, is key to change.

Remember how you felt when you first learnt how to ride a bicycle or drive a car? Everything felt difficult and weird. You probably felt incompetent or stupid when you fell over or stalled. Over time however, the more you practiced, the more competent and comfortable you felt. Eventually riding the bike or driving the car became automatic and you could concentrate on other things such as your environment around you or chatting to a passenger. This is what we want for the core capabilities we wish to build.

3.5 Being conscious of our daily thoughts and habits

Many researchers and neuroscientists have estimated the number and type of thoughts we have in a day. Taking an average view, here are some surprising numbers. We have about 50,000-70,000 thoughts a day. Of these, 90% are automatic and the same as yesterday. And 70% are more negative than positive.

> *"95% of who you are by the time you are 35 years old is a set of memorized behaviours and emotional reactions that create and identity subconsciously. 5% of your conscious mind that is plugged into reality is working against 95% of what you've memorized subconsciously".* –Dr Joe Dispenza[17]

Think about a typical day. We wake up, check our devices, roll out of bed (maybe greet our spouse), bush our teeth, make our way to make tea or coffee, feed the dog, get the kids up, pack lunches, shower, dress and make our way to our place of work using the same mode of transport, using the same route. We have the same thoughts about what to expect that day. We know who we are going to meet or talk to and how we feel about them. We may be nervous or excited about any possible changes in our day. We feel the same frustration, achievement, tiredness, enthusiasm, or insecurity that we feel most days, even if the players in the play are slightly different that day. We feel the same stresses, release the same chemicals and return home not much changed from the day before.

To change deeply engrained default behaviours, we need to unlearn and create new, more effective ones. We cannot create the body of our dreams if we only lie in bed and imagine ourselves getting fitter

---
17 Dispenza, 2012.

and stronger. We need to make it a priority. We need to be clear on the target, assess where we are starting from, stay informed about the latest research in body sculpting, believe we can achieve it, and then invest time in daily mental and physical practices and habits. As Angela Duckworth says in Grit: **Enthusiasm is common. Endurance is rare!**[18]

We used to believe it takes 21 days to change a habit. Other research in the European Journal of Social Psychology[19] shows that it takes from 18 to 254 days to automate a new chosen habit, depending on how consistently the behaviour was repeated in a certain context. When we are learning something completely new, in which we have no previous experience, e.g. driving a car, it is actually easier than un-learning and re-learning a new behaviour or habit which is hard-wired, e.g. wanting to change procrastination or give up sugar!

4. BRINGING BACK CHOICE

Not only can you change your natural responses (e.g. being more calm, courageous or curious), but you can use these techniques to build new neural pathways of possibility. You can programme your brain to imagine a future you in a future reality. The brain does not know the difference between imagination and reality! Once this vision has been formed, stored and believed subconsciously, your brain will then use every ounce of stored knowledge, experience, intuition and available energy to help you achieve it. Many times I have found myself achieving something I dreamed of (starting my own company, building a house, my first international client, eating pizza in Tuscany or hiking to Everest Base Camp), that I suddenly remember where the dream started. I remember how I made it part of my future picture of myself and how many times I paid attention to ideas and opportunities leading to it and followed them (and I have been looking at it on my vision board for years). It works!

---

18 Goodreads, 2020.
19 Lally, van Jaarsveld, Potts & Wardle, 2009.

The greatest power to influence or shift our behaviour and habits comes at the **point of CHOICE**. If we can recognise a potentially stressful situation and pause before we react – we give ourselves the space to choose an appropriate response. We need to become fit at rethinking the possibilities and outcomes of events, AND reprogramme our physical and emotional reactions to keep ourselves in the CREATIVE brain state to make effective and rational choices to achieve the results we really want. A simple process, to shift your mental, emotional and physical state from a SURVIVAL STATE to a CREATIVE STATE, using the science of the brain, is as follows. Work on cultivating an identity (I am), a belief (I believe), an emotion (I feel) and a habit (I act).

An **identity** determines the state that you are creating from, e.g. an anxious controller or a courageous adventurer. When you feel courageous you are more likely to **believe** that you can do it AND therefore **feel** confident and optimistic. When we feel this way, we are more likely to make a **habit** of acting with confidence and courage.

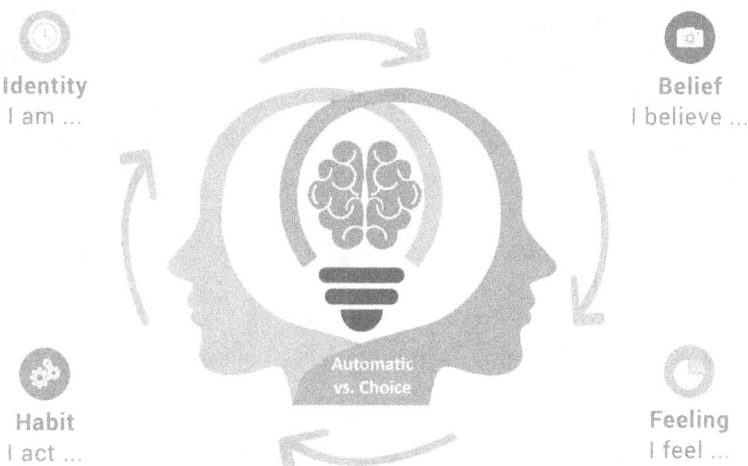

Start with just one aspect of yourself that you wish to develop, e.g. be more courageous. Assess what your old pattern used to be and choose a new one. See the visual example.

Place this visual up somewhere that you can see it regularly, e.g. on your desk, pin board, screen saver or fridge. After a while, remove the old self pattern and just keep the "new self" pattern.

In order to bring back CHOICE, I have picked a few of my favourite GO TO activities based on the most recent understanding of how the brain makes lasting change: establishing new thought patterns and neural paths, mindfulness and alpha state, cultivating identities, shifting beliefs, maintaining emotional coherence and creating new habits. This is the also the basis for how each of the eight core capabilities can be built.

4.1 Establishing new thought patterns

As we learnt above, establishing a new neural path (or thought pattern) requires regular repetition. Each repetition enhances the connections and ease of information flow between neurons, which become automatic over time. The opposite occurs when we consciously unlearn something – like kicking a bad habit – through just not doing it anymore. The stickiness between the neurons reduce and the neurons eventually drift apart and shrivel up (this is called synaptic pruning) – just like an overgrown path that starts to disappear through lack of use. For a real live view of neurons making connections during a learning process. (See the resources below.)

There are many techniques to stimulate neuron growth and plasticity, including:

- repetition of positive affirmations or beliefs that help you feel confident;
- use visual cues such as words, quotes, pictures or a vision board for sub-conscious programming;
- learning new things – a language, musical instrument or yoga;

- experiencing different things such as travelling to a new country, dancing, bungy jumping or connecting with people who are different from you;
- cultivating learning brainwave states through breathing and mindfulness practice;
- being in flow when working on something you really enjoy; and
- guided meditation to reprogramme your mind and body at a subconscious level for effortless change.

You can also gain benefits from intermittent fasting, non-dominant hand exercises, art, dancing and sleeping.

4.2 Practicing mindfulness

We can consciously shift our neural pathways with energy and effort (which is limited), or we can enable change at a subconscious level. "Mindfulness is a moment-to-moment awareness of your own experience without judgment."[20] Mindfulness can be practiced when sitting quietly, walking in nature, praying, meditating or doing practices such as yoga and tai chi. We can also learn to practice mindfulness while sitting in traffic, cooking, gardening, running or even washing dishes. Mindfulness enables us to become more aware of ourselves, our bodies, our thoughts and our state of being – using our meta-cognition ability. It is an intent to be aware, a slowing down and deepening of breathing, and a slowing down our brainwaves from Beta to Alpha State.

There are many scientifically researched benefits of mindfulness. These include improved capacity to regulate emotions; improved quality of thinking and decision-making; reduced negative mindsets; enhanced empathy, intuition, inspiration, self-insight; a reduction in negative moods, depression, fatigue, confusion and heart rate; and an improved quality of life and sense of well-being.[21] (See resources below.)

---
20 Davis & Hayes, 2012.
21 Davis & Hayes, 2012.

Alpha waves (relaxed focused mode) are the door to the subconscious mind and to your body, and are one of the most effective ways to rewire and cultivate neural paths and intentions for success and well-being. Beta waves, on the other hand, when we are rushing, analysing and worrying about life, is rapid mental activity which can be productive (low beta). High beta waves or high alert, on the other hand, can result in fear-based over-thinking, ruminating over and over again about an incident or general anxiety. Alpha has been associated with the brain state when you are in "flow" or "in the zone", as with high performance athletes, artists or performers. It has also been shown to boost creativity and resilience to stress and reduce anxiety and depression. The NeuroClinic explains our brainwaves as follows[22]:

THE RANGE OF BRAINWAVES IN THE HUMAN BRAIN

INFRA-LOW FREQUENCY .0001 Hz	DELTA Less than 4 Hz	THETA 4-8 Hz	ALPHA 8-12 Hz	SMR 12-15 Hz	BETA 15-20 Hz	HIGH BETA More than 20 Hz
Core Calmness & Stability	Sleep	Creative State Drowsiness	Relaxed Focus Daydreaming	Body Calmness Mental Alertness	Active Thinking Problem Solving	Excited Irritability

Hertz=cycles per second

There are many techniques for slowing down your brain waves which you can get better and better at with practice:

- You can sit or lie quietly and slow your breathing, thoughts and brain activity down.

- You can use guided meditation or subliminal music aimed at eliciting the Alpha State.

- You can use the Hawaiian Hakalau technique which uses a focus and diffused focus with your eyes and awareness to attain alpha state.

- You can use meditation apps, such as Headspace or Calm.

- You can use technology with a device such as Muse for biofeedback on your brain state.

---

22 Neuroclinic, 2020.

- A fun way is staring into a moving Kaleidoscope image.

(See links in the resources section.)

Once you are in Alpha State you can use affirmations, visualisation or lucid dreaming to imagine a future you that has mastered the areas and goals you wish to achieve. Once the programme has been initiated, the rest runs on automatic.

4.3 Cultivating identities

Many of our beliefs, behaviours and habits combine to form our "identities" – our distinguishing characteristics. What comes to mind first when you describe a new boss or colleague? When you think of your family members, what characteristics make them memorable and unique? These are usually a combination of what we might associate with "positive" traits, e.g. friendly, outgoing and caring AND "negative" traits, e.g. uptight, aggressive and narrow-minded. When combined, a batch of traits or ways of being in the world can form an identity.

Two extreme examples on the opposite ends of a continuum could be the **self-saboteur** on one end and the **self-master** on the other. The self-saboteur is often unaware of their thinking, emotional state or impact on others; can struggle to control their emotions, words and actions; and tends to be reactive to triggers in their environment and easily distracted from their goals. The self-master on the other side of the spectrum is very aware of their thinking, emotional state and impact on others, and is disciplined in managing their emotions, words and actions. They generally choose the appropriate responses to people or triggers in their environment, which leads them closer to their goals or intentions.

If we take a familiar example of driving in chaotic traffic and running late, the self-saboteur might get frustrated, shout, swear and hoot at the other drivers. They might blame the other drivers, the weather or the government for causing traffic jams. Their heart rate goes up, cortisol floods their systems and they feel flustered and angry by the time they reach their destination, most often loudly proclaiming their difficult drive over and impacting others' mood. The self-master ,on the other hand, breathes deeply, listens to some calming music or an audiobook, smiles at other drivers or passers-by, and appreciates the time to think, listen or just be. They may make a call to let people know they could be late, but just with the key details without making a drama of it. They arrive at their destination, calm and collected, with suggestions for catching up the time if needed. There is an acceptance that life happens and whilst we do our best to be proactive and prepared, sometimes it doesn't work out that way, and that is ok. There is a general attitude of calm, a humble yet confident approach to life in the pursuit of own intentions, and a contribution to common purpose and goals.

Do you recognise some instances in your life where you have temporarily slipped into the self-saboteur or had the wisdom to choose self-mastery? We will be playing with various identities throughout this book, so that you can actively choose what works for you – most of the time.

4.4 Shifting beliefs

Many of our automatic brain programmes are founded on beliefs that we developed through experiences growing up. A belief is a strong opinion or conviction not necessarily based on facts or proof, e.g. a belief in the tooth fairy, a belief that we are "better than" some people, a belief in the rightness of only one religion or approach (leading to many conflicts and wars over centuries), or a belief that we are not worthy of love. We accept a belief as true until we are shown or experience otherwise. Some people take a long time to shift their beliefs even when confronted with overwhelming evidence, as demonstrated through various scientific discoveries over the years e.g. members of the flat earth society! We have beliefs about ourselves and others, money, health and the world around us, and it is these beliefs that drive our responses to events and stimuli at a subconscious level.

If we want to change our reality or learn something new, we need to identify and shift our beliefs to those that serve us and our goals the most. Here are some beliefs that you might have seen or heard before – from others or from your inner voice – that you may be able to relate to. Read through the beliefs below, and imagine how you might think, feel or act if you truly believed these statements.

• I can't help how I think, feel, act • I have no control – life just happens to me • I expect other people to make my life better • I have to fight for limited resources • Nothing I ever do is good enough • I am so afraid of failing	• I choose my thoughts, feelings, actions regardless of circumstances • I create my reality through the choices I make • I am the change I want to see in the world • There is always enough and we can grow abundance together • I am enough and doing my best every day • Failure is part of learning and life

The more regularly we rehearse empowering useful beliefs, mentally, in writing and out loud, the stronger the new neural paths will get. This weakens the hold of the old beliefs and old reactions to life. You will have many opportunities throughout this book to examine your beliefs sitting at a subconscious level and start the process of shifting and choosing them to enable your future fitness and skills.

4.5 Emotional coherence

For us to become masters of our choices and destiny, we need to become masters of our desires and emotions and practice emotional intelligence.

The HeartMath institute[23] has done ground-breaking research over many years and has established the importance of emotions in our ability to think clearly, remember, learn, reason, and make effective decisions. Our ability to sustain a positive, constructive and empowered emotional state or "heart coherence" also fundamentally improves our ability to connect with and listen to others, tune-in to our intuition and sustain healthy relationships over time. This could include being in a constant state of gratitude, confidence, compassion or openness to learning, and avoiding being pulled into a more negative emotional state through triggers around you that could create worry, frustration, sadness, etc.

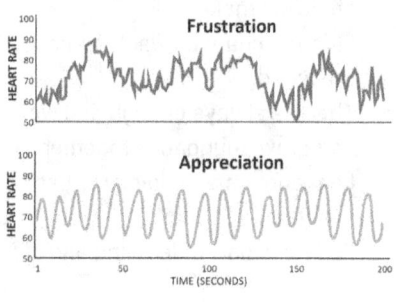

In general, emotional stress — including emotions such as anger, frustration, and anxiety — gives rise to heart rhythm patterns that appear irregular and erratic (or incoherent). Uplifting emotions such as appreciation, joy and love cause our heart rhythm pattern to become highly ordered, looking like a smooth, harmonious wave (coherent). (See diagram.) Physiologically, incoherence indicates that our sympathetic and parasympathetic nervous systems are out of sync with each other. This can be likened to driving a car with one foot on the gas pedal (the sympathetic nervous system) and the other on the brake (the parasympathetic nervous system) at the same time — this creates a jerky ride, burns more gas, and isn't great for your car, either! For our bodies, this means that stressful emotions can cause our body to operate inefficiently, deplete our energy, and

---
23 HeartMath, 2020.

produce extra wear and tear on our whole system. This is especially true if stress and negative emotions are prolonged or experienced often.

One of the simplest and most powerful ways to adjust our stress response, calm our brains and bodies down, and tap into our wisdom is the art of breathing fully and deeply. Most days, and particularly on more stressful or difficult days, we tend to breathe a fraction of our full breaths. Breathing affects our autonomic nervous system that carries out the vital functions of the heart, lungs, circulatory system, and glandular system without our conscious control. Deep slow breathing stimulates the relaxation response and automatically decreases heart rate, blood pressure, and skeletal muscle tone, and has been proven to increase organ and overall physical health, reduce anxiety and insomnia, and result in greater calmness, presence, and acceptance. There are many advanced breathing techniques that you can learn through breath, yoga or meditation schools. However, you can start immediately and safely by being conscious a few times a day and breathing deeply four to five times and notice the change. Extend the time and start using time in the car, watching TV, in meetings etc. to practice your breathing and increase your health and energy. (See resources below.)

4.6 Creating new habits

Another very useful approach is building new habits to replace less-effective ones. As discussed earlier, we now know that the brain is very effective at reducing effort and resources by creating automatic programmes or "habits". This allows it to direct energy toward repairing, creating, learning or managing life. We therefore rely on habits (which drive us to action without conscious thought or choice) to free up our limited amount of conscious attention and working memory. We receive and must respond to thousands of stimuli throughout the day, but our brains can only process a minute percentage of these. So, our brains delegate most of our responses to the subconscious using these pre-existing strategies or programmes.

Can you imagine trusting your executive personal assistant to deal with most of your correspondence, clients or urgent family matters while you are in meetings? The quality of the personal assistant and their alignment to your style and intentions will determine your satisfaction with the results. Would it not make sense to invest the time and energy in training your personal assistant (sub-conscious mind) in how you would like things to be done? Do you want him or her being deeply respectful to important clients or being rude and dismissive?

Charles Duhigg, in his book *"The Power of Habit"*[24], says a habit is a physical structure of neurons in your brain that can only be overridden by conscious willpower or a new, deeper habit. Habits can never be completely erased and are prone to relapse. The problem is that willpower is limited in both capacity and endurance (like a physical muscle). For example, we can only lift three times our maximum weight once or 60% of it for three hours. Willpower can be strengthened through patient practice (but only within limits). Eventually, and particularly in times of uncertainty, change or stress, we become overwhelmed and suffer a relapse in resolve.

This is so typical of a diet or exercise programme we attempt. It goes really well until we have a long, difficult day, get bad news or have a late night dealing with crazy friends or sick kids and then we just give in to old habits and grab that glass of wine, cigarette or chocolate and forego the planned gym session. Once we give into one craving, we most often lose our willpower and give in to them all. This is the habit cascade effect. The more we do this, the harder and harder it becomes to get back on the proverbial wagon.

> *"Habits are the choices that all of us deliberately make at some point, and then stop thinking about but continue doing, often every day".* –Charles Duhigg

Duhigg shows that habits consist of a cue, a response or routine, and a reward.

---

24 Duhigg, 2013.

- Cues are combinations of stimuli (sight, smell, taste, touch, sound, thought).
- Responses are chains of thoughts and/or actions.
- Rewards are increases/decreases in pleasant/unpleasant sensations, emotions or thoughts.

In our diet and exercise example, a typical old habit might look like the picture on the left, and a newly created positive habit could look like the picture on the right.

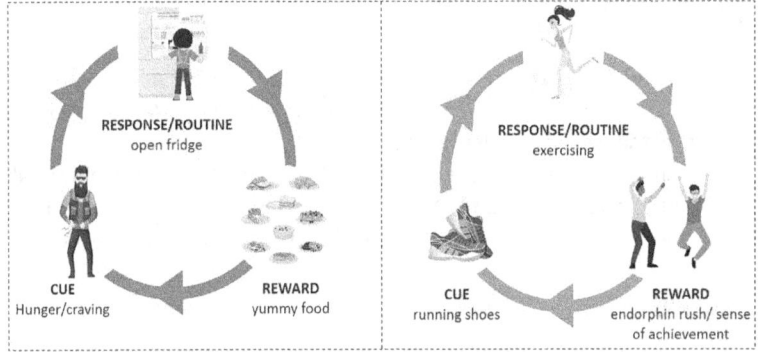

To change an old habit, we must address an old craving, keep the old cue and deliver the old reward, but then feed the craving by **inserting a new routine**... and then practice that new routine until it becomes a reliable and automatic habit. Repetition triggers long-term changes to the brain's structure. It changes as it learns. With time, the brain begins to expect and crave the reward as soon as the cue arises.

This works equally well with physical things we want to change AND with mental or emotional habits we wish to change, e.g. reacting to criticism, feeling insecure, being more courageous, trusting well-intentioned people, unleashing your creativity or becoming more curious. There will be many opportunities in this book to practice the habits to build the 8Cs so that we can be more **curious, creative, courageous, conscious, critical thinkers, collaborative, change navigators** and **contributors**.

"We are what we repeatedly do. Excellence, then, is not an act, but a habit." –Aristotle

5. TIPS, TOOLS AND RESOURCES

If you are interested in exploring and learning more, here are some of our favourite tips, tools and resources to accelerate your journey to knowing your brain and owning your CHOICES. (See https://catalystconsulting.co.za/power-up8-resources/).

Blogs

Proper Breathing Brings Better Health – Christophe André January 15, 2019: https://www.scientificamerican.com/article/proper-breathing-brings-better-health/

What are the benefits of mindfulness? – American Psychological Association, Daphne M. Davis, PhD, and Jeffrey A. Hayes, PhD, July/August 2012. https://www.apa.org/monitor/2012/07-08/ce-corner

Videos

Learn How To Control Your Mind: https://www.youtube.com/watch?v=v7KQsS2kLM4

Discover How to Rewire Your Brain with Neuroplasticity: https://www.youtube.com/watch?v=bbLP-as1ABk

Neuroplasticity – neurons connection – learning process: https://www.youtube.com/watch?v=xFKvX_LKV2I

After Watching This, Your Brain Will Not Be the Same by Lara Boyd: https://www.youtube.com/watch?v=LNHBMFCzznE

The Heart's Intuitive Intelligence – a path to personal, social and global coherence: https://www.heartmath.org/about-us/videos/the-hearts-intuitive-intelligence/

How Meditation Can Reshape Our Brains: Sara Lazar at TEDxCambridge 2011: https://www.youtube.com/watch?v=m8rRzTtP7Tc

What is the Alpha State and How do I reach it? https://www.youtube.com/watch?v=BwVviLgfwn0

Books

Breaking the habit of being yourself – Dr Joe Dispenza, 2013

Leading With Conscious Awareness: a narrative of personal insights, Dr Ian Weinberg, 2018

Mind to Matter – Dawson Church, 2018
Thrive – Ariana Huffington, 2015
The power of habit: Why we do what we do and how to change – Charles Duhigg, 2013

Tools

Calm – sleep and meditation app: https://www.calm.com/
Meditation tool – kaleidoscope – Get into Alpha State: https://www.youtube.com/watch?v=gA-KxnVQJwY

CURIOSITY

"The important thing is not to stop questioning... Never lose a holy curiosity." –Albert Einstein

1. CURIOSITY IS ACTUALLY A SECRET SUPER-POWER

Can you think of any famous inventor, innovator or high achiever who was not curious? No matter who comes to mind when you think of curiosity, whether someone in the recent press like Elon Musk, Jack Ma, Jeff Bizos or Richard Branson, or some icons of the past such as Steve Jobs, Thomas Edison, Leonardo da Vinci or Albert Einstein. They all have some common characteristics; they have an underlying curiosity about how things work, what is possible, how to solve a problem, or just a drive and desire to try something out of pure inquisitiveness and a sense of adventure. They also have an ability to engage and collaborate with a wide variety of people and ideas to stimulate ideas and options. They apply critical thinking to ask the right questions, as well as a bucket load of courage and creativity. They have a healthy sense of self and how to manage around their individual personality strengths and derailers. Curiosity is one of those foundation mindsets for many of the other critical capabilities necessary for succeeding in this crazy world of ours.

Many people will say that they are curious and will explore various aspects of their world with some sense of curiosity. I always believed that I was curious and interested in how the world worked. A lot of this came from my dad, who loved to take us travelling when we were young, and mom who was a Geography teacher and was always explaining the formation of mountains, clouds, oceans or river systems around us.

The day I realised that I was not as curious about others was during my first leadership assessment centre, where we had a group discussion to agree a way forward on a business dilemma. I was feeling pretty chuffed that I had got the group to agree, only to get feedback later that I had barged my way through it with little empathy or curiosity on what the others really thought or felt about the matter. This was a real wake-up call which got me reflecting deeply on empathy, and curiosity and why my focus seemed to be more on things than people or my inner world. I started searching for answers about personality and behaviour and how to achieve tasks WITH other people rather than have my own view of how things should be. It has also led to a love of wondering why, asking questions and learning. This enables me to keep options open, listen for a bit longer, and get a few more diverse ideas before making important decisions. Many years later I am so glad I received that lesson (although a bitter pill to swallow at the time) to remind me to tap into my empathy and curiosity.

> *What are you curious about? Where are your potential blind spots? How can you learn from curious inventors, artists and entrepreneurs that have shown us what is possible? In which circumstances, or about which topics, are you less curious or less willing to learn new things?*

Academy award-winning producer and best-selling author of "A Curious Mind", Brian Grazer, says: "There are many kinds of curiosity. Curiosity comes in a whole variety of qualities and wavelengths, flavours and intensities." He believes that it is his regular curiosity conversations with people from all walks of life

– from presidents to FBI agents, from supermodels to sports stars or young entrepreneurs – that have inspired him to create some of the world's most iconic movies and television shows, such as Splash, Apollo 13, A Beautiful Mind and Frost/Nixon, which have been nominated for 43 Academy Awards and 187 Emmys. He states that it is not just the curiosity of novelty, trying new things or learning a new subject, but different kinds of curiosity that can fundamentally change your experience of life. "Curiosity is actually a secret super-power that all of us can cultivate."[1]

Our definition of curiosity is as follows:

> Curiosity requires going beyond the obvious and actively seeking new information and ideas – not just about the world or things but about people, relationships and our own potential. It is about questioning, experimenting and taking risks for accelerated learning and innovation.

2. DID CURIOSITY KILL THE CAT?

Curiosity is particularly important in our exponentially changing world, which requires high speed innovation, accelerated learning, rapid relationship building and an open and resilient mind to stay ahead, survive and thrive. A mindset of curiosity enables original ideas, unique questions, rapid learning and connecting with people to unleash our own and other's potential.

Francesca Gino, in her Harvard Business Review article, "The Business Case for Curiosity", outlines research that shows how curiosity is vital to an organisation's performance. Her findings show that we make **fewer decision-making errors** by avoiding confirmation bias (looking for information that supports our beliefs rather than for evidence suggesting we are wrong) and stereotyping people (making broad judgements, such as that women or other minorities don't make good leaders). Curiosity has these positive effects because it leads us to generate

---
1   Grazer & Fishman, 2015.

alternatives. A curious mind also results in more ideas, greater work improvements and expanded creative solutions to problems or customer concerns. She shares an INSEAD study by Spencer Harrison, which demonstrating that a 1-point increase in curiosity on a 7-point scale was associated with 34% greater productivity. This can be applied even in call centres where jobs tend to be highly structured. Curious people also tend to be more resilient in that they view tough situations more creatively and are less defensive or aggressive under stress. Finally, we tend to perform better individually and in groups when we are curious. A higher level of curiosity results in reduced group conflict as people are able to put themselves in one another's shoes (empathy) and take an interest in one another's ideas rather than focus only on their own perspective (my own lesson again!). This results in more open communication, more sharing of information, better listening and overall better team performance.[2]

Despite these proven benefits and so many amazing examples, there are still many barriers to curiosity at both an individual and an organisational level. In these lean and economically uncertain times, we are often challenged with tough short-term goals, leaving us little free time to research and explore alternative approaches to work, learn new skills and stay relevant. Some leaders are worried that curiosity and experimentation will lead to a costly and hard to manage mess, and so they slow down decision-making. Many organisations have rigid, hierarchical structures, which do not support curiosity with quick decision-making. Others seek efficiency to the detriment of exploring new ideas, and so put the brakes on innovation. There are leaders who are threatened by smart questions from people younger or more junior than them, and so tend to avoid engaging with them. Many individuals are just as afraid of making a fool of themselves by asking "stupid" questions or exploring a different way of engaging with customers, communicating with their teams or processing workflow. They are stuck in the 'curiosity killed the cat' mode.

---

[2] Gino, 2018.

Our curiosity usually declines the longer we're in a job as we start to run on automatic pilot and assumptions more and more often. If we do not actively focus on a mindset that creates space for curiosity and agile learning and exploring, it is unlikely we will prioritise this on a daily basis, leaving us and our businesses stale, unskilled or irrelevant for the evolving world of work. Maybe a **lack of curiosity** killed the proverbial cat is closer to the truth!

3. HOW CURIOUS ARE WE?

Curiosity is primarily a mindset and an identity driven by underlying beliefs and views about ourselves and the world. We can build skills to enhance our curiosity and practice these with effort and planning, however the more efficient route to a natural effortless curiosity is to shake up and shift some of the programmes we learnt through our role models, experiences or personality styles as we grew up.

Remember when you were a child, or if you have children, you will have to agree that they are naturally curious. They start exploring the world around them from the moment they open their eyes in the morning. They touch, they feel, and they want to taste everything. They are **curious explorers**. This behaviour changes as they learn through trial and error what to do and not to do, what hurts or keeps them safe. They form beliefs about their world, and many of them lose their instinctive curiosity over time and learn how to manage their natural fascination with the world in a more structured, controlled and cautious manner. They can become more of a **safe spectator**, letting others take the risks that curiosity can bring.

We are seldom either curious or not curious, but rather move up and down a continuum depending on our personal attitudes and life circumstances. We have created some interesting characters to illustrate the two opposites of curiosity so that you can explore which character you can identify with, and where you tend to spend most of your time, or if you are somewhere in the middle. You can choose some characteristics you would like to adopt to help you navigate the future.

Welcome to the **safe spectator** and the **curious explorer**.

Safe spectator	Curious explorer
Spectator	Seeker
Opinionated	Engager
Cautious	Experimenter

Curious explorers are seekers, engagers and experimenters

Curious explorers are **seekers** of knowledge and understanding of themselves, the world and others. They are inquisitive, open, life-long learners who strive for building their skills to adapt, be ready for change and be relevant in the ever-evolving world. They read, research and explore widely on topics of interest and ask many questions both inwardly and outwardly to find answers to the not yet known or understood. They are willing to question everything they read or experience, digging deeper into what is below the surface.

Seekers are curious about themselves and what makes them tick. They investigate and assess their personality preferences, strengths, talents, fears, weaknesses and blind spots. They actively seek feedback and compare their versions of themselves with other's perceptions to ensure they don't fall into the delusion trap of self-importance or irritate others with their lack of self-awareness. They have what Carol Dweck calls a "growth mindset" and believe that their basic abilities can be developed through dedication and hard work, i.e. they don't just think that they are born "smart" or "dumb" with no choice in the matter.[3]

---

3   Dweck, 2016.

Curious explorers actively engage with diverse people and different perspectives on how people think and see the world so that they have a well-rounded view on life. They are intensely curious about their current and potential audiences, stakeholders or customers. They are open-minded and avoid hard wired labels or stereotypes when interacting with different people. They are curious about other's feelings, and life experiences and can truly listen without judgement and filters. They have the capacity to hold space for other's emotions, even when hard to hear without becoming defensive or aggressive in return. Too often, we get "comfortable" in a close relationship; we may switch off our emotional curiosity and assume we already know how our spouse/friend/child thinks and feels.

> *"Familiarity is the enemy of curiosity. And when our curiosity about those closest to us fades, that's the moment when our connection begins to fray. It frays silently, almost invisibly. But when we stop asking genuine questions of those around us—and most important, when we stop really listening to the answers—that's when we start to lose our connection."* –Brian Grazer[4]

Finally, they are experimenters who love to figure things out and test new and different ways of doing things to see what or how something works. They are not afraid to explore unchartered territory or be perceived as slightly weird or crazy to breakthrough old ways of doing things. Experimenters make it their mission to become comfortable with uncertainty and ambiguity, and are not afraid to fail and get feedback. They trust in their own resourcefulness to navigate any challenges and see failure as an opportunity to learn and try again. They know that life is full of ups and downs, and that venturing into the unknown can be daunting and result in some bumps and bruises but also some exhilarating and breath-taking moments. They like to meet new people, taste new foods and travel to new destinations. They often have a strong connection with **trust in life itself** and can stay calm and curious when things get crazy.

---

4   Grazer & Fishman, 2015.

They **believe** that curiosity helps them grow, that trying and failing fast is better than not trying at all, and that learning is critical to adapt to change. They generally **feel** excited, enthusiastic and open to new ideas, topics, people and opportunities.

They use **language** like, "I wonder if ...", "I am curious about ....", or "Let's try ...."

They have daily **habits** like reading, viewing, reflecting, questioning, trying something new, practicing, connecting with different people, and creating (new) meaning through their habits.

> ### William Kamkwamba: The boy who harnessed the wind
>
> A fabulous example of an amazingly curious young man, in circumstances that we can only imagine, is William Kamkwamba, known as The Boy Who Harnessed The Wind. Despite his desperate situation of poverty, drought and lack in Malawi, William, at the age of 14, taught himself how to build an electricity generating windmill with a library book and scrap metal, to have light to study and power to charge village cell phones, giving hope to and changing the lives of many in his village. The windmill became an icon for curiosity, creativity and resilience in the face of adversity, not just in Malawi, but throughout the world as William's story became famous through TED Talks, a book and then a movie in 2019. William has since gone on to achieve an international Engineering degree through scholarships and his own hard work, curious mind and dedication to a result.[5]
>
> Watch the movie, "The boy who harnessed the wind" or see additional links in our resource section below.

Safe spectators are opiniated, cautious spectators

On the opposite side of the continuum are the safe spectators who tend to sit on the side-lines, in the stands or in their easy chairs,

---

5   The Boy Who Harnessed the Wind, 2019.

taking no risks and commenting about the game from their place of safety.

Spectators prefer to stay with their certain, tried and tested view of the world and live in their own bubble of what they have been exposed to without questioning too much. They avoid involvement and tend to be less interested in the world beyond their immediate surroundings, job or social group. They are, however, quick to criticise others or people who are different from them (including opposing sports teams, different work functions, different cultures or locations). In turn they end up being highly critical of themselves.

They can be seen to be **opiniated** if they don't engage actively in exploring the merits of other views. They often have a fixed mindset and avoid learning or trying something new for fear of getting it wrong and then beating themselves up. With limited new inputs and learning they can be in danger of being out of touch with the evolving world, new skills and younger generations. Due to their strong views and sensitivity to criticism, they can get defensive when challenged.

Spectators often believe that the world doesn't tolerate too many questions or new ways or different behaviours, and so limit their exposure to new things. They are overly **cautious**, possibly due to having been severely criticised, socially excluded or rejected in the past. They prefer the path of least resistance and avoid taking action or making decisions in times of uncertainty or ambiguity for fear of getting it wrong and being exposed. External criticism (even if just perceived) can feel devastating. For this reason, they will be extra careful to minimise risks (to their person, their sense of self, their social status or their livelihood) and may take a long time to be convinced that risky change can be positive.

Overall, these **safe spectators believe** that curiosity is risky, requires too much effort and is unnecessary. After all, it's all been tried before. They generally **feel** cautious, all knowing or detached.

They use **language** like "I know what I know", "Curiosity killed the cat", "Why rock the boat?" or "Why fix it if it isn't broken?".

They have daily **habits** like being critical, procrastinating and staying safe from the side-lines.

Being a safe spectator may keep you out of the firing line or give you time to rest and recharge, but it can also keep you isolated with a narrow view of what is possible. This can mean losing relevance in the rapidly shifting world around you. It is important to find your own unique balance and timing. Are there some of the curious explorer characteristics that you can acknowledge in yourself or some that you can embrace more? Are there some characteristics of the safe spectator that you recognise in yourself that you would like to evolve or spend less time in? Take the opportunity to become aware of your strengths and possible blind-spots or derailers and where you would like to play – now and in the future. Sometimes it is easier to identify these in a colleague or one of your current or past managers, teachers or sports coaches. Where have others been labelled as the cynical blocker or resistor to new ideas or change? Have you noticed where someone always needs special attention in a change project and feels threatened by outside views and possibilities? Who often delays progress because they are overly cautious or stuck in their ways? It's always good to check that it isn't you!

4. WHAT HAVE MY BELIEFS GOT TO DO WITH IT?

Growth and change start with how you think and what you believe. It then develops further with the daily practice of habits, skills or tools that build your curious explorer muscle. It is reinforced when we see the fruits of our new beliefs, behaviours and choices. We learnt in Chapter 3 that many of our daily routines run on automatic pilot and leave us complacent and comfortable. How often do you change your morning routine or your conversations with your family or co-workers? How many times do you take a different route to or from work?

If we **think** (believe) it is not safe to explore, we will **feel** anxious and **react** with caution to the new or uncertain, and avoid taking **action,** resulting in things staying the same.

If we want to become more curious, we need to disrupt our routines of thinking and doing and experiment with some different beliefs. Have a look at what beliefs might be sitting in your sub-conscious mind that may be determining how you see yourself and the world. Balance being overly critical with noticing some realised strengths. See this as an exercise in curious awareness giving you the power to choose useful beliefs to set you up for success. This list is just an indication of beliefs. Please feel free to add your own.

Safe spectator beliefs	Curious explorer beliefs
• Why fix it if it isn't broken? • It's all been tried before • Don't rock the boat • I am who I am – I know what I like • I know best – it's worked for me before	• Let's keep on improving • Let's explore what else could work • Challenge the status quo • I am open to learning and evolving • More heads are better than one

Lumka Msibi – young South African rocket scientist

I had the privilege of listening to the story of an amazing young South African who is another role model for her beliefs and actions as a curious explorer – not just of this world but of the universe beyond. Lumka Msibi, originally from Soweto, Johannesburg, has imagined, strived, studied and worked her way to become an award-winning rocket scientist and Senior Aerospace Systems Engineer with an international qualification and over five years of global experience in

AeroSpace, including a stint in Antarctica and a position at NASA in the USA. At the age of 24 she had travelled to six continents, won numerous prestigious awards and spoken alongside many notable leaders. At 28, she is the youngest board member appointed to a government entity, the South African National Space Agency (SANSA), and is credited with providing a unique perspective to the board alongside her knowledge and expertise in engineering, strategy, innovation and technology. She shares her story to build the belief that you can achieve your dream with the right attitude and actions, which has led her to be a wonderful role model to young people in South Africa and all over the world. She says her success has been based on her intense curiosity for how and why things work the way they do, a belief in her ability to achieve what she sets out to, and a determination to find the path to her destiny, no matter what it takes. We can only imagine what her inner world of beliefs, self-talk and emotional resilience is like, but I can imagine it is built on some very strong beliefs about questioning, exploring, experimenting, learning and always being curious.[6]

5. DAILY HACKS AND HABITS FOR CURIOSITY

There are so many hacks and habits that we can explore to build our curiosity muscle. Sometimes we can start with shifting our beliefs, and sometimes we can start with taking action, which in turn helps us create the new beliefs. Working on both will help you accelerate your learning. Here are some of my favourites. There are many more ideas and links in the resources sections if you wish to explore more.

5.1 Habit #1: Quick questions

Build your repertoire of quick questions to ask before taking action:

---

[6] Space in Africa, 2019.

For self:	For others:	For work:
• How curious was I today? • What did I do differently? • Did I ask enough questions today? • How did others experience me today? • What did I learn today? • What assumptions or biases do I need to challenge? • Did I get some input or feedback today?	• How does this impact others? • Have we considered or included everyone impacted? • Who else should be involved? • Have we communicated clearly? • What is going on for them? • What is not being said?	• How else could we do this? • Is there a better way? • Have we got all the information we could get? • Who else could add a perspective or input? • I wonder how ABC would approach this? • What can we learn from past projects or people?

Tip: Sometimes our thinking and personality preferences can influence our curiosity. Some of us instinctively ask more questions, explore or act quickly. Others may naturally take time to consider, reflect and be cautious to minimise risk. Explore your own thinking and personality preferences and practice leaning into the areas you are least comfortable with to expand your options (e.g. Insights, Enneagram, Myers Briggs, Herman Brain Dominance). Learn to balance questioning, exploring and learning with taking action.

5.2 Habit #2: Down the rabbit hole

Expand your curiosity through daily trips down the rabbit hole. As you are reading or viewing an article, YouTube video or post, allow a bit of time to explore beyond what you see in front of you. Validate stories or facts, click through to other recommended sources and ask Google, Siri, Alexa or Quora for answers to questions you have on your mind. Start a conversation with an interesting colleague about their thoughts on a topic, new trend or gadget. Reach out to new contacts to network and share. Subscribe to newsfeeds or forums from diverse sources to expand what you take in. Look up interesting facts about movies, people or companies you are about to engage with. Play Trivial Pursuit or online quiz games to expand your general knowledge.

> **Tip:** Allocate specific time to this so that you don't completely forget about time and miss other important priorities (the Rabbit Hole effect).

5.3 Habit #3: Fail fast

Get used to small experiments, getting it only half right or getting it terribly wrong. Use every opportunity to get feedback and input and see it as progress and try it again differently next time. I am on a continuous (and totally hilarious) learning journey as I have tried to master the basics of yoga. Years of sport can never prepare you for feeling like a spastic pretzel as you stretch and strengthen your body in new ways. You could learn to do public speaking, or practice speaking a new language. Speak up at a meeting, write a blog. Make a decision and take a step in uncertainty or ambiguity. Engage your audience in your experiment. Ask them if they mind being guinea pigs for something new. They love being first, seeing new things, and respect curiosity and courage.

> **Tip:** Learn to laugh at yourself and see all outcomes as learning opportunities.

5.4 Habit #4: Listen beyond the obvious

Engage in conversation with diverse people. Strike up conversations in the lift, at a coffee bar, over lunch, in waiting areas, with conference attendees or with people in service roles (shop keepers, waiters, receptionists, car guards) by commenting on something interesting or asking them about themselves. When travelling, stay with local people, have a meal with them, find out about their lives. Get yourself invited to quick ideation or feedback meetings of another team or department. Show interest and ask questions that link your area of interest with theirs. Check assumptions and biases of your natural filters. Get into dialogue about the country or the world with young people. We are often surprised by conversations with our own children on their views on country, politics, fashion, emigration, careers etc. Say yes to conversations with connections (friends of friends, social media, etc.) that make business sense. Dig a bit deeper in personal relationships. Show some genuine interest with some curious questions such as how did that feel, tell me more, what else are you thinking/feeling, what is really going on for you?

Tip: Avoid the temptation to pre-judge a situation or imagine being ignored, rejected or thought of as being over-friendly. Avoid projecting your own relating style onto others. Many life-long friendships, a marriage and business relationships have started this way for me. My motto is a "no rejection policy". Give others the opportunity to say no thanks, instead of wondering if!

5.5 Habit #5: Make time to learn

Many of us want to learn new things, but don't make the time. Make it a priority to learn something new every day. Book time in your diary or wake up a bit earlier. Complete that online course, read that book or use that new digital tool. Join a forum, attend a webinar or learn a new language before an exciting trip (Duolingo is a cool tool). Find a coach or mentor. A buddy system or learning circle for collaborative learning is great for motivation and accountability. My consulting company, Catalyst, has experimented with a variety of learning circles and innovation days. We invite our clients and specialist network to events to share topics of interest to deepen our knowledge and capability. Start Learning or Problem-Solving

Fridays at work to discuss a topic of interest or tackle a hairy problem and learn from each other. Many innovative companies such as Google or Atlassian allow 10-20% of an employee's time to work on a pet project, as long as they can justify a proposed benefit to the company.

Tip: Organise your learning into topics so that you can find them again. Create mind maps and summaries to capture the key take-aways, so that you can embed the learning in your memory for future recall.

5.6 Habit #6: Do it differently

There is nothing better to take you out of your comfort zone than doing something differently and getting off auto pilot mode. Take a different route to work or to the gym or to a friend's house – don't always just follow your navigation app (unless you are on a deadline). Try a different place for a social get together, a weekend or holiday. Sit with someone different at a meeting, lunch or workshop/conference. Try new food choices. Use your non-dominant hand to do something. When I travel, I love wandering and even getting lost, often meeting up with people or finding places I would not usually encounter if I just followed the guidebooks. At work, go the extra mile to find out more and bring something more back to the team. At home, vary your routines and conversations to see what happens.

> *"Curiosity is hard-wired in the brain, and its specific function is to urge us to explore, discover, and grow. It is the engine of our evolving self. Without curiosity, we are unable to sustain our attention, we avoid risk, we abort challenging tasks, we compromise our intellectual development, we fail to achieve competencies and strengths, we limit our ability to form relationships with other people, and essentially stagnate."* –Todd Kashdan

6. TIPS, TOOLS AND RESOURCES

If you are interested in exploring and learning more, here are some of our favourite tips, tools and resources to accelerate your journey to becoming a curious explorer. (See https://catalystconsulting.co.za/power-up8-resources/).

Articles/Blogs

6 kinds of curiosity by Brian Glazer: https://www.porchlightbooks.com/blog/changethis/2015/six-kinds-of-curiosity-and-how-you-can-use-them-to-change-your-life

Lumka Msibi story: https://africanews.space/sansa-8-meet-28-year-old-lumka-msibi-who-sits-on-sansa-board/

Books

Mindset: The New Psychology of Success, 2016; Carol S. Dweck

Richard Branson – Losing My Virginity or Screw It, Let's Do It – Lessons In Life

Elon Musk – How the Billionaire CEO of SpaceX and Tesla is Shaping our Future

Videos

Jack Ma – Jack Ma's Ultimate Advice for Students & Young People – HOW TO SUCCEED IN LIFE: https://www.youtube.com/watch?v=bXGhtjezJPY

Moving Windmills: The William Kamkwamba story: https://www.youtube.com/watch?v=arD374MFk4w

The Movie: Boy who harnessed the wind: https://www.netflix.com/title/80200047?s=a&trkid=1374225&t=cp

The first 20 hours – how to learn anything | Josh Kaufman | TEDxCSU: https://www.youtube.com/watch?v=5MgBikgcWnY

The Curious Person's Guide to Learning Anything | Stephen Robinson | TEDxUAlberta: https://www.youtube.com/watch?v=VoecD4my4_4

Tools

Britannica curiosity compass assessment https://curiosity.britannica.com/

For some questions that will expand your curiosity and potentially change your life: https://www.forbes.com/sites/jasonnazar/2013/09/05/35-questions-that-will-change-your-life/#244607345660

Insightful card pack of questions that assist individuals and teams to have meaningful discussions: http://www.3stickmen.com/product/discussion-cards/

CHAPTER 5: CREATIVITY

"Creativity is putting your imagination to work, and it has produced the most extraordinary results in human culture."
—Sir Ken Robinson

1. CREATIVITY IS NOT A COMPETITIVE SPORT

"Robots may help us get to where we want to be faster, but they cannot be as creative as humans (yet)". —Alex Gary, World Economic Forum[1]

The exponential rate of technological evolution is reshaping economies, merging industries, fusing technologies and reinventing the customer and employee experience.

Creativity is trending at #3 in the World Economic Forum report on future skills (up from #5 in 2018).[2] A computer or robot lacks the imagination or creativity to dream up, connect or co-create a vision for the future that it has not yet been programmed to think of. It also lacks the empathy, compassion, and collaborative ability of humans.

---

[1] Gary, 2016.
[2] World Economic Forum, 2018.

Most organisations today are facing major disruption requiring serious overhauls of their strategies, operating models, technology, processes and customer interfaces. Leaders, employees and suppliers are reeling from the sudden and drastic changes happening without much notice or consultation. Paul Hobcraft in the Innovation Blog says, "Innovation has become increasingly complex, connected, and contextual".[3]

Organisations need people who can not only think out of the box, but break boxes, build new boxes, travel between boxes and invent new shapes (not boxes) if they want stay ahead of the change curve or at least ahead of their competitors. We need people who can imagine a possible future, overcome constraints, identify potential and bring diverse ideas and people together to create something of value.

Most of the unicorn companies (privately owned businesses valued at over $1 billion) started with a customer need, a creative idea and an emerging technology (as outlined in Chapter 1). Original ideas typically develop through collaborative design, visionary funding, a fierce passion and commitment to long hours and early failures from its founding members and early team.

THINK OUTSIDE THE BOX

Established brands with an innovative flair such as Apple, Tesla, Alibaba and Amazon started the same way, but have continued to grow and innovate through their ability to harness the creative energy and ideas of their workforce AND expand the idea search through crowdsourcing and collaborative partnering. Amazon Studios uses crowdsourcing to find original stories and feedback from their customers. Waze allows users to share driving conditions to work out best possible routes. "The Samsung Strategy and Innovation Center" is world's largest crowdsourcing

---

3   Hobcraft, 2018.
4   Basinski, (n.d.).

service to connect start-ups, technology and AI professionals to develop new products.[5]

Creativity is no longer an individual competitive sport. It is essentially the ability to bring diverse ideas, people and possible solutions together and test them in a fast and efficient way. Creative thinking is needed in designing, marketing and delivering new products or services, in unique and differentiated ways. In addition, strong project management and organisational skills are needed to take creative ideas to market (our conscious and critical thinking skills). We also need to combine creativity with the ability to influence others to join a cause, a team or a purpose – our change navigator role.

2. MOST ADULTS HAVE ONLY 2% CREATIVITY LEFT

George Land – Creativity Test Results

98% (5 years old)
30% (10 years old)
12% (15 years old)
2% (280,000 adults)

For most of us, creativity has been educated out of us. George Land developed a creativity test which was used to select the most innovative engineers and scientists to work for NASA. The assessment was successful, so he decided to try it on children. "What we have concluded," wrote Land, "is that non-creative behaviour is learned." Land's longitudinal research study tested the creativity of 1,600 children at 3, 5, 10 and 15 years of age and found a drastic decrease in creativity through the years. The difference between 10 and 15 years old is 18%. The same test in 280,000 adults found a dismal 2% creativity left in them.[6] This is well explained in Sir Ken Robinson's popular TED Talk, "How schools kill creativity". He states that many "problem" children with likely learning, focus or behavioural difficulties have many other talents, that if encouraged and nurtured would lead to

---
5   Lets Techknow, 2019.
6   Land, 2015.

amazing creative genius being released into the world. Unfortunately, many of these outliers get belittled, side-lined, or controlled into conforming to the majority and mainstream school "rules" and lose their creative edge.[7]

Most adults end up not even using the "small amount of creativity" left in them, due to fear, risk avoidance or just a general lack of motivation, time and energy dealing with day-to-day realities and crises. Our safe spectator can keep us protected from the risk of creative expression. In addition, social structures and organizational barriers drain adults' creative inspiration and creative power.

I remember signing up for a 3-day programme called: "Disappear into the Painting"[8] at a meditation centre in India many years ago. I did this intentionally as I had never really seen myself as "artistic" and thought it might stimulate some openness to this neglected area in my life. I imagined learning how to paint a pretty picture. What I discovered in the 3-day immersion was a part of myself that had been locked away in a little box from school days when I was encouraged to be neat, use the materials given and colour within the lines, impress the teacher (or in this case my mother who was also my teacher) and finish on time. This programme created an environment of expression, with plastic covering over the floor and walls, old painting smocks and a range of artistic materials, music, nature and activities to stimulate creativity. We were encouraged to paint, splash, smear, use our hands, collaborate, sing, paint over, paint with a blindfold and change our paintings many times over. Over the three days I was able to let go of my very controlled "definition" of painting or art and access my

---

7 Robinson, 2007.
8 OSHO International Meditation Resort, 2013.

soul's colours and energy into a totally unexpected result – which still hangs in my house today. The process to get to this result was enormously empowering (after numerous moments of frustration and tears) and stays with me today when I get "stuck" and need to find a way out in any area of my life – work, relationships, and financially.

Sir Ken Robinson says that creativity is not just about the arts. He says, "you can be creative in anything – technology, math, anything. Creativity is the process of having original ideas that have value."[9] All original ideas have to be subjected to some sort of a process and critical judgment, whether crafting a poem or plotting a business plan or developing a scientific experiment. If we can learn how to unleash more of our natural creativity AND understand the conditions and process to make it come alive, we can make ideas into something valuable to others.

> "You can't just give someone a creativity injection. You have to create an environment for curiosity and a way to encourage people and get the best out of them." –Sir Ken Robinson

3. CREATIVITY CAN BE LEARNT

The good news is creativity is not just for the artists, painters, musicians or poets, but for anyone who wishes to solve complex problems, invent original things and create something new for the improvement of our society. Creativity is a skill that everyone can learn, re-learn and improve on. However, it cannot be learned through a course or reading a book, but by investing in new habits, thought processes and beliefs – to create a creative way of life or culture. It requires people who are willing to be a bit unorthodox, different and rebellious, and those who are willing to listen and embrace different thinking in order to bring a fresh perspective to ways of work. It requires colourful thinking, reimagining problems, breaking through imaginary boundaries, stereotypes or "rules", connecting

---

9   Strauss, 2015.

the unlikely dots, and seeing new patterns. It requires challenging the obvious, discarding the irrelevant, anticipating scenarios, an openness to being wrong and a passion for seeking to understand – a product, a market, a customer, a function, a skill, a perceived value. Creativity is also about acting a bit insane and persisting despite seeming dead ends. Creativity, ultimately, is an attitude.

Elizabeth Gilbert, author of "Eat, Pray, Love", says in her TedTalk, "Your elusive creative genius", that the second hardest thing for a creative person is staying with the process, especially when you are not feeling inspired.[10] The hardest thing is believing that you have what it takes to be creative again, especially after a big success (and after a big failure!). This is all about attitude. Writing this book has been a creativity attitude challenge, especially being thrown the curve ball of COVID-19 right in the middle. Finding my authentic voice and stories and overcoming self-doubt of my unique value has been a life-long journey. I had to just dive in and do it, allow my own special creativity to emerge, and learn through the experience!

Our **definition of creativity** is as follows:

> Creativity is about harnessing our own and others' unique ideas and beyond ordinary thinking to create collaborative and innovative approaches and solutions to risks, dilemmas, and opportunities that new technology, business models and global challenges bring.

There are many ways to use creativity at work and at home:

- Design packaging for a product, a logo, or a new look for your business.
- Brainstorm ways to cut energy use, improve quality or cut costs.
- Find new ways to engage and communicate with your clients online.

---
10 Gilbert, 2009.

- Design a more efficient assembly line robot or computer programme for automation.
- Develop a social media platform for a cell phone.
- Write a book or a blog.
- Create a YouTube Channel or Instagram Page.
- Figure out a complex issue with your child or your health.
- Resolve a conflict with a friend, colleague or loved one.
- Find smart ways to do more with less – less time, money, equipment or people.

Times of crisis seem to accelerate the rate of innovation and creativity as people are forced to reimagine how to do business when business-as-usual is disrupted.

A little while ago, in our consulting business, a number of long-term client projects had come to an end and we were struggling to secure new contracts at a time when our country's economy, politics and legislation was making it particularly difficult to do business. We were contacting our database, sending proposals out and getting interest, but nothing was being signed and our cash reserves were running low. Everyone seemed to be waiting... for elections, budgets, quick fixes or a bit more economic certainty. We kept asking the question... how could we let our clients (and their friends) know more about our creative, innovative and engaging people strategies and solutions in a more personal and tangible way? We decided to take a risk and invite our top clients to a day of exploration into our offerings, case studies, games and immersions at our offices. To our surprise, we received many bookings, had an overflowing house and received many positive comments about learning and networking. And so, our Innovation Day was born... leading to a number of new relationships and contracts in the next few months.

4. AN ATTITUDE OF CREATIVITY

Many supremely creative innovators have been ridiculed for their ideas by their peers. Thomas Edison was ridiculed in his quest to make an electric light bulb. The Apple Newton was a spectacular flop, until it evolved into the iPad. The Amazon Fire smartphone failed, as did Amazon Destinations travel service. Amazon CEO Jeff Bezos, now one of the wealthiest people on any continent, says multibillion-dollar failures are actually a good thing: "If the size of your failures isn't growing, you're not going to be inventing at a size that can actually move the needle".[11] Before these products or services changed the world, people asked, "Why would we ever want that?!" Today, we can't imagine living without them – the iPhone, Post-it notes, Google, Siri, Waze, Instagram, Spotify, UberEats, and many more.

All of us have probably, at some stage, experienced some level of ridicule, criticism or pain associated with our unique creative attempts – leading to the sad reduction in our natural creative thinking to some 2% of our potential. So how do we bring back the spontaneous and original creativity of our pre- five-year-old selves? What underlying beliefs and views about ourselves and the world could nurture more creativity? What habits can we cultivate to build new neural pathways to enhance our capacity and courage to think and express ourselves creatively? What identities could we adopt to face potential criticism or failure with grace and learning and continue with a different approach or the next idea? Let's explore some answers to these questions.

Have a look at the two opposite ends of the continuum below. Where might you be spending most of your time, more as a cautious dreamer, or more time as a possibility connector? Under which circumstances do you slip further to the left? What encouragement do you need to create more possibilities at home or at work? Sometimes it is easier to notice friends, colleagues,

---

11 Gilbert, 2019.

or family members (or politicians, bosses or movie characters) on the continuum than ourselves. If you are prepared to step out of your comfort zone, show these definitions to a good friend and get some feedback so that you know where to focus your attention.

Cautious dreamer	Possibility connector
Follower	Ideator
Pretender	Authentic
Dreamer	Connector

Possibility Connectors are Ideators and Authentic Connectors

You can often spot a possibility connector by their original and sometimes off-the-wall ideas and adventures. If given the freedom to express themselves and their ideas, possibility connectors will be **ideators** and the source of many new ideas and options in a team. Sometimes they talk differently, dress differently and even behave differently to the norm. To a cautious dreamer, some of these ideas may seem intangible, impractical and down-right silly. However, this is part of the creative process that allows **the imagination** to free-wheel unrestrained, so that one awesome idea can emerge. Being in an inclusive environment that embraces **authenticity** and constructive differences is critical for creatives to shine. It is also important for them to explore ideas through initiatives or experiments to test their merit without getting shut down too soon. Lastly, possibility connectors are **connectors** of ideas to create new value. They keep an eye on trends and seem to have an uncanny ability to know what or where is hot or happening. They don't only talk about their ideas, adventures and dreams, but they actively seek to implement and create value out of them. Where a cautious dreamer may come up with more and more dreams and ideas, the possibility connector will turn those ideas into activities, products or experiences that others can benefit from.

They **believe** in the power of imagination, ideas and exploring possibilities to solve problems and unleash potential. They believe in the value of diversity and embracing differences. They believe in keeping options open and testing them until the best one emerges for real value.

They **feel** excited about new challenges and confident in their ability to come up with a solution. They can also feel playful and young at heart to tap into their creative genius. They may also feel proud of what they have contributed to a situation or team.

They use **language** like, "Let's try something different", "It's ok if we fail", "How else can we view this?", "There must be another way" and "Who or what else can we get ideas from?"

They have daily **habits** like keeping a creative journal or dream diary, viewing trend tracking forums or influencers, taking time to reflect and imagine, mind-mapping ideas or drawing pictures, starting Pinterest boards for new projects, and sharing their ideas with others.

Turning art into creative learning

A colleague of mine, Lita Currie, left the corporate world a few years ago and was trying to figure out how she was going to earn an income, do what she is passionate about and be able to spend time with her children. She had a background in training, she loved drawing and art, and loved to simplify things so that people would remember. She started offering her service as a visual artist at workshops and conferences to capture key messages and images that people could take back to the office or take photos for their personal records. She spent time after each engagement asking for feedback and suggestions, joined forums,  connected with people, researched tools and ideas online and continually improved her skillset. She also offered training courses on how to do visual art for communication and training. A few years later, she is now so in demand for her visual artistic services, training, card sets, posters, tools, animations and writing that she is turning people away. Lita is the illustrator for this book and helped to bring these characters to life. See her work at https://www.3stickmen.com

Cautious Dreamers are Followers, Pretenders and Dreamers

On the opposite side of the continuum are the cautious dreamers who are Followers, Pretenders and Dreamers. Their deep need to be protected and feel safe, are some of the underlying reasons for being cautious, following the crowd and pretending everything is ok. Cautious dreamers are more sensitive to pain, fear or criticism than others, perhaps due to receiving a fair bit in their early years and not developing the coping mechanisms for dealing with this. Fear of pain, humiliation or being reminded of our shadow-sides where they feel insecure or inadequate can result in cautious dreamers feeling stuck and afraid to step out of their comfort zones. They prefer certainty and so may limit their choices to the known and resist change. They may portray an image of confidence and success but are actually very self-critical and insecure. They tend to imagine the worst and will do everything in their power to avoid failure or ridicule. They will tend to imagine or **dream** of what they would like to do or be, but not find the self-confidence to try it out without a lot of encouragement and risk management, and so they become known as dreamers rather than doers. Cautious dreamers can be perfectionistic and less trusting of others, and therefore stay under the radar and share fewer details about their ideas for fear of judgement or ridicule.[12]

These cautious dreamers **believe** that it is safer to follow others than be the first. They believe it is risky and humiliating to fail and that it's not safe to trust others or share how you feel. They also believe that their ideas and talk are valuable but may expect others to make them happen.

They generally **feel** stuck, defensive, pessimistic, resistant and cynical.

They use **language** like "I'd rather not", "Not now", "It's too risky", "Let's wait and see" or I'm fine".

They have daily **habits** like convincing themselves they are better off being safe, noticing risks, and other people's failures, thinking of ideas but not acting on them.

---

12 Vullings, 2013.

Have a look at the Idea Killer's poster[13] for more underlying thoughts and beliefs that may just be killing yours or other's ideas.

> "Creativity is the way I share my soul with the world."
> –Brené Brown

5. BELIEVING I STILL HAVE IT

If you are still not sure about where you may be spending your time and which character is in charge of your creativity, explore the following beliefs. Which resonate and make sense if you look deeply into your upbringing, role models and programmes? Could some of these be playing out without your awareness? How could some of these beliefs be protecting you or limiting you? Is the trade-off worth it? Which ones could you adopt for a while and notice how it feels and what it enables you to do? Feel free to add your own beliefs that could enhance your creative value and be more of a **Possibility Connector** when it counts.

FROM believing…	TO believing…
• It's safer to follow or copy others	• My original ideas add unique value
• It's risky and humiliating to fail	• Failure is feedback and learning
• It's not safe to trust others or share how you feel	• My true power lies in my authentic ideas and voice
• I like doing it this way – I work better alone	• What possibilities and perspectives we can try?
• I love thinking or talking about creative ideas	• I love creating unique value from converging ideas

I remember a key shift I became aware of in India during my soul painting experience. Once I let go of my belief that it is risky and humiliating to fail (and by extension, to get it wrong, not perfectly

---
13 Vullings, 2013.

right, not please others) and started messing with my "perfect" image of the painting I was creating, I could relax and enjoy the experience. I opened up to other possibilities and perspectives. I allowed interruptions, spontaneous splashes, different colours and other people coming along to join in the fun. Life can be like painting – full of colours and expression as it emerges, never quite knowing how it will turn out. And if it's a real mess, you can always paint over it and create another!

6. DAILY HACKS AND HABITS FOR CREATIVITY

There are many stimulants of creativity that get our creative juices flowing. Possibility Connectors have daily habits, rituals and tools that flex their minds, expand their brains, stretch their imagination, harness their emotions, engage their senses, activate their bodies and connect with others… to come up with unique thinking and ideas to contribute value to society. In true possibility connector style, we will share some of our favourites with you. There are many more ideas and links in the resources section if you wish to explore more. Have a look at www.creativebrainmovie.com for some inspiration or do your own creativity test to see how you compare to the average at www.testmycreativity.com.

6.1 Habit #1: Playful imagining

The biggest challenge to our creativity is the hardwiring in our brain. Here are some things to try to soften and even unravel some of the wiring to give yourself more room to create.

- Imagine you are a five-year-old child with no fear of play or being "silly". Play allows free reign, where there are no stereotypes, preconceptions, or boundaries. Draw, laugh, dance, cry, be silly, dream, play with toys, roll in the grass, act out a scene or build a blanket fort.

- Imagine you are a supremely creative genius and act "as if" or imagine you had a council of creative geniuses on call. What would they suggest?
- Imagine yourself 10 or even 20 years from now. What could be possible?
- Imagine if you had all the time and money in the world, what would you do?
- Imagine you could wave a magic wand and bust all the barriers to your creativity – beliefs, fears, myths, rules, what you think you can and can't do, e.g. draw, paint, create, innovate.
- Imagine what is the worst that can happen with your new ideas – and perhaps find out that it is not so frightening, especially if we keep in mind all of the famous people we know today who had many failures and rejections before they succeeded.
- Imagine that the assumptions you have on a topic or problem need to be challenged. Ask "What if ..... was not true?"

Tip: Really immerse yourself in the experience and forget about how you usually think and behave.

6.2 Habit #2: Energy in motion

Another big barrier to creativity is our self-limiting emotions that hold us back from stepping out, being different, trying something new and being our authentic selves. Notice what emotions come up when you do something silly, new, weird, etc. and identify and reframe. Consciously shift your feelings from insecurity to interest, from fear to fascination, from self-criticism to self-love. Passion is a powerful emotion to inspire creativity.

Do things which stimulate different senses. Be aware of what happens when you:

- listen to a specific song (goose bumps);
- taste interesting or unusual food (distinguish different flavours, textures, etc.);
- tune into the sounds and smells of nature;
- really absorb the colours of a favourite painting; and
- feel the fabric of a favourite shirt, the grass under your feet or the fur of a pet.

What do you notice, or experience, or feel? These emotion and sensing activities are very powerful for unlocking existing neural pathways and create space for a different experience if we consciously cultivate a comfort with the new.

Tip: Close your eyes when you want to tune into feelings or senses to enhance the impact. Even when using your visual sense, close your eyes for a few minutes before and then open them to see in new and deeper ways.

6.3 Habit #3: Let's get physical

Our bodies are our connection with our sub-conscious and when we move and get physical, we can effortlessly programme new possibilities into our awareness. Here are some options to explore:

- Move your body through dancing, exercising with awareness, gardening, or walking in nature.
- Role-play a creative scenario with a friend or make a fun, quirky video or "TikTok" clip.
- Eat a meal starting with dessert and working backwards to starters, or eat with a blindfold on.
- Use your non-dominant hand for doing things.

- Create a physical space for creativity (work or home) with colours, pictures, sounds or quotes.

- Travel to another neighbourhood, city or country.

- Get creative in the bedroom and surprise your partner with initiating something new.

- Immerse yourself in a problem without interruption for a few hours or days.

- Learn something new that requires you to physically do something, such as learn to play a musical instrument, design a software programme or robot, erect do-it-yourself furniture or make a piece of art.

Tip: Set up some morning rituals to open your mind and build your emotional resilience. Spend a few minutes in the alpha brain wave state to imagine your day, anchor the positive feelings you want to retain for the day, write down your dreams, do some deep breathing or physical exercises or jump into a cold shower. Mix it up daily to keep on surprising yourself and keeping you out of automatic.

6.4 Habit #4: Diversify Perspectives & Paradigms

"If you change the way you look at things, the things you look at change." Dr Wayne Dyer

More perspectives make for more diverse ideas and options. Opening our minds requires questioning, challenging, and testing different perspectives and paradigms that may be our only reference point in our life experience so far. Whenever you catch yourself thinking: "But I know this will or won't work, or this is the only way, or it's obvious", it may be time to investigate some different ways of thinking. Here are some ideas for expanding and diversifying your perspectives.

- Invite a bunch of people from different industries, functions or walks of life to a design thinking session or a learning circle to share ideas on a specific topic.

- Send out a mini-survey or poll to your friends and colleagues for ideas on diverse subjects or opinions.

- Join an international online forum or group to see how other people and organisations think and do things.

- Hang out with or speak to different people, imagine standing in their shoes or look up highly creative people or experts and imagine how they would think.

- Follow any ideas, leads or contacts that you get from others or reading, trust your intuition, reach out, have a conversation, learn something – follow the rabbit hole.

- Visit your own office as if you are a stranger or competitor. Notice things with fresh eyes, like Undercover Boss. Visit a friend or competitor's office and notice what they do differently.

- Learn from nature through biomimicry, a method which studies nature's best ideas and then imitates these designs and processes to solve human problems, i.e. studying a leaf to invent a better solar cell. Velcro is the most famous example of biomimetics which imitated burrs clinging to dog's fur.

Tip: When you think you are right, think again! Listen, learn, experiment and adapt in a continuous flow of evolving your ideas and worldviews as you get exposed to more.

6.5 Habit #5: Test the tools

There are many creativity tools out there. Most of us might be familiar with some of the old favourites such as brainstorming, mind-mapping, SCAMPER or 6 hats thinking. If not, go and explore these. Some interesting creativity tools I have come across and are worth taking a look at are introduced below, with more in the resources section.

Moon-shot thinking: is imagining a solution that is exponentially (or 10X) bigger or better than what you have now or that will make an exponential impact. Singularity University's moon-shot mission for their 12 global challenges is "How will we impact a billion people?" It requires radical thinking and often radical risk to imagine and shoot for a moon-shot, such as solving for climate change, poverty, water and health.

Retrocast: is about designing a story of sometime in the future when you have solved your problem or achieved your vision. What were the milestones, ideas, decisions, skills and attitudes that it took to get there? Divide it up into time periods working backward to imagine what needed to happen in each year. Use a large chart and Post-it notes to work backwards from the future to now. Have a look at a full SCiFi by Design process in the resources section.

Bad ideas: is about brainstorming all the bad ideas you can come up with for your project or problem. Many an innovation came through initially ridiculous ideas or by accident, e.g. matches, penicillin, safety glass, X-Rays and Post-it notes. Start by generating the worst possible ideas you can imagine, which then shatters the existing paradigms and may actually lead to some original options that could actually work. Brendan Boyle from Ideo says; "Big Innovation Lives Right on the Edge of Ridiculous Ideas."

Mash-up: brings odd or unexpected things together to spark fresh ideas. Start with a "How might we" question, e.g. how might we better support patients' families in the hospital? Pick two broad but unrelated categories like hospitals and hotels or waiting rooms and schools. Think outside your industry. Then generate as many ideas as you can in two minutes. Finally combine items from the two lists to ideate as many new products, services or experiences as you can. This process helps us start down the path from the ridiculous to the radical solution.

Tip: Check out our resources section for more tools and amazing resources such as 27 creativity and innovation tools – in one-pagers! Or MoreInspiration.com, a website that gathers innovations in products and technologies from all possible sectors and domains which can inspire you to innovate your product or technology.

6.6 Habit #6: Space to flow

Often original or inspired ideas stem from creating a space for your brain and body to free-flow and transcend beyond the day-to-day thinking and activities. My previous book, *Accelerated Learning,* was an idea on ice that I didn't have the time or energy to engage with, until I went trekking to Everest Base Camp and spent 8-9 hours a day, for 12 days... just walking. No computer, no input, no people... just me, my body and the gorgeous mountains. Something happens inside you when you are still long enough and do the extraordinary. You start reaching parts of yourself that had been silenced by responsibility or the noise of life in the fast lane. Somewhere on that mountain I found the vision, the inspiration, and the energy to create the new book, which was born only nine months later. This book gained momentum through a seven-day advanced meditation retreat in Malta, where I was totally out of touch with anyone back home and practicing moving into inner spaces to allow flow. Some ideas to get you into that space follow.

A beginner's mind: is, according to "Zen Mind, Beginner's Mind" by Shunryu Suzuki, a beautiful way to approach life – with an open, empty, non-expert, non-judgemental mind; with the innocence of first enquiry, being present, and to accept and see things as they are without your preconceived ideas, expectations or comparisons. This can be very refreshing in approaching a meal, a new relationship, or a new creative project without the baggage of past successes or failures. There are a number of guidelines to practice this, which you can find in an animated summary in the resources section, which include Right Practice, Right Attitude and Right Understanding.

The Einstein Technique: is a mental simulation technique used by many scientists and inventors over the years to model their craft in their heads, including the greats such as Tesla, Einstein and Elon Musk. It entails consciously building a mental model of how your field actually works (e.g. an architect has a mental model of a new building) and then testing the mental model in your mind by mentally simulating different scenarios (e.g. how people will walk in and interact with the building). The best mental state to do the simulation is of course Alpha state, when your analytical mind is lowered in volume and you can access more imagination, intuition, and flow of original thought.

The Power-Nap: is another habit of many of the great inventors and artists throughout history, including Einstein, Aristotle, and Salvador Dali. They seemed to realise that the moment just before dropping off to sleep was the brain's most creative state (i.e. the doorway between the alpha and theta brainwave states). Salvador Dali, the master of surrealism, is known to have sat in a chair with a key in his hand and an upside-down plate below it. The moment he fell into a deep sleep, his hand released the key which clanged onto the plate and the painter awoke with a start, refreshed and ready to get weird with his art.[14]

Invisible Counsellors: Napoleon Hill, in his book, *Think and Grow Rich*, describes his 20-year study of the most successful people of his age — including Andrew Carnegie, Henry Ford and Thomas Edison. He learnt one of their secrets was to imagine what other successful people would say or do. He called his favourites into imaginary meetings in his head and called this group his 'Invisible Counsellors'. Tesla also developed an aptitude for conjuring imaginary people, societies, and worlds to stimulate his inventions.

---
14 Baer, 2013.

Tip: Make it a priority to take time-out from day-to-day work and activities — at least two weeks once a year, with some smaller breaks in between. Get to a wild beach, walk in nature, climb a mountain, do a creative art or cooking experience. Nurture the belief that time for playing or day-dreaming is productive, (as long as it is not used and abused as an excuse for procrastinating).

"Massive innovation comes not from solving what we know how to solve but from radical, crazy, forward-thinking ideas."
—Peter Diamandis, Singularity University

7. TIPS, TOOLS AND RESOURCES

If you are interested in exploring and learning more, here are some of our favourite tips, tools and resources to accelerate your journey to becoming a possibility connector. (See https://catalystconsulting.co.za/power-up8-resources/).

Videos

Do schools kill creativity — TED talk. Sir Ken Robinson: https://www.youtube.com/watch?v=iG9CE55wbtY
Thinking in New Boxes: Alan Iny: https://www.youtube.com/watch?v=-oCN7A8E3Bc
Success, failure and the drive to keep creating | Elizabeth Gilbert: https://www.youtube.com/watch?v=_waBFUg_oT8
Tim Brown urges designers to think big: https://www.youtube.com/watch?v=UAinLaT42xY
Creative Courage — Jason Silva: https://www.youtube.com/watch?v=wQL1_dyS1wQ
Creative Brain Documentary: www.creativebrainmovie.com

Blogs

The Innovation World is Changing Due to the 4th Industrial Revolution by Paul Hobcraft 2018: https://blog.hypeinnovation.com/innovation-fourth-industrial-revolution

Books

Thinking in new boxes – Alan Iny A new paradigm for business creativity
Can you learn Creativity? Yes, here's how – Igor Ovsyannykov
Lateral Thinking : A Textbook of Creativity, Edward de Bono
Creativity is the Future of Work – Declan Wilson
Sci-Fi by Design
https://singularityhub.com/2018/05/09/how-to-leverage-the-power-of-science-fiction-for-exponential-innovation/

Tools

http://www.testmycreativity.com
https://www.ideo.com/tools
https://www.3stickmen.com/
http://www.moreinspiration.com/
27 creativity and innovation tools – in one-pagers! – SlideShare https://www.slideshare.net/ramonvullings/27-creativity-innovation-tools-final
How to Invent Radical Solutions to Huge Problems: A Guide to Moonshot Thinking: https://medium.com/singularityu/how-to-invent-radical-solutions-to-huge-problems-745d8207649a
How to use 'Bad' Ideas to find the Best Ideas! 2019: https://myndflo.com/blogs/news/how-to-use-bad-ideas-to-find-the-best-ideas

Chapter 6

COURAGE

"Daring greatly means the courage to be vulnerable. It means to show up and be seen. To ask for what you need. To talk about how you're feeling. To have the hard conversations." –Brené Brown

1. THE COURAGE TO BE VULNERABLE

If the one constant in life is change, then the antidote to the fear of uncertainty and perceived loss is courage. I don't think it is within the reach of most of us ordinary folk to have no fear. Fear is a natural part of our psychology and survival instincts – our in-built fight, flight or freeze brain response.

One of my all-time favourite authors on courage is Susan Jeffers who wrote "Feel the Fear and Do It Anyway".[1] I love the idea of noticing and acknowledging the fear AND then still continuing toward your goals. It is knowing that you might fail, look silly, or lose things that are important to you along the way AND still courageously doing what is right for you and your future vision. She describes bravery as taking full responsibility for our responses to life.

> Bravery: *"Taking responsibility means never blaming anyone else for anything you are being, doing, having, or feeling."* –Susan Jeffers

---

1   Jeffers, 2006.

Franklin D. Roosevelt's view on courage was that "Courage is not the absence of fear, but rather the assessment that something else is more important than fear."[2] It takes courage to face tough times with pragmatic honesty AND with the optimism that comes with knowing and trusting that everything will work out in the end, and that we grow most through challenges. It also takes courage to be authentic, share both your strengths and your struggles, ask for support, and speak up with bold ideas or requests. Courage is a skill that can be built with patience, practice and a willingness to fail, knowing that you can get back up and bounce back.

I realised through personal discovery workshops and books that FEAR was going to be THE limiting factor of my life unless I found a way to conquer its debilitating impact on my life. I spent many years choosing high adrenalin activities to try and master my fear. These included white water rafting, bungy jumping, parachuting, climbing mountains and diving in caves and with sharks. I even took a job facilitating outdoor adventure teambuilding sessions in the bush in my early 20s.

I remember a moment, during a teambuilding event, in which the objective was to build relationships between employees of different races, in a context of much racial tension in South Africa at the time. I was leading a rafting trip where people shared a two-person raft and had to figure out how to communicate and work together to make their way down river. There was a real mix of rafting or swimming experience and comfort with being in the water. This led to a fair amount of frustration on the part of those competitive individuals who wanted to get it right and look competent. There was a river guide in front, and I was sweeping at the back of eight rafts. I came around the corner to find one of our team (Peter) sitting on a rock in the middle of the river while his companion, Jabu, was crying out in terror from the raft that was now bouncing down some rapids into the distance. With the lives of all 16 participants in my hands, I faced a tough choice. Do

---

[2] Quotespedia, (2020).

I leave Peter alone (knowing that we couldn't paddle upstream and fetch him) and go after Jabu or do I leave Jabu in the hands of the team and the river guide already at the bottom of the rapids and go and talk to Peter? My instincts kicked in and I chose to anchor my raft on a rock next to Peter (in the middle of the roaring river) and listen to him. He was extremely frustrated and angry with Jabu who just wasn't listening, with me for making him do this and with his company for sending him on this stupid exercise. He had had enough and refused to go any further. In a moment of stupendous boldness (I am still not sure where this came from at the tender age of 22, talking to a man at least double my age), in a calm voice, I explained his options. He could walk the 12kms out or join Jabu in the raft until we got to our next rest point when I could swap him out. After much swearing and limited options, we made our way down the rapids and he climbed with a scowl back into the raft with Jabu, who looked at me with wide-eyed surprise. I honoured my word and let him swap at the rest point. I have no idea what happened in those 20 minutes, but it was some sort of breakthrough. Peter came to me at the end of event to thank me for an experience that had opened his eyes more in three days than in his 45 years. He was returning with a new attitude to help build this country with his fellow South Africans in a new way. From that moment on I knew that those moments we fear the most, can be the most transformational of our lives – for us and for those we serve.

I survived my early experiments with fear, much to the horror of my parents at the time. Whilst I now feel more prepared for crazy moments, and my tolerance for fear is perhaps a bit stronger, inner fears are still a constant companion, particularly in times of stress, uncertainty and change. It still takes conscious effort to choose my courageous adventurer voice when I feel the lurking fear of potential judgement, hurt, loss, getting old or not being able to provide, etc.

Courage for me is the self-belief and self-confidence to learn from failure, to persist in a problem, and to have grit (tenacity). Courage is also about being humble enough to listen, to learn, to take on feedback and to accept ourselves fully. Courage starts with how we think, feel and respond to life's shocks, surprises, challenges, hurts, losses and failures. It is also about the daily mindsets and habits that we cultivate to build resilience and continue to learn and grow regardless of circumstances. The old perception of courage being for heroic or brave deeds is shifting. Brené Brown talks about the courage to be vulnerable and the inner strength it requires to speak openly about who we are and our experiences –

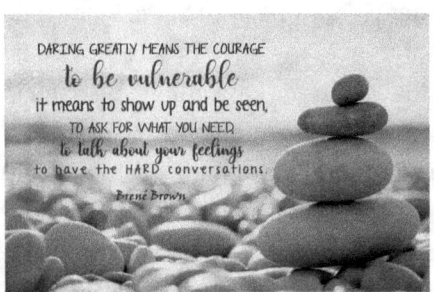

good and bad. If you have not viewed her TED Talk "The Power of Vulnerability" | Brené Brown, it is a must watch and one of the most popular TED Talks in recent years.³"

There have been many moments that I have had to face my own vulnerability. Writing my first book, starting a business, failing at a marriage and getting divorced, internet dating in my mid-30s, getting married again, running workshops in China and speaking to my first audience of 400 people on stage. I have also been through many difficult conversations (and some counselling) with loved ones, friends, colleagues and partners, some of which I had the humility to truly listen and acknowledge my faults, and some of which I lost through my own arrogance and lack of empathy at the time.

---

3   Brown, 2011.

> **Just beyond yourself: the poetry of robust vulnerability**
>
> The poet David Whyte says, "there are very practical reasons for understanding the role of vulnerability in human resilience. We human beings do not have a choice whether or not we are vulnerable. Whether we feel we are on top of the world or confined and traumatized by it, vulnerability is the abiding undercurrent of our natural state. We do not have the luxury of choosing between an untouched, invulnerable interior self and the necessary vulnerabilities of achievement or disappointment in the world. Our response to vulnerability is often to run from it as fast as we can. And yet, to attempt to run from vulnerability is to attempt to run from the essence of our nature, immobilizing the tidal, conversational foundations of our identities. In refusing our vulnerability we also refuse the visible and invisible help needed at every turn of our existence, in effect closing off our understanding of the grief of others. Let's explore how to bring our vulnerable yet undefeated and robust selves into the world—in order to do, achieve, and, above all, in these times, to find the generosity to give."[4]

Our **definition of courage** is as follows:

> Courage is about self-belief; our willingness to learn, change, believe in possibility and move through fear despite ambiguity and uncertainty. It is the willingness to fail fast, be vulnerable and have honest conversations with yourself, at work and at home for meaningful growth focused relationships

Courage is also....

- speaking up in a meeting or to your boss when you know it is the right thing to do;

---

[4] Whyte, 2020.

- confronting a friend or loved one who has been pushing into your boundaries;
- asking for honest feedback about how you are showing up;
- saying no to friends or a lover when you are not in the mood for food, drugs, sex, alcohol or company;
- dealing with your own frailty through illness or an inability to do or achieve something;
- coping with let-downs, disappointments and failures, but still taking the next step; and
- reaching out and helping a friend or stranger in need and being willing to sacrifice something of yours (time, plans, money, convenience).

Courage is particularly **important** because the increasing levels of disruption, change and uncertainty in the world requires courage – to face fear, to risk, to fail, to be real, to be vulnerable, to have honest conversations about what matters. It also requires the self-belief that we can bounce back, in case things don't seem to work out the way you intended. Famous basketball star, Michael Jordan said: "I've missed more than 9000 shots in my career. I've lost almost 300 games. 26 times, I've been trusted to take the game winning shot and missed. I've failed over and over and over again in my life. And that is why I succeed."

2. ARE THE RISKS OF COURAGE WORTH THE REWARD?

When we read about courageous deeds or watch our favourite movie heroes, we are filled with hope and inspiration. We also want to be bold, explore the unknown or stand up for those less fortunate than us. It may help to focus on the personal rewards for practicing courage. Courage can help you develop inner strength, reduce anxiety and find your own authentic voice, passion and purpose. Courage can help you be noticed, speak up and make a difference. Courage can also deepen your personal relationships and help build trust by taking risks to share how you really feel or say I am sorry.

Despite these benefits and many amazing examples, there are still many **barriers to courage**. The movies often misrepresent the costs of courage with the hero somehow managing to survive many near death experiences, and still getting the money and the girl (or guy).

Fear is the major barrier to bold action and there are many fears that keep us awake at night – usually associated with loss of some sort. **Material loss** and the thought of not being able to provide is a deep instinctual fear. What if we cannot pay the bills, keep the house or afford basic necessities for our survival? This primal fear gets us imagining worst case scenarios – even though consciously we know that it is highly unlikely.

Fear of being judged by others when we fail to provide or perform or deliver the goods also runs deep. The thought of unimaginable **embarrassment and humiliation** of letting our loved ones down or having to ask to help from family or friends is not everyone's happy place. This taps into another major fear of **social rejection**. In the past, you would not survive unless you were part of a social group that would work together to ensure that food, protection, love and healing was available. In our modern, more independent lifestyles and micro-families, we may not need our community in the same physical way, but **belonging** is a basic human need. On a subconscious level, we still instinctively react when we are criticised or judged harshly, broken up with, retrenched, fired, voted out or told in some way that we are not good enough to stay in the social group. That is why **loss of status** is also so painful. Status or power in a group used to indicate more material means for you and your family to survive. When we lose status through a restructure, change in role, demotion, public criticism or failure, fear surges through our bodies as we imagine disasters before we can even counter it with positive self-talk.

There is of course **existential fear** – not achieving our highest potential. We compare ourselves to role models who seem to have it all. Not living up to expectations of ourselves at particular points in life (often at the time of a big birthday) can be very painful. The transparency of life on social media, carefully filtered to the positive, can bring up all kinds of comparisons of lack or feelings of not being good enough.

Often the very nature of life itself that is evolving at warp speed creates fear through the **uncertainty and ambiguity** of change. How can we stay "safe" when we don't know what is round the corner or the new rules of the game? A perception of safety comes from predictability, planning and control. This is next to impossible in today's world which is **unpredictable and volatile**. An amazing, client, bonus or business profit this year could turn into a life changing retrenchment, end of contract or financial loss the next.

Many people in places where persecution, crime and poverty are rife also fear for their **physical and psychological safety**. In South Africa, the statistics for home invasions, hijackings and violent crime are staggering. The South African College of Applied Psychology estimates that over six million South Africans could be suffering from post-traumatic stress disorder (PTSD)[5] and many suffer from anxiety, depression, or substance abuse problems. Many people face potential threats in their communities or navigating the daily route to school or work and home again. This is exacerbated by being a victim or witness to a traumatic event or on-going circumstances. There are many other fears such as fear of ill health, getting old, a broken heart, death of a loved one or despair.

So how do we build courage and resilience in the face of so many potential dangers and threats? Our focus in this book is on what you CAN do to understand your fears, where they might come from, which are real vs. imagined, and how to manage them a

---

5   South African College of Applied Psychology (SACAP), 2019.

little differently for a better quality of life. If you learn to feel your fear, face it, make friends with it and take the next step despite it... then you can bravely embrace life with enthusiasm and a sense of freedom. As Susan Jeffers asks:

> *"What if you knew could handle anything? What would you have to fear?"*

3. WHERE DOES FEAR COME FROM?

It is helpful to figure out where fear comes from and what we have learnt about being brave in our life experience so far. Most fears are to protect us and come as a precondition of being human. They can be from outdated evolutionary survival responses (fear of snakes, bugs, wild animals), natural fears for dangerous activities, (fear of heights, loud noises, water), through our mother's fears in utero (fears around birth, finances or relationships) or learning about life through experiences (fear of strangers, abandonment, connection, etc). Most of our fears are learnt fears from painful physical and emotional experiences and now we do everything we can to avoid those feelings again.

These deep and traumatic experiences are also known as core wounds. According to Lise Bourbeau in her book "Heal Your Wounds and Find Your True Self", the five primary core wounds that we may have experienced are rejection, abandonment, humiliation, betrayal and injustice.[6] Every time we are triggered and feel emotionally upset today, our brains bring up memories and pain of past events to protect us, i.e. this situation could be harmful. Move away! This leads to us overreacting to something "small" and getting caught in a loop of uncontrollable feelings. Only when we grow in awareness and the ability to protect ourselves, can we shift sub-conscious reaction to rational, mature choice. It can be very empowering to explore some of our foundational life experiences and resulting core beliefs and figure out which are more or less relevant as an adult today.

---
6   Bourbeau, 2002.

4. WHO DO I WANT TO BE?

We are seldom either courageous or not at all, but rather move up and down a continuum depending on personal attitudes and life circumstances. Have a look on our opposing characters to identify which aspects of each character you resonate with and at which times in your life you might gravitate to one or the other – the **Anxious Controller** or the **Courageous Adventurer** – or most often somewhere in between. Once you are more aware of your choices in any moment, you can choose who you want to show up as more often.

Anxious controller — Anxious Vigilant Controller

Courageous adventurer — Resilient Optimistic Adventurer

Courageous Adventurers are Resilient, Optimistic Adventurers

You immediately know when you meet someone with an inner strength of character, optimism and confidence. They are warm, open and engaging, and make you feel somehow safe and relaxed. They look comfortable in their skin and talk about their mistakes and fears with as much energy as their achievements and adventures. They are tough minded, resilient, determined and they bounce back from disappointments with renewed energy. They are **optimistic**, believe in a positive future and see possibilities. They are **adventurers** who bravely leap into the unknown despite fear. They step up, speak up, take calculated risks and stretch their limits to achieve meaningful goals or purpose. They are not afraid to build on other's ideas and encourage them to flourish.

They share stories with passion and conviction and yet come across as humble and compassionate. They stick with projects and relationships with grit and determination. When things don't work out, they feel the heaviness of disappointment and failure. But they get right back up, figure out what they learnt, adjust their approach or plans and get back out there on a revised route or a new adventure – believing that they have what it takes to succeed in the end.

> *"It is not what happens to you, but how you react to it that matters."* –Epictus

Courageous Adventurers are not free from fear. They feel it, often intensely due to the risks they face. They have, however, learnt to face their fear, manage their physical reaction to it, learn from it, and take action despite it. They are the kind of people you want leading an expedition into unchartered territory (up a mountain, or a breakthrough project) – not just brazenly brave, but continuously weighing up choices and consequences, listening to and consulting with others, and then being decisive and focused when required – particularly in a crisis situation. You will find many Courageous Adventurers on the road as you travel off the beaten track or participate in sporting events, exploring, learning, testing and stretching their wits, guts and bodies for new frontiers of what is possible. You are not likely to find a self-made entrepreneur without a lot of courage. You will also find many adventurers busy with personal or spiritual development courses, retreats or journeys as they adventure into their inner worlds and learn how to optimise their impact, effectiveness, health, wealth and happiness.

Courageous Adventurers **believe** that life is an endless adventure and that they can achieve anything they put their minds to. They have a healthy trust in themselves to handle life's curveballs. They also believe that they are their most powerful, unique, talented selves when they are authentic and willing to be vulnerable in a conscious way.

They generally feel passionate, courageous, determined, optimistic and brave.

They use **language** like "We can do this", "What can we learn from this?", "Let's try again", "What else is out there?", "What doesn't kill us makes us stronger", "When the going gets tough, the tough get going", "Fail fast, learn fast", "It's okay to be scared", "Feel the fear and do it anyway".

They have daily **habits** like internal affirmations to build confidence, speaking up when it is important, taking the next steps even when it is uncomfortable, questioning their fear to see if it is real or imagined, staying calm in the midst of chaos, trusting their intuition, and reaching out to people to connect and for support.

> ### Courage Heroes
>
> Some of my courage heroes include:
>
> **Brené Brown**, who faced much criticism in her early public life, but courageously continued her quest to help millions of people own their vulnerability and shame and live a whole-hearted life.
>
> **Saray Khumalo**, the first black African woman to reach the summit of Mount Everest in 2019 despite several failed attempts. She has also summited five other mountain giants.[7]
>
> **Lewis Pugh**, an endurance swimmer and ocean advocate who was the first person to complete a long-distance swim in every ocean of the world, and frequently swims in vulnerable ecosystems to draw attention to their plight and advocate for change.
>
> **Lady Gaga**, who has achieved exceptional fame through her music, movies and an Oscar, has taken many big risks with career, her image and her music. She has faced many hardships, hard times and personal struggles in order to stay true to herself. She says: "To be a star is to have the courage of the human spirit."
>
> **Who are your heroes and why?**

---

[7] Wikipedia, 2019.

Anxious Controllers are Anxious, Vigilant, Controllers

When we forget that we are Courageous Adventurers we may slip to the opposite side of the continuum and show up as **Anxious Controllers** who are **Anxious, Vigilant, Controllers.**

When we are stressed or scared, we could feel **anxious**, highly strung and nervous. We may be emotional and easily rattled. We imagine the worst, are hyper-vigilant and are on the constant look-out for possible threats. In this state we can be negative and limit or shut down other's ideas to stay safe and in **control** – to the point of manipulating others to follow our desired outcome. We may over-analyse and avoid decisions to minimise the possibility of shame or pain – often struggling to rest or sleep well.

It may not be easy to see yourself on the left of this continuum, but I know for sure that I have been there many times in my life, particularly when things are not working out and my dreams are under threat. I was a horrible person to be around just prior to my ex-husband being sequestrated and losing everything. My finances, my marriage and my ego (status) was under threat. Just to notice the possibility that we can at times play here is useful for self-awareness. Sometimes specific areas of your life bring up more anxiety such as money, love, parenting or career challenges.

The Anxious Controller **believes** that life is dangerous and that any form of humiliation, pain or failure should be avoided at all costs. They believe they need to be continuously on guard, organised and in control to be safe.

They generally **feel** anxious, nervous, fearful, worried and doubtful.

They can use **language** like "I can't do it", "It is too risky", "What if we fail?" "Let's keep to the known route", "Let's have a definite plan for all eventualities", "Let me gather more data", "I am not ready".

They have daily **habits** such as worrying, withdrawing, playing small, procrastinating, making excuses, justifying non-committal behaviour, postponing, criticising (self and others) and planning obsessively for eventualities.

Some people take this to the extreme. We love to read about highly strung celebrities who resort to unhealthy mechanisms to exert control in their lives, including overachieving, over planning, over-exercising or becoming addicted to drugs, shopping or sex. It is not only public personalities who have shared their struggles with anxiety; (Oprah Winfrey, Kim Kardashian-West, Demi Lovato, etc.). There are many people all around us who are trying to balance fear and courage to become their best selves.

5. WHAT DO I BELIEVE?

Anxious controllers and courageous adventurer behaviours show up due to life experiences and what we believe at the time. Many of these beliefs are hard-wired into our operating system as a protective mechanism to keep us safe. In order to start the shift, we need to build trust in ourselves that "WE CAN HANDLE ANYTHING!" The more we say these beliefs, feel the feelings AS IF we already believe them, and then act on them... the quicker we can build new neural paths that can become new thinking habits. We can also write these shifts in our journal daily to embed them in our sub-conscious mind. Here are just a few beliefs as examples. Cultivate your own set of empowering beliefs. Write them on Post-it notes and place them around your house to re-programme unconscious patterns from the past.

FROM believing...	TO believing...
• Life is dangerous, risky and hurts • It's best to stay in control, stay safe • Vulnerability is weakness and people can judge me • I'll stick to the path of least resistance • Fear is a warning to back off	• Life is an endless adventure • Those that dare greatly, achieve greatly • Vulnerability is strength and builds trust • I choose courage over comfort • Feel the fear and do it anyway

6. DAILY HACKS AND HABITS FOR COURAGE

You can also practice these daily habits that can empower you to identify, understand, work with, confront and act with courage and a spirit of adventure, despite your fear.

6.1 Habit #1: Own the 5 Truths About Fear

Practice these truths from Susan Jeffers[8] in addition to your belief shifts above:

1. The fear will never go away as long as you continue to grow!
2. The only way to get rid of the fear of doing something is to go out and... do it!
3. The only way to feel better about yourself is to go out and... do it!
4. Not only are you afraid when facing the unknown, so is everyone else!
5. Pushing through fear is less frightening than living with the bigger underlying fear that comes from a feeling of helplessness!

---
8   Jeffers, 2006.

Tip: Remember this. "What if you knew you could handle anything? What would you have to fear?"

6.2 Habit #2: Fool the FEAR

Make a list of your fears. Aim to confront and reframe them one by one. Enrol the support of a friend or courage buddy so that you have back-up and accountability when you want to rather run a mile. Before you embark on this quest, identify the cause of each fear. Is it from a real past experience, an imagined future experience, or someone else's belief about fear? Use some critical thinking to validate the truth of the fear and potentially reframe it into a much smaller probability or impact from your adult mind and let go the baggage of the past and claim back your power.

Is your fear REAL or is it **F.E.A.R. = False Evidence Appearing Real.** Learn to examine and unpack the evidence.

Fears	Causes	Action to confront	Support needed

Confront with critical questions to reframe your fear:

- What am I actually afraid of?
- Is it the right thing to be afraid of?
- Should I be this afraid of it – or rationally, should I be less or more afraid? (Is it a huge deep ocean… or just these few square meters of water?)
- What harm can this actually do to me or others?
- What could happen as a result of my actions and/or inactions? The best… the worst?

Tip: Remember to recognise all your **capabilities of courage** that you have built up over your lifetime. Make a list of all the times you have been courageous or stepped out of your comfort zone. What helped you take the action or do the right thing? Reaffirm these abilities in yourself and practice doing these more often to build the courage muscle.

6.3 Habit #3: Calibrate the FEAR

Identify where you could possibly be feeling fear out of an over-developed need for **control, perfectionism and "being good enough" or a pleaser**. Ask yourself these questions to check on this.

- Control: where do you like to stay in control and how could you let go more?

- Perfectionism: where do you like things or your results to be perfect and how could you let it be?

- Not good enough: where do you feel not good enough and how could you appreciate who and where you are now?

- Pleaser: where do you do more to please than is necessary or required and how could you gain more balance in giving and receiving?

Practice vulnerability and asking for and receiving feedback. Offer some constructive feedback in return. Have an honest conversation with a friend, colleague, spouse, boss. Calibrate your own version of how you show up with how others experience you. The more we do reality checks on our inner reality with a variety of external inputs, the more we are aware of our strengths, weaknesses and identity... and the less frightened we are of hearing about these again or from others.

Tip: Learn the skills of having **difficult conversations** and giving and receiving feedback. Learn to gain permission, chose the right timing, activate your empathy and curiosity, and acknowledge your own impact in what has unfolded. I have too often given feedback without permission or at the wrong time or in an emotional state – not a good idea if you want to build lasting friendships. Too often, I have taken feedback too personally and sensitively and made a huge issue out of something small. Courage also means admitting to admit when you are wrong and asking for forgiveness when needed. Afterall, we are all doing the best we can with the awareness we have.

6.4 Habit #4: Make Friends with FEAR

Do something you are afraid of:

- Travel on your own.
- Start a business or community project.
- Reach out to network or build a friendship with someone at the risk of being rejected.
- Have the courageous conversation when a colleague lets you or the team down.
- Stand in for your boss or colleague to present or facilitate at a meeting or session.
- Apologise publicly for an error of judgement and ask for help.

Learn to say NO or Not Now – with grace. Be willing to say no when requests cross boundaries that are clear. Learn to ask for what you want or need. Learn to share how you feel without apologising for your needs and feelings. Stand up for yourself and your beliefs and be ok with being alone in that or being the one who rocked the boat. Courage means that you are supporting your own authenticity.

Fail on purpose. Learn to laugh at yourself and with others. How many times did Edison try his light bulb? How many times was he told he is ridiculous with his ideas? Until he proved them all wrong! Courage is persevering toward a dream after failure or not getting that deal, or that promotion, or that relationship, or that business.

Tip: There is a fine line between courage and stupidity. When you courageously defend your view, but it is completely and obviously wrong, courage becomes stupid! It's not about just winning an argument; it is also about taking your brains with you.

6.5 Habit #5: Become FEAR... LESS

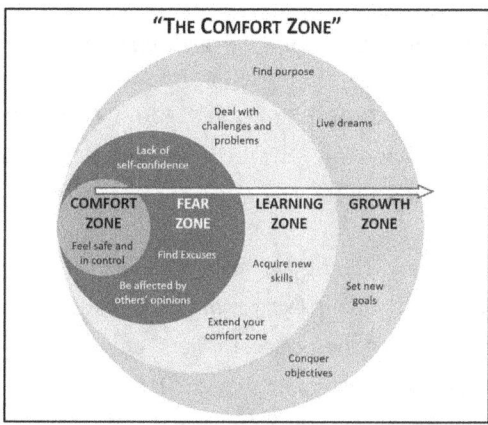

Get comfy out of your comfort zone.[9] Notice where in your life you are stuck in a comfort zone. It may feel safe and in control, however nothing grows there! You have to move through your fear zone and start being open to learning new skills and coping with new and challenging problems or situations. Only then can you truly enter the growth zone in which you are continually learning. Practice feeling fear and becoming used to it without freaking out. Use emotions (fear) as energy – as a tool to achieve your purpose and your dreams.

Check and shift core beliefs. Susan Jeffers says the worst fear is not the fear of the actual event or feeling of something bad happening to you – it is the fear that you will not be able to handle it, i.e. you will go crazy, collapse, become depressed, lose everything, etc. If you truly believed that you could handle anything that came your way – retrenchment, illness, loss of a loved one, a failed business, etc., – what would you have to fear?[10]

---

9   RethinkandFocus, 2019.
10 Jeffers, 2020.

Practice new scripts for different scenarios:

- I can handle anything!
- I am enough, I have enough.
- I am always safe, protected and guided.
- Fear = separation from source. Love = connection with source.
- F.E.A.R. = Free ... Empowered ... Agile ... Resilient.

Tip: Put up affirmations, pictures and examples about courage. Read about or view movies of famous people who have failed many times and persevered to become great.

"Your time is limited, so don't waste it living someone else's life. Don't be trapped by dogma – which is living with the results of other people's thinking. Don't let the noise of others' opinions drown out your own inner voice. And most important, have the courage to follow your heart and intuition." –Steve Jobs

7. TIPS, TOOLS AND RESOURCES

If you are interested in exploring and learning more, here are some of our favourite tips, tools and resources to accelerate your journey to becoming a Courageous Adventurer. (See https://catalystconsulting.co.za/power-up8-resources/).

Articles/Blogs

The Five Truths About Fear by by Susan Jeffers, Ph.D.: http://www.susanjeffers.com/home/5truths.cfm

Books

Feel the fear and do it anyway, Dr Susan Jeffers
Daring greatly, Brené Brown

Videos

The power of vulnerability | Brené Brown: https://www.youtube.com/watch?v=iCvmsMzlF7o

Movie Netflix : Brene Brown The Call to Courage: https://www.netflix.com/title/81010166

Vulnerability – Patrick Lencioni video on vulnerability: https://www.youtube.com/watch?v=pbWEDk8fbBU

COURAGE – Best Motivational Video Speeches Compilation: https://www.youtube.com/watch?v=cVNW9bx5SK8

COURAGE is the KEY to LIFE Itself | Nobody is FEARLESS...: https://www.youtube.com/watch?v=LTJsjradIK8

Tools

Courage self-assessment: https://daretolead.brenebrown.com/assessment/

Chapter 7
CHANGE NAVIGATOR

"Change will not come if we wait for some other person or some other time. We are the ones we've been waiting for. We are the change that we seek." –Barack Obama

1. HOLDING ON TO A WORTHWHILE VISION

As the world speeds up and we face many disruptions, we need to adapt our thinking, behaviour and habits at a rapid pace. Many changes are happening simultaneously in our personal, work and social lives. This requires daily prioritisation, focus and decision-making to make the best of our circumstances.

Many years ago, I was hiking to Everest Base Camp in the midst of a regional super storm which resulted in flight delays, snow storms, avalanches and not knowing whether we would be able to achieve our life dream of getting up to base camp. We were already committed and two days up the mountain when we heard the news of eight people dying in an avalanche and the closure of base camp. I had also injured my foot exploring Kathmandu in the rain before we left for the trek and was facing many days of painful walking. We faced a choice. Do we turn around and go back home, or do we continue for the next six days in the hope that we avoid any avalanches and that the path would be opened before we got there?

The journey to get to base camp was five years in the making. I had injured my back to an extent that doctors said I would never run or do serious hiking again. I was in the prime of my life with so many dreams of travel and physical adventures, that it was a real blow. I spent a while in despair and trying to adjust my dreams in my head. And then one day I decided NO! I would spend as long as it took to prove the doctors wrong. The next five years I tried all treatments and activities I could find to "fix" my back. These included all kinds of Western physical therapy – physiotherapists, chiropractors, biokineticists – as well as many personal transformational experiences and Eastern practices at mediation and healing centres in India and beyond. There were many moments of hope, which were only dashed away a few days or weeks later. Eventually I was able to peel the layers of conditioning away and strengthen my physical and emotional core with the help of a very gifted wellness coach. I was ready to take on the challenge, only to find these extreme conditions and difficult choices in our path.

We chose to continue and navigate the changing conditions, holding on to our dream, knowing what it had taken to get this far. Despite facing deep snow, icy paths, detours, collapsed bridges, daily foot therapy, altitude sickness and freezing weather, we had an unforgettable adventure. Moving into the unknown with a pack on my back, my life partner, a guide, my trained body and my optimism was very empowering. I have called upon that trust and resilience many times over, as I have navigated other different challenges.

Recently we have faced the Coronavirus pandemic and its aftermath, with the media drumming up a storm of fear and worst-case scenarios. We are being forced to reflect, stay informed and adapt our everyday behaviours. We are grappling with how to stay safe and financially viable. We are having to work hard at managing fear and stress (which depletes our energy and immune systems) and aiming to stay in a state of creative adaptability (which recharges our energy, boosts our immune systems and enables us to make critical decisions).

Our choice is react to uncertainty as a **passive resistor** with much anxiety, or respond as a **change navigator** who looks for opportunities to learn and make a difference. Change can be fun and exciting when we choose the change (e.g. moving to a new house, starting a new job or learning a new skill). When change is forced upon us from outside and we feel we have no control over it (e.g. organisational restructuring, clients cancelling, new procedures or skills), we can feel insecure and out of our depth.

It is in these times that we need to become greater than our circumstances, our challenges or our old habits of fearful, limited thinking, and be adaptable, optimistic and influence positively while we navigate sudden curve balls and complex frightening change.

> *"Change is not merely necessary to life – it is life."* –Alvin Toffler

Our **definition of a change navigator** is as follows:

> Change navigators hold onto a worthwhile vision through rapid change and disruption, with determination, resilience and agility in their approach. They bounce back from disappointments and failures and try again, despite external judgement or ridicule. They engage the hearts and minds of others and help them navigate the scary journey of necessary change. They commit and follow-through to get results.

Developing the heart of a change navigator is particularly **important as we face so many unknowns and 'unexpecteds' every day.** To lead at the speed of change, we need to continually adapt to emerging competitors, shifting client expectations, new technology, restructuring, different leaders, virtual teams and different ways of thinking, learning and working. We have to be willing to experiment, learn and fail fast with both ourselves and in business. We also need to positively influence those we work and interact with to confront their discomfort and come with us into the unknown future towards a worthwhile vision.

> **Nelson Mandela**
>
> Nelson Mandela has been one of the greatest change navigators of our time. Not only was he able to overcome his bitterness and resentment of being imprisoned for 27 years of his life, but he was able to hold onto the vision of a united, free South Africa, and influence people way beyond the prison walls globally to become part of his dream. He was able to get diverse, previously intolerant groups of people to work towards a fundamental policy and belief change in a country that had faced years of racism, separate treatment (apartheid) and cross-cultural hatred. He then continued to lead the nation through the most disruptive years of change with strength and humility, by building hope for a better and brighter future for all.

We can easily recognise the change navigators around us. They stay positive and optimistic despite challenging times. They speak up, are creative and seek alignment to a joint plan of action. They are part of the solution rather than part of the problem. They listen, ask for feedback, learn and adapt quickly. They bounce back from disappointments quickly, avoiding blame or dwelling on the past. They are the people we go to when we need some positive guidance on where to and leave with insight and a sense of hope. They stop negativity firmly and gently and minimise drama wherever they can to focus energy and resources on adapting. They are the leaders of the future that we would follow without hesitation.

2. TO RESIST OR TO NAVIGATE?

When we adopt the identity of a **change navigator** and take on all life's adventures with a spirit of optimism, trust, openness to learning, resilience and teamwork, we experience more energy and less anxiety. We are also able to build inner resilience, meet fabulous people and make meaningful achievements and connections.

When we fall into the trap of being a **passive resistor**, we can succumb to fears and insecurities that tempt us to hold back, play it safe, resist and avoid change. We get left behind, miss opportunities, delay our learning curve and are not prepared when the impact of change hits us. We may also find that there are less people around us willing to help as they have moved on, leaving us isolated or in the company of other pessimists or victims of change.

The biggest downside to playing the passive resistor is the impact of the stress response on our physical health and energy. As we learnt in Chapter 3, we are designed for short-term stress for our survival. But when we find ourselves in a continual loop of anxious thoughts, "what if" scenarios, frustration, fear, judgement or powerlessness, our nervous systems and stress hormones go on high alert, we struggle to relax or sleep, and feeling exhausted, burn out or get sick.

We become masters of our own destiny by recognising our stress loops and building resilient coping mechanisms and support systems to stay effective without falling over or burning out. Our work colleagues and families rely on us to be there for them too. In these difficult situations do you want to be the supporter or the needy? Are you open to being both the giver and receiver of support to build an interdependent community around you?

3. CHOOSING IN THE MOMENT

Because our brains are wired for short-term survival, it is only natural that we will sometimes fall into the **passive resistor** reaction. When we remember, however, that we have a more advanced forebrain and conscious choice as our human gifts, we can move beyond our initial reactions and choose more **change navigator** habits. You may find that you have more choice and less reaction in different areas of your life. For example, you may be very accomplished at managing work related change, but kick and scream your way through personal conflicts. Or you may be the calm in the storm in family crises, but quiver at the thought of presenting your innovative ideas to a group of senior managers. We invite you to honestly assess yourself and see where you might spend most of your time on the continuum below. Remember not to be harsh on yourself but rather see a learning opportunity for continuous growth towards achieving your highest potential. This exploration into the beliefs and habits of a **maze navigator** will build upon many of the learnings from previous chapters. You may need to call upon your curiosity, your creativity and your courage. This will also be a very useful core capability to pick up as you navigate your journey and meet other interesting characters throughout the rest of this book.

Passive resistor

Resistor
Passenger
Dramatizer

Maze navigator

Embracer
Navigator
Influencer

Maze navigators are embracer, navigators, Influencers

Maze navigators are embracers of change. They see change as an opportunity to test themselves and reinvent the future. They look for the reasons "why" or "how" rather than argue for "why not". They are able to **sift through the noise** of overwhelming demands and change initiatives and create an intentional and **inspirational vision** for the future. This requires **optimism** and a sense of **hope** that we will be able to navigate the uncertain and uncomfortable disruptions, turmoil and changes around us. They **believe** that they and their teams will **emerge victorious and stronger** for the journey, and help people believe that the bigger purpose is ultimately **worth the effort** and struggle along the way.

They are **navigators** who are **committed** to their vision and **determined** to find a way under, over or through perceived and real barriers to achieve it. They are **swift** in their response to the conditions or ground shifting beneath their feet, and can quickly **adapt** their approach or route on their way to the vision. They are **resilient** when initial plans don't work out, and are quick to pause, reflect, learn and be curious about what else could work. They don't give up but are resourceful and proactive. They **persevere** through the tough times.

They are **influencers** who have an incredible ability to **tap into other's fears and motivators** and **engage** them in a way that makes sense to them. This takes **awareness, empathy** and deep **listening** with an interest and curiosity to understand. They are able to **articulate** their vision with **passion and energy**. They outline the **journey of adventure and risk** and the unique **benefits** to different groups in a way that stirs some **meaning and hope** deep inside. They have a large **network** of people they engage with, share and contribute to, who are **willing to follow** them into the exciting unknown.

A change navigator in a murky space – Caster Semenya

Caster Semenya, a South African middle-distance runner and Olympic gold medallist, is a wonderful example of a maze navigator. She spent years under scrutiny and threats of her right to belong in her gender and her sport, in her pursuit of her vision to become the fastest female athlete sprinter in the 400, 800 and 1500m events. She has been subjected to gender testing and racism due to her high levels of natural testosterone and has had to legally defend her right to compete in international courts. Despite these difficult challenges, Caster has continued to train and compete to show the world that she will not give up or disappear without a fight. She has since won the South African Sportswoman of the Year award three times and been chosen as the Discovery Vitality Ambassador and speaker at their Leadership Summit to inspire others through her attitude and her journey. She has been called "Mokgadi", 'the one who guides'. She knew, even at an early age, that she was destined to lead, to drive and to run the race of the swift and strong.[1]

Some of her quotes:

> "Your strength lies in your ability to cast the weight off your own shoulders."
>
> "What defines you is how you rise up"[2]

Maze navigators believe that change creates opportunities, that the path will reveal itself if we stay committed and focused, and that there is always a way. They believe that *attitude determines altitude* and that together we can achieve more. They believe in openness and transparency and know that acknowledging weaknesses or fears enable others to step up and offer support, which in turn empowers them.

They generally **feel** confident, inspired, motivated, determined and agile.

---

1 Wikipedia, 2020.
2 Discovery, 2018.

They use **language** like "We can do this", "Let's keep our eyes on the prize", "Change is an adventure", "The wisdom is in the room", "What could it be like if we all worked together on this?".

They have daily **habits** like courageous visioning; passionate sharing; logical arguments; grit; willingness to be wrong; weird or criticised; seeing the bigger journey; planting a seed; calibrating ideas; and celebrating small wins

> *"You cannot control what happens to you, but you can control your attitude toward what happens to you, and in that, you will be mastering change rather than allowing it to master you."*
> —Brian Tracy

Passive Resistors are Resistors, Passengers, Dramatisers

On the opposite side of the continuum sit those who can be Resistors, Passengers and Dramatisers. Of course, this will not be you all the time, but there may be times when you have played this role. Identify it and acknowledge it… so that you can empower yourself to make proactive choices next time around.

Resistors unconsciously resist change, resulting in subtle or passive resistance to change. They find change uncomfortable and threatening to their ego identities that may hang on the known past.

To sabotage change efforts, they find fault in the change. They may smile and nod in agreement in meetings but then engage in corridor talk to seed doubt and derail decisions that have been made.

Passive resistors can be **passengers** on the journey of change, preferring to let others take all the risks and pay the costs while they sit back, just following the masses and avoiding any personal risk or public failure. They are non-committal when buy-in is sought and wait for instructions before contributing to the change.

Passive resistors can be **dramatisers** by over-sharing their concerns and worries publicly. They can personalise the change, having a "woe is me" face if they have to give up something as a result of the change (e.g. time, team members, budgets, status). They can tend to become hyper critical of change leaders, be active nay-sayers and can influence the fence sitters merely with their negativity even, without intending to.

In my early years, as a natural extrovert, I was energised by conversations and "drama" and used to love to engage with my peers over lunch on how the organisation could lead better, invest more time on developing leaders or communicate better. And then I received the call to a one-on-one with my manager at the time, who assertively (it felt brutally at the time) explained how I would need to "tone it down" if I was to help build the culture rather than criticise it. I needed to realise the impact of my unfiltered "blabbing" and ask myself the question, "Was I being part of the solution or part of the problem?" I will always remember that conversation and still today need to be reminded to be a bit more conscious with my words and filters when speaking to others in my own or client organisations.

When we become less aware or feel more threatened by a particular change, we can come across as passive resistors who **believe** that change is hard and scary and exhausting, and that we can only take so much change. We believe that is better to stay with what we know, take the easier route and rather watch and wait than take action too soon. When things don't go our way, we believe that life sucks and is not fair.

We generally feel discouraged, apprehensive, wounded and victimised.

We use **language** like "Let's not bother", "It's always/never worked before", "I'll go with the majority", "Yes...but, this idea is a non-starter", "It's too risky", "Let's wait and see".

We have daily **habits** like being sceptical, criticising, sabotaging, managing our image, avoiding commitment, and creating unnecessary drama.

> **Change navigator or rebel?**
>
> When does initiating or driving too much change become a detractor rather than have a positive effect?
>
> Leaders who are very energetic and experimental with a high change threshold might rush off into the future at a pace that leaves people behind. Their teams may try to keep up but may not have the mental or emotional processing speed or physical stamina required for rapid and sustained change. This is where empathy and checking in with the people around you is critical for sustainable, effective change. Other people initiate change through less constructive or consultative ways by rebelling against the system and demanding faster change than is possible in the current context. These change agents can be labelled rebels or troublemakers and lose their power to influence as they are side-lined by those in power. This is where diplomacy and political savvy are important to tread the fine line between being a change agent or a saboteur. Learning to balance a perceived urgent need for change with the common sense of what is possible within a space of time with the people you have, is the difference between a master change navigator and those who burn out or get ousted.

4. WE ARE WHAT WE BELIEVE

Leadership (whether of self or others) starts with a belief that you can influence others positively. Each one of us is unique and has wonderfully diverse strengths and talents to contribute to the world. What if we believed that our special mix of personality, ideas and skills could help others around us in some way? Wouldn't we want to share them for the benefit of all? What if we believed we could make a difference to our own and other's health and energy through our thinking and actions? What if we believed that life was a playground to learn and grow, not a place of threat and danger? Each of these possible beliefs determine the way you think about situations and the actions you take. Let us examine our beliefs about change and influencing to see where can cultivate some beliefs that can fundamentally shift our sense of purpose and impact and how much fun we can have dancing with change.

Have a look at some underlying beliefs of a passive resistor and a maze navigator and notice where there are opportunities to take on and practice some different beliefs. Beliefs get formed through past experiences, listening to and watching others. We can shift our beliefs through creating new experiences and finding different people to listen to and watch – those who have been examples of positively influencing and navigating change. The more we practice making choices from an empowered state of belief, the more we create and reinforce the neural hardwiring in our brains and create new habits that over time become automatic and without effort.

FROM believing…	TO believing…
• Change is painful and exhausting	• Change is necessary for growth and survival
• I hate change. I'm not good at change	• I love the adventure of change
• I'll just go with the flow	• If it's to be it's up to me
• Why bother, let's just chill	• Our attitude determines our altitude
• This is a waste of time and will never work	• We can make this work if are agile and adapt

5. DAILY HACKS AND HABITS FOR NAVIGATING CHANGE

Here are some daily questions that Maze Navigators ask, and habits they practice to build their ability to deal with disruptive, unexpected change and to encourage others to embrace the opportunities and possibilities that change brings when we stay in a positive, creative state. For a quick way of remembering these, try the 4Ps – **Perspective, Pivot, Purpose** and **Perseverance**. Check out our resources section for more in-depth explanations and tools.

5.1 Habit #1: Empathetic Perspective

To be great change navigators we must become adept at empathetic perspective. The big questions to ask on a regular basis, with empathy, are: Where am I? Where is my team or key stakeholders? How will I know?

A good definition of empathy from Greater Good Science Center at UC Berkeley is: "The ability to sense other people's emotions, coupled with the ability to imagine what someone else might be thinking or feeling."[3]

If we can sense and imagine, we can respond with more insights and compassion than just operating from our perspective.

Where am I?

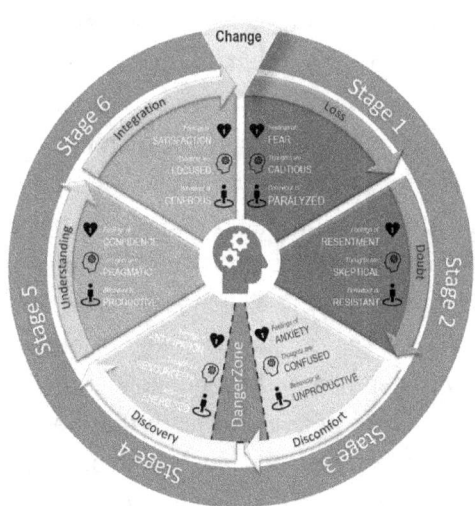

The first person to tap into is YOU. If you are conscious of your own feelings and reactions to change, you are more likely to be able to tune into others – and avoid being blind to your own reactions that can impact others subconsciously. There are many diagnostic tools that help us understand where we might be in our cycle of reacting or adapting to changing circumstances.

---

3   Greater Good Magazine, 2020.

One of these is the change cycle.[4] Use this cycle to identify where you are and how you might be feeling on the change cycle below. Are you at the stage of loss, doubt, discomfort, discovery, understanding or integration? You can be at more than one stage at a time, especially when the change is complex or there are many changes happening simultaneously. This allows you to manage yourself and your reactions first without projecting your own feelings or insecurities onto others. Aim, with the help of a coach, colleague or friend, to see how you can move through the phases beyond the danger zone to discovery and then through to understanding and integration over time. You can also use this tool to guess where some of your colleagues might be.

Where is my team or key stakeholders?

Another great diagnostic tool for understanding your own and other's reactions to stress or change is David Rock's SCARF model. Research by the NeuroLeadership Institute has shown that our brains seek rewards and certainty, avoid threats and pain, and aim to minimise their energy use.[5] A current day reward such as increasing status, certainty, autonomy, relatedness, fairness or SCARF factors can activate the same emotional brain response of our ancient survival elements of food, sex or shelter. In a similar way, a current day threat such as social rejection, decreasing status or unfairness can generate as strong an automatic response as being confronted by a wild predator or an armed attacker. When one of the SCARF factors are under threat during a change process, they can bring up intense and sometimes irrational fears and emotions. If you are aware of these, you can respond accordingly. Use the following table to identify possible needs and fears that you or people you know might be experiencing, and learn how to optimise your response to them and address their fears and needs.

---

4   Change Cycle @ CCMC Inc., 2020.
5   Rock, 2009.

FACTOR	Needs	Fears	How to optimise
Status	Relative importance to others.	Fear of criticism, exposure, failure, loss of power/status	Recognise incremental growth, change the comparison
Certainty	Being able to predict the future	Fear of uncertainty, chaos, not knowing, loss	Find the patterns, normalise, over-communicate
Autonomy	Sense of control over events	Fear of authority, loss of control, loss of freedom	Provide choices, give parameters
Relatedness	Sense of safety with others, of friend rather than foe	Fear of rejection, disappointment, betrayal, not being accepted	Connect people together, reduce social threat
Fairness	Fair exchanges between people	Fear of unfair treatment, inequity, not being recognised	Be transparent

Another aspect to watch in a team environment under change is TRUST. Trust is the foundation to team effectiveness and when it breaks down due to insecurity or a need to compete for survival, team spirit and the ability to maintain results and energy crumbles. Patrick Lencioni, one of the leading experts on building high performing teams, has found that healthy teams trust team members, have unfiltered debates, commit to decisions and plans of action, hold each other accountable and focus on the achievement of results.[6] Unhealthy teams, on the other hand, demonstrate the

---

6   Lencioni, 2002.

opposite of these traits as shown below. Use the definitions below to help you identify where you or your team might be struggling and what is required to get you back to facing the change as a cohesive, supportive, trusting team. When we are working more virtually, as in recent times, opportunities for personal engagement often suffers, and trust is tested. Make the time and space to help your team to identify the team and trust challenges, encourage them to share some of their underlying stress responses, and then explore how they can contribute to navigating the change as a team. See assessment tools and guides below.[7]

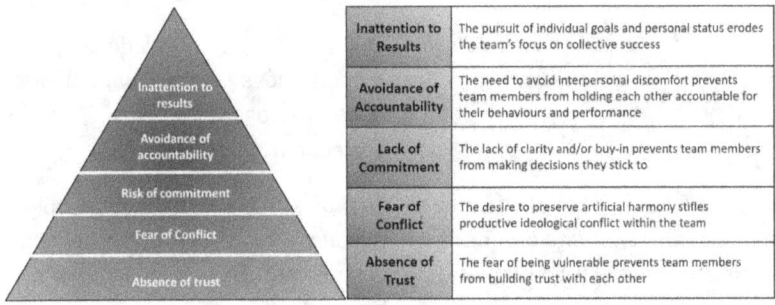

As the world around us is changing rapidly, it will be important to navigate the dynamics of team effectiveness. Korn Ferry, in their article, "Accelerating through the turn: Preparing for a future beyond the crisis"[8] say that "it is not enough that leaders build agile teams. They also have to build "smart teams" – diverse, inclusive, and configured for a precise purpose. They feature not only a mix of skills, expertise, and viewpoints, but also a blend of gender, racial, and cultural backgrounds. They require leaders who can establish trust through empathy, recognise their own cultural preferences, and gather different viewpoints to achieve organisational goals.

In the midst of a crisis, "true influencers" aren't the usual suspects but often unexpected, emerging leaders who can help connect leaders to different groups, teams, and areas of the organisation,

---

7   Lencioni, 2002.
8   Korn Ferry, 2020.

including those who may be resistant to change, and gather information and feedback to create real-time cultural agility. Korn Ferry data shows that "true influencers" can increase the speed of change by as much as 25%, improve engagement initiatives by up to 30%, and even reduce communications costs by around 15%.

When you, your team, your organisation or your family is facing significant change, it is a good idea to identify who is impacted the most, and who you might need to prioritise to support during the change. This can be very tricky in situations that impact you both personally and professionally, for example the global COVID-19 pandemic. Many people are caught in the middle of job role and family role as they navigated this change and tried to keep their families and work teams safe. Think about all the people who are impacted by you or who are impacted by, and include those that might require your communication or support during the change. Typical stakeholder groups in business are executives, managers, staff, team, change influencers, internal customers, external customers, suppliers or external stakeholders (e.g. board, media, government). Typical stakeholder groups in personal lives might be immediate family unit, parents, siblings, extended family, friends, neighborhood or community.

How will we know?

When assessing the change impact and needs of ourselves and others, it is best to access our **intuition** and **empathy.** Tapping into our intuition enables us to pick up energetic, emotional or body language signals that are not directly communicated. Empathy allows us to see things from another's perspective (as if we walked a thousand miles in their shoes) and not just through our own personality, filters, preferences, biases, and assumptions. When we are in the stress response, our ability to access our intuition and empathy is severely compromised as all our energy and resources are occupied in readiness for flight or flight. Take some time to breathe deeply, calm your brain and connect with your heart and become the conscious observer to notice what is really going on and how you can be of highest service to that person or group at that time.

5.2 Habit #2: The Agile Pivot

Agility = the ability to move quickly and easily AND also to think and understand quickly.

Pivoting = the ability to change direction quickly when the chosen approach is no longer working – while still remaining focused on the ultimate goal or purpose.

When we combine the terms 'agility' and 'pivoting', we get a sense of what is needed to adapt in these crazy, interesting and disruptive times. We think of soccer or netball players pivoting, but also many companies have pivoted their strategy when their current tactics were not working. Eric Ries, author of *Lean Start-Up* says a pivot is a change of strategy without a change in vision. He gives a number of great examples of company pivots in his Youtube link, *Eric Ries explains The Pivot.* Pivoting for entrepreneurs, as defined by Entrepreneur.com, is also the art of recognising that the pursuit of a specific idea, direction or product – in which you've invested significant time, money and energy – is no longer the correct path to follow.[9]

Have a look at the following aspects of agility and see where you might have some opportunities to think about this in new ways. The first five of the below agilities are adapted from the HFMtalentindex Learning Agility Assessment.[10,11]

---

9   Ries, 2012.
10 Abrahami, 2014.
11 HFM Talent Index, 2020.

AGILITY & PIVOTING reflection tool	OPPORTUNITY
Change Agility Constant curiosity, fueled by new unknown things and an interest in investigating, experimenting and learning. Embraces change and sees change as an opportunity to learn new things and test own abilities.	
Mental Agility Analyses, thinks out of the box and uses new ideas to create new insights when things are complex or unclear. Recognises and makes sense of patterns quickly and suggests a way forward despite ambiguity.	
People Agility Open and constructive to people with different backgrounds and opinions, taking others' needs and opinions seriously and adapting approach accordingly.	
Results Agility Ambitious, self-confident and success-oriented. Able to set and adjust goals in new and unfamiliar situations and maintain focus and calm during pressure and change.	
Awareness Agility Knows own strengths and weaknesses, self-aware, self-critical and self-correcting, with high willingness to learn and improve. Able to shift perspectives and adapt approach quickly as new information or feedback is received.	
Pivoting Agility Recognises that the pursuit of a specific idea, direction, product or relationship – in which you've invested significant time, money and energy – is no longer the correct path to follow. Humility to listen to other's advice and admit mistakes, embrace the learning from the past, and pivot quickly with available resources toward a new direction.	

5.3 Habit #3: Purposeful stories

We all need a sense of vision and purpose to know where we are going and why. "If you don't know where you're going, any road will do." Change navigators take time to create their own vision boards and co-create courageous and inspiring visions for their teams, families or organisations. It is not just the end goal, which is important to share, but the journey and roadmap with key milestones to get there, i.e. the narrative or story. This includes the acknowledgement that the journey will likely be a windy adventurous one with many twists and turns, but that together we will make it to the worthwhile destination. Some great vision examples are given below.

- Nelson Mandela: "Equality and justice, freedom and multiracial democracy built on the premise that people are created equal."
- Tesla: "To accelerate the world's transition to sustainable energy."
- Google: "To organize the world's information and make it universally accessible and useful."

Change navigators excel at inspiring others through the art of storytelling. They communicate a new way forward in a simple, clear and exciting way. This requires good communication skills and storytelling techniques. When thinking about communication, include verbal, written and digital communication as well as speaking to groups in a public forum. You need to understand rapport, body language, presence, preparation and how to create logical arguments in which the benefits outweigh the risks of change.

In "7 Storytelling Techniques Used by the Most Inspiring TED Presenters"[12], Nayomi Chibana explains that "our brains are hardwired to process and store information in the form of stories.

---

12 Chibana, 2020.

So, when we hear that "once upon a time" there was a certain character in such and such place, our minds are immediately transported to this imaginary scene. Stories are irresistible to the human mind because they activate our imaginations and so we have no choice but to follow the mental movies created in our heads." In his insightful book *The Seven Basic Plots*[13], author Christopher Booker finds that there are seven basic story plots that have universal appeal. These include the story of the hero defeating a monster, the rags-to-riches tale, the quest for a treasure, and the voyage of a hero who comes back a changed person. Practice building your stories and presentations with a few key tips:

- Immerse your audience in a story – with bold words, emotive aspects, sensory details and graphic images.
- Tell a captivating personal story – of triumph over extreme adversity or pick one of the seven plots above.
- Create suspense – keep them guessing, "What will happen next?"
- Bring characters to life – with three-dimensional detail and unique traits, fortunes and misfortunes.
- Show. Don't tell – transport them to a scene, rather than tell them about it.
- Build up to a S.T.A.R. moment with "Something They'll Always Remember".
- End with a positive takeaway – a "spark" or key piece of wisdom in a short, memorable phrase or sound bite.

5.4 Habit #4: Empowered Perseverance

One the images that sticks with me that defines **resilience** and **perseverance** is that flower or tree that grows in inhospitable places, and despite the lack of fertile soil, regular rainfall or a nurturing environment, still

---
13 Booker, 2004.

grows and reaches for the sun and shares its beauty or shade with others. Resilience for me means knowing and believing at a deep soul level, that we will all be ok in the end. I love the quote from Sonny Kapoor in the movie "The Second Best Exotic Marigold Hotel": "Everything will be all right in the end and if it's not all right, then it's not yet the end."[14] Resilience is facing falling, failing, disappointments and painful experiences and not giving up. It is finding the gift, lesson or silver lining behind every dark cloud. It is reaching a place of acceptance of what happened, and bouncing back after a difficult time and starting afresh and seeing all experiences as learning experiences rather than good or bad. As Edison, the inventor of the light bulb, famously stated: "I have not failed. I've just found 10,000 ways that won't work."[15] Resilience is telling the story of your past in a way that empowers yourself and others, rather than blames or shames. It is also not falling into the toxic traps of cynicism, skepticism or denial. It is keeping the vision alive despite seemingly insurmountable odds. Some **empowering thoughts** and words as we hear disturbing news are:

- Ok, so let's recalibrate our expectations.
- What can I or we do now?
- Let's try a different approach and be willing to be wrong.
- What opportunities or learning could come out of this?

For a really good overview of the power of resilience, or in this case grit, watch "Grit: the power of passion and perseverance" by Angela Lee Duckworth[16] listed in our resources section.

When things seem tough, the outcomes are uncertain, or after a disappointment or failure, it can be hard to muster the motivation each day to get up and try again. To start over or try a different approach, especially when those around you are feeling drained,

---

14 The Best Exotic Marigold Hotel, 2011.
15 Brainy Quote, 2020.
16 Duckworth, 2013.

disappointed and demotivated. This is the time for the change navigator to break up the task ahead of regrouping, pivoting and revising the plan into small steps that can feel like small wins and be celebrated. This also the time to overcome procrastination, by committing to a few small actions a day and setting up buddy time with someone who will hold you to your commitments. During our first 21 day lock down during the COVID-19 pandemic, my family drew up a large 21 day visual calendar with key commitments such as yoga, writing a blog, doing some core exercise or some neglected personal admin, and spent time each day updating it to see how we were doing. If we fell off for a day, the others would motivate us to start again the next.

A big fear driving passive resistors is the fear of being humiliated, embarrassed or criticised for trying new things when they are not sure how they will turn out or how they might come across. The high need for control and certainty (deeply embedded for protection from harm) keeps them away from trying new things and adapting to change with ease and flow. One of the most powerful shifts I was lucky enough to experience in my early years was the invitation to adopt the mantra: **"Willing to be wrong."** This can be extended to "willing to be judged or criticised to be unusual, unique, weird, crazy, stupid, incompetent, etc." When we are willing to be wrong (or any of the above) we develop the capacity to be authentic (not bound by society's expectations or fitting the mould rules) and to laugh at ourselves when things don't work out as planned. It is a capacity to approach challenges and difficulties with a lightness of spirit and an inner knowledge that it will all work out in the end (or at least be an amazing adventure with lots of learning and laughs).

When we feel stuck or hopeless, it is sometimes useful to help someone who is worse off than you. Reach out to someone who is struggling with resources, skills or dire circumstances. Support, donate or give of your time. This puts our own misery into perspective.

6. TIPS, TOOLS AND RESOURCES

If you are interested in exploring and learning more, here are some of our favourite tips, tools and resources to accelerate your journey to becoming a Maze Navigator. (See https://catalystconsulting.co.za/power-up8-resources/).

Blogs

Managing with the brain in mind – David Rock, Psychology Today: https://www.psychologytoday.com/sites/default/files/attachments/31881/managingwbraininmind.pdf

3 Rules for Making a Successful Pivot, Entrepreneur Mag: https://www.entrepreneur.com/article/235168

7 Storytelling Techniques Used by the Most Inspiring TED Presenters – Nayomi Chibana: https://visme.co/blog/7-storytelling-techniques-used-by-the-most-inspiring-ted-presenters/

Videos

Staying stuck or moving forward | Dr. Lani Nelson Zlupko: https://www.youtube.com/watch?v=sHLpOUZe388

5 ways to lead in an era of constant change | Jim Hemerling: https://www.youtube.com/watch?v=urntcMUJR9M

Patrick Lencioni – 5 dysfunctions of a team: https://www.youtube.com/watch?v=GCxct4CR-To

Eric Ries explains The Pivot: https://www.youtube.com/watch?v=1hTl4z2ijc4

TED's secret to great public speaking | Chris Anderson: https://www.youtube.com/watch?v=-FOCpMAww28

Grit: the power of passion and perseverance by Angela Lee Duckworth[3:] https://www.youtube.com/watch?v=H14bBuluwB8

Books

Influence: The Psychology of Persuasion, Robert B. Cialdini

The Hero's Journey: Joseph Campbell on His Life and Work, Joseph Campbell; 2014;

Wired for Story: The Writer's Guide to Using Brain Science to Hook Readers from the Very First Sentence Lisa Cron; 2012

Who moved my cheese? Spencer Johnson

Tools

Learning Agility Indicator: https://www.hfmtalentindex.co.za/product/learning-agility/

Ennea 5 lens assessment – Catalyst Consulting: https://catalystconsulting.co.za/wp-content/uploads/2019/06/Overview-Assessments2.pdf

Self-disruptive leader – Korn Ferry: https://www.kornferry.com/self-disrupt

Change cycle: https://changecycle.com/change-cycle/

The five dysfunctions of a team model and summary: https://www.tablegroup.com/download/the-five-dysfunctions-model-and-summary/

Chapter 8

CONSCIOUSNESS

"Remember that your perception of the world is a reflection of your state of consciousness." –Eckhart Tolle

1. ARE YOU PAYING ATTENTION TO YOUR INTENTION?

One of my favourite insights I wrote down in a talk I attended by John Kehoe is: *"What we intend to... and pay attention to... become our reality."*[1]

It makes a whole lot of sense that if we set our intentions clearly (what we want to be, do or have), and then pay attention to our thoughts, choices and actions to support these intentions... in every moment of every day... that we will have a pretty good chance of achieving them. For example, if we want to learn a new language or skill, the more mind time and physical time we spend practicing a new skill, the more likely we are to succeed.

But how often have you found yourself being side-tracked by your intentions? I can just kick myself sometimes, when I realise that I have lost my awareness and realised my negative impact

---
1   Kehoe, 2011.

or lost time. There are many small moments I realise my lack of awareness after the fact. The time I dived straight into task mode in a meeting and forgot to check on how everyone was doing. Or when I shared feedback in the wrong way at the wrong time. Too often I get frustrated with a colleague's lack of delivery and make an unnecessary jibe. There are also many bigger intentions that I have forgotten about by being too busy, impatient or expedient, or justifying it is not that important. I have employed the wrong person, client or friend knowing the risk and ended up losing the client or the friend. I have pushed my body beyond its limits and got seriously sick or injured. I have started many a gym, diet or book project only to get distracted along the way. Most of us want to show up as our best selves, be respected and have a positive impact on others. Why do we forget?

The trick is training our brain to pay ATTENTION and maintain FOCUS! Every day we are bombarded with emails, WhatsApps, social media feeds, likes and calls. We are continuously pulled in different directions by our bosses, family, colleagues, customers, and the personal chores we just have to get done. We also face multiple challenges daily which disrupt our to do lists – new leaders, roles, technology and products; sudden school meetings or projects, car issues, health challenges, friends in crisis, home or childcare issues and traffic jams. We also face so many juicy temptations such as Netflix and fun social events – and why shouldn't we be allowed to chill and have a life? So how do we maintain our attention and focus in a world of overwhelming distractions AND find that perfect balance of achieving goals AND enjoying the sweetness of life?

The first step is to assess how you feel about yourself as you move through your daily choices. **Are you motivated, satisfied, proud and energised by your choices OR are you feeling frustrated, guilty, anxious or depressed about your progress? Are you clear on your intentions? Are you allocating attention to them?**

As Daniel Goleman says in his book *FOCUS*, "If your life feels like a series of quick hits and dopamine fixes, it's time to put the smartphone on airplane mode for a while. Relying on these devices more than on our minds has left us with an attention span that's less than that of a goldfish. Now that's something to worry about."[2] We live in a world of constant connectedness, in which we tap or swipe our phones over 2600 times a day.[3] As our real and digital lives merge, we receive many benefits of convenience, speed and connection. We also face the risks of false news, inaccurate data, digital avatars posing as real people, chat bots or robots programmed by unethical humans, cyber-attacks, digital predators, brain overload, human isolation, and many others. We need the savvy to consciously create and contribute to our digital footprint in a conscious manner and learn to filter, discern and detox to stay healthy safe, and sane. Inc.com states that over 60% of college students are addicted to their phones. Aside from the many physical dangers of cell phone addiction (eyestrain, headaches, accidents) there are many psychological effects such as sleep disturbances, depression, Obsessive Compulsive Disorder (OCD), relationship problems and anxiety.[4] Over 73% of people experience anxiety over losing our phones[5] and our pre-occupation with smart phones leads to a decrease in empathy, presence and connection in relationships. "Our phones make us physically present, but emotionally absent."[6] McKinsey says that in times of crisis, empathy is critical for managing relationships and staying connected.[7]

---

2 Goleman, 2013.
3 Brandon, 2019.
4 PsycheGuides, 2020.
5 Brandon, 2019.
6 Dahl, 2014.
7 D'Auria, & De Smit, 2020.

> Nomophobia is a term explaining fear of being without a mobile device or beyond mobile phone contact. Among today's students, it's on the rise, with an increasing number of college students now showering with their cell phone.[8] But as our digital engagement goes up, so does our personal sense of loneliness.[9]

If we want to manage our attention and focus, we need to be self-aware. According to Goleman, being self-aware means: "understanding your own thoughts and emotions and how they impact your performance."[10] It's having an accurate sense of your strengths and limitations and understanding how others see you. It is being able to observe your inner dialogue and notice how much attention you are paying to the critical, doubting voice or the motivating, "we can do this" voice. It is noticing your impact on others, especially when you are feeling stressed or down. It is about listening to your conscience and doing the right thing, not just following the masses. Consciousness is about being a conscious leader of self and others by focussing on people and inspiring and drawing out the best in others as a path to success, and not just focussing on short-term results or self-interest.[11]

Our **definition of consciousness** is as follows:

> Consciousness is about being constantly aware of our intentions, attention and impact. It's about focusing our minds to get meaningful and original work done, relationships built, growing our potential and making wise choices. It includes conscious consumption (what we allow into our awareness and bodies), conscious being (how we think, feel and act) and conscious impact (who and how we impact others).
>
> *"Through life I have learned that the most important critic whose judgement of my actions matters most is my conscience."*
> –Thuli Madonsela

---

8 Psychology Today, 2014.
9 Amatenstein, 2019.
10 Goleman, 2013.
11 Dawn, 2020.

2. **OVERWHELMED OR FOCUSED?**

There are many benefits to consciously choosing how we live moment to moment and develop our self-awareness. People who are consciously working at improving their operating systems achieve goals faster, prevent problems, make more appropriate decisions, feel more fulfilled and have a healthier self-esteem. They also seem to have greater courage and confidence to take action, have a growth mindset, learn to let go of past hurts and have better quality relationships. Healthier life choices also lead to healthier bodies with more energy to do the things we love.

Many longitudinal studies, the most famous being the Stanford marshmallow experiment on delayed gratification in 1972[12], show that children (and adults) who have the inner mental strength to delay immediate gratification (distraction) for a greater reward in the longer term show significantly enhanced life results than those who can't. This includes income, education, relationships, health and happiness. For a quick overview you can view *The Marshmallow Experiment – Instant Gratification,* on YouTube[13]

There are also many downsides of our conscious minds remaining underdeveloped and stuck in our past programmes and beliefs. These can include cluttered and unfocused thinking; low self-esteem; procrastinating; and feeling stuck, overwhelmed or distracted. People in reaction to life often feel anxious, afraid, depressed or ashamed, with recurring problems or drama. A life full of inaccurate observations, false beliefs, negative emotions or assumptions can feel like an emotional roller-coaster as short-term or difficult relationships play out and impact health and energy levels. Poor decision-making can also lead to financial troubles, business failures or poor work performance. Relationships are fraught with conflict, with more than half of marriages ending in divorce. Many people don't look after their health or save for

---

12 Wikipedia, 2020.
13 FloodSanDiego, 2010.

their retirement. Most people admit they don't get work-life balance correct and many people get duped into online, phone or relationship scams. Others go through life oblivious to the hurt and damage they create for others due to their insecurities, unexpressed pain or lack of awareness. I have fallen into many of these traps as I have navigated life and become unconscious at times. What about you? Would you like to experience more of the benefits and less of the downsides?

The good news is that consciousness can be developed. We don't need to feel bad about some of the traps we fall into; just decide how much you want to change your results by changing your approach. Just like a computer programme can be upgraded, so can we update and upgrade our minds – with understanding (learning how to), practice (making new neural pathways) and persistence (continuing and repeating until it is a new habit).

> *"Directing attention toward where it needs to go is a primal task of leadership."* –Daniel Goleman

3. WHERE IS YOUR TIME (AND LIFE) GOING?

Being conscious is a mindset and skill that anyone can master, if they believe it is a worthwhile pursuit. It is a skill, however, that takes constant awareness, practice and discipline. It takes much less effort to follow juicy distraction, quickly check social media activity, eat that chocolate, take that drug or sleep in, instead of getting up to follow-though on your morning mental and physical routine. Only once neural pathways have been built through consistently choosing the best response for you over time does it become a habit that requires no more effort. Mel Robbins' 5 second rule TED Talks video on YouTube is very good and relevant!"[14]

---

14 Robbins, 2018.

To make the shift easier, let's explore the different identities that you may be able to relate to. Remember that you are not only the one or the other of these identities, but move between them on good and bad days depending on the amount of awareness and energy you can muster. Some days (or parts of days) you may find yourself falling into the trap of being the **distracted operator.** Other times or days you are able to call upon the **wise discerner** and notice bad choices before acting on them and stay focused on the most important things. Wouldn't it be great if we could spend most of our time in our wise discerner identity with a little break every now and then to just float and go with the flow for a bit?

Distracted operator	Wise discerner
Drifter	Discerner
Deflector	Decisive
Distracted	Focused

The major difference between these two states of being is whether you are operating a default old operating system (instilled through your upbringing and social conditioning) or whether you have upgraded your original software through a conscious effort to create new neural paths and faster, more powerful processing capacity that is relevant for your age and this time. Let's use this opportunity to level up our options and rewards.

Wise discerners are Focused, Decisive, Discerners

As a **wise discerner**, we set clear goals and take intentional action toward those goals. We are mindful of our internal state, our energy, our choices and invest our time and energy wisely every day. We can observe ourselves, be the "witness" and think about our thinking. For example, we can watch ourselves getting angry in an argument, feel the rush of blood to our heads, and yet still have the wherewithal to manage our emotions, take a deep breath and prevent ourselves from saying or doing things we may later regret.

As Wise discerners we can distinguish facts from fiction, consciously discern what we are consuming (news, words, information, nutrition, energy), and how that impacts us and those around us. We can more easily avoid the "noise", gossip, false news, scams or other negative influences – or at least not pay them too much attention. This includes what we view or watch on our social media feeds – and what we pass on to others. This level of awareness expands our choices and helps us avoid the trap of being caught in unnecessary fear or subconscious dysfunctional habits, like getting into unnecessary arguments, procrastinating, self-criticism, self-sabotage or carrying baggage from the past.

Our Wise discerner make good choices and thoughtful, appropriate, timeous decisions that take us closer to our goals. We tend to ask more questions and check assumptions to avoid making rash, reactive, emotional decisions without having thought through the impact and ripple effect or unintended consequences of those actions or decisions. We can tune into our intuition (inner wisdom) and determine what is best for us right now (take that job, drive that road, enter into that relationship, listen to our heart etc.). We are also able to tune into our bodies to sense when to rest or recharge, detox or change our nutritional or exercise rituals. We make decisions even in times of uncertainty or incomplete information to move things forward. We take responsibility for our decisions and commitments, and manage expectations when things change and we can't meet them. We can also manage unreasonable demands in an assertive way (managing upwards or outwards) without getting overwhelmed, dropping the ball or affecting our health.

Our wise discerners are focused, organised and digitally diligent. We keep an eye on our goals, our principles and our health, and avoid being hijacked by less important people, emotions or things. We balance our time in a busy office with quiet space for deep focus or creative work. We are effective, not just busy, and avoid ineffective multi-tasking. In a Thrive Global article, *"Is busy the new stupid? You can't buy time..."*[15], Nunzio Presta says "the bottom line is that there needs to be results tied to your busyness", or you're just haemorrhaging time! If we run ourselves ragged chasing the ever-increasing opportunities and demands, and bounce between meetings, networking events, webinars, projects, out of town conferences, we can feel really good about being productive and busy. But are we really effective? Are the meetings, mails, documents etc. really adding value by an objective measure? This requires us to set healthy boundaries (not working in family time), ask useful questions (purpose and agenda of meetings) and have honest conversations to manage expectations and priorities. We manage our dopamine fixes from our digital devices and juicy distractions and balance intense focus with space for spontaneity, connection and flow. View on YouTube: *"How I Tricked My Brain To Like Doing Hard Things (dopamine detox)"*.[16]

> **Too busy**
>
> I remember a time a number of years ago when I was so proud of my "achievements" for the year, which included our first year long international project in China and South East Asia, a simultaneous project in Cape Town and Durban (I lived in Johannesburg), planning a wedding, building a holiday home in the Drakensberg mountains (4.5 hours drive away) and getting married. My year included six – international two to three week trips, over 20 two to three day local work trips, over 100 flights (and many a weekend in the mountains). I was flying high on adrenalin and ego and dreams coming true. Whilst that is nothing to sneeze at, and it was wonderfully exciting at the time

---

15 Presta, 2019.
16 Better Than Yesterday, 2020.

> and a significant learning experience, I paid the price with multiple jaw spasms, a torn calf muscle and an on-going back injury that was not improving (especially with international travel and exceptionally hard beds and strange environments in China). I also ended up in conflict with a good friend and some family members due to lack of time to engage and deal with certain issues. Looking back, I realise how crazy and out of balance this was. My optimistic, efficient, "I can do anything" driver didn't know when to slow down or listen to my body and my friends. I have to stay really conscious and remember how important down time is for recharging my body and brain and nurturing important relationships.

> *"We live in a culture that says you should be able to power through anything. Life will very generously remind you that you cannot, and it will very generously break you at times and very generously show you."* —Elizabeth Gilbert

Wise discerners **believe** that their intention (goals) and attention (focus) will determine their energy and their results. They believe they can watch and choose their thoughts, emotions, behaviour and how they spend their time. They believe in consciously developing their minds, programmes and power to make wise choices. They believe they should be guided by their conscience.

They generally **feel** focused, calm, patient, reflective and healthy.

They use **language** like "Let's focus", "What is important here", "How will this impact", "What we can do differently", "Let's be wise here".

They have daily **habits** like planning and prioritising; pausing to reflect; mindfulness practice; managing focus, attention, time and energy.

> **Time Optimisers**
>
> In a CNBC.com article [17], Ashton Kutcher says he used to lose two hours of his morning responding to emails, or as he puts it, "everyone else's to-do list for you". Now he says before he opens his computer or smart phone in the morning, he spends time writing down what he wants to get accomplished for the day. Then he deals with his outgoing important mail before responding to what others want from him.
>
> Read about other successful time optimisers such as Brian Tracy, Oprah Winfrey, Tony Robbins and Elon Musk in: *How These 7 Successful People Manage Their Time And What You Can Learn*.[7]

Distracted operators are Drifters, Distracted, Deflectors

Many of us have some work to do to become masters of our attention, our energy and our conscious choice, and often fall into the trap of being a **distracted operator**. There is just so much information and so many opportunities coming at us from all sources, particularly in times of high change, that we desperately want to stay informed, in touch, in the know and not miss out (fear of missing out, FOMO, is real). Particularly when we are overwhelmed, tired, emotional or bored it is all too easy to **drift** into effortless distraction and be absorbed for hours in activities that we may question later – but why did I do that? We forget about our goals or boundaries and just go with the flow. We can easily be **distracted** or influenced to join someone else's interesting project or scheme and so become overly busy, stressed, drained and disorganised. Our FOMO makes us say yes to things or people we should rather say "no" to or "not now".

It can be a vicious cycle because when we catch ourselves drifting, we can also fall into being a **deflector** and making up excuses or blaming external factors for unmet commitments. We would prefer to avoid responsibility, confrontation, or big decisions at

---
17 Connley, 2017.

these times, and can thus become part of other people's stories rather than the writers of our own. We can end up chasing our tail or bouncing from one drama to the next.

Distracted operators tend to believe that it is better to be spontaneous and not rock the boat. They believe being busy and multi-tasking makes them efficient and important. They believe they have very little control over their thoughts, feelings, or lives or believe they can catch everything up later.

They generally **feel** overwhelmed, flustered, tired and distracted.

They use **language** like "I am overwhelmed", "I can't help it", "I can't seem to get things done", "There's too much to do", "I'm so drained, why me, who cares?"

They have daily **habits** like procrastinating; blaming; multi-tasking; being distracted with social media, or conversations or problems; and bouncing between urgent issues or dramas.

4. TAKING THE ROAD LESS TRAVELLED

Becoming more of a wise discerner is a journey of conscious intent, practice and repetition. Firstly, you need to believe that wise discerners achieve more in their life at a faster pace. Secondly, you need to cultivate the neural paths of conscious awareness and choice until they become automatic programmes. Then you need to build discerner habits into your daily routines for effortless achievement of your goals.

Have a look at some of the differing beliefs below and choose some to focus on to shift your choices. This list is just an indication of beliefs. Please feel free to add your own.

FROM believing...	TO believing...
• I can't change how my brain works or who I am • I like to be spontaneous and take what comes • I am busy therefore I am important • I have FOMO and proud of it • I am overwhelmed, stressed, tired, just surviving • I do what I feel like	• My thoughts, feelings and habits create my personal reality • Where my attention goes, my energy flows • Busy is the new stupid • My time is my life and I need to choose wisely • I am focused, energised, organised and thriving • My conscience is my guide

Here is an example of someone who is caught in some belief traps, but also consciously shifting them.

A Proud Master Procrastinator

I have an amazing friend who is one of those special people that is almost always there for you when you need an ear or some help. He is wonderful when he is present with you, but then so often doesn't follow through on what he offers or commits to in time. He is continuously lamenting that he isn't getting to the most important things in his life (setting up his new business with marketing material, training material, his website and contacting potential clients, etc.), because he overcommits to too many things. He wakes up with so many things to do, goes into overwhelm, and then just gives up getting anything done and spends the day allowing anything to distract him – including the internet rabbit hole, gardening, daydreaming or calls to "help" his friends. He is almost proud to say he is a master procrastinator. Only when he remembers his goals and who he has the potential to be does he set and communicate healthy boundaries with others and get stuff done. I am seeing more of that recently and hope to see it continue! Look on YouTube to see how a typical procrastinator rationalises his actions: "Procrastination Tales of Mere Existence"[18] or "Inside the mind of a master procrastinator" by Tim Urban.[19]

---

18 AgentXPQ, 2006.
19 Urban, 2016.

"In our consciousness, there are many negative seeds and also many positive seeds. The practice is to avoid watering the negative seeds, and to identify and water the positive seeds every day." –Thich Nhat Hanh

5. DAILY HACKS AND HABITS FOR CONSCIOUSNESS

Wise discerners have daily habits that help them to be aware and continuously raise their level of conscious choice, and therefore increase their effectiveness, happiness and goal attainment. See our resources section for more information and tools to enrich each habit.

5.1 Habit #1: Conscious intent

Make your intentions very clear and visible – write them down and display them visually for regular reminders of what is most important to you. Include intentions for all areas in your wheel of life to strive for a healthy balance over time, e.g. wealth, health, career, learning, relationships, social or community and spiritual aspects. Create a vision board for the wall or door or a digital board on Pinterest or a screen saver for your computer or mobile. You can also set up daily or weekly tasks that pop up to keep you focused. There are also new technologies available that enable a digital Mind Movie with pictures, videoclips, affirmations, music etc. that are extremely effective for bringing your dreams and goals closer using brain science. (See https://www.mindmovies.com or https://www.subliminalvisionboards.com)

5.2 Habit #2: Conscious attention

Make it a habit to pause every hour or so and check in on where your attention has been for the last hour or so. Initially set a timer and after a while it will become a habit. Notice where your attention goes and what pulls you away from what is important. Make a list. Is it noise, people, texts, notifications, daydreaming, FOMO, saying yes to last minute requests from others, craving food, coffee or nicotine? Do you know what the payoffs are for these distractions? What is the underlying need or fear or emotion that is taking your attention? Notice how much attention you give to the distractions versus your intentions or goals for the day. Is there a healthy balance or is some mental discipline required? Remember that **busy is the new lazy**. Make your time count. Make the consequences for the distractions immediate so you can manage them more actively. Create space in your day for both focused work and spontaneous flow time which is also important for creativity.

5.3 Habit #3: Conscious being

Practice the skill of becoming the Witness; the state in which you watch yourself thinking, feeling, doing while you are doing it. Quieten your mind and be still long enough to stop the incessant chatter of the analytical mind and become aware of a part of yourself beyond the mind. Try the "2 columns" exercise in a journal or digital note pad and write down the moments you fell into distracted operator mode and where you stayed focused as the wise discerner.

Distracted operator	Wise discerner
e.g. Got caught up in social media for 30 mins and was late for an appointment	e.g. I stayed focused and didn't respond to WhatsApps until I finished my document

5.4 Habit #4: Conscious time[20]

	URGENT	NOT URGENT
IMPORTANT	Quadrant #1 "NECESSITY" Your Key Action: "MANAGE" **Common Activities** • Crises • Deadline-driven activities • Medical emergencies • Other "true" emergencies • Pressing problems • Last minute preparations	Quadrant #2 "QUALITY & PERSONAL LEADERSHIP" Your Key Action: "FOCUS" **Common Activities** • Preparation and planning • Values clarification • Empowerment • Relationship-building • True recreation
NOT IMPORTANT	Quadrant #3 "DECEPTION" Your Key Action: "USE CAUTION" or "AVOID" **Common Activities** • Meeting other people's priorities and expectations • Frequent interruptions • Most emails, some calls • Urgency masquerading as importance	Quadrant #4 "WASTE" Your Key Action: "AVOID" **Common Activities** • Escapist activities • Mindless tv-watching • Busywork • Junk mail • Some emails • Some calls

Time is the one thing that is finite in our three-dimensional world and that everyone has equal amounts of. Time operates differently in the quantum world but that is another topic not for this book. It is amazing how some people just seem to get a whole lot more out of their allotted time – a day, a year, a decade or a lifetime. Watch Jay Chetty's motivational YouTube clip, "Before You Waste Time – WATCH THIS".[21] A brilliant tool that has stood the test of "time", is Stephen Covey's *Urgent vs. Important matrix*. Use it to analyse where your time is going. See Covey's Timecounselor.com or the book *First Things First* for a detailed description. Other excellent resources for mastering your time include *The 4-Hour Work Week* by Tim Ferriss[22], *Getting Things Done* by David Allen[23], and *Eat that Frog* by Brian Tracy[24] listed in the resources section.

5.5 Habit #5: Conscious space

Effective multi-tasking is a myth. It has been proven that people who try to switch between tasks are significantly less productive than those who are able to focus and complete something first. Juggling too many things at once means fewer resources, less

---

20 The Time Counselor, 2020.
21 Shetty, 2018.
22 Ferriss, 2009.
23 Allen, 2015.
24 Tracy, 2017.

attention and less quality thinking. The brain can move in and out of different tasks but leaves "empty holes" where that information should be, leading to the "swiss cheese" effect and an incomplete recollection of a topic or conversation and an exhausted brain. It takes the brain on average 23 minutes once distracted to get back into a space of deep, creative thinking.[25] People need space to do "deep work" as outlined in the book *Deep Work* by Cal Newport. He says that those who can master their focus can get more and higher quality output in less time... and therefore stay ahead of the competition. He distinguishes between shallow work (e.g. mails, calls, social media, meetings, light documents) and deep work (where we can focus for four to five hours at a time to write, innovate, design, solve complex problems).[26] You can watch a summary on YouTube listed in the link in the resources section below.

A few tips for conscious space are:

- Plan your day to ensure you have space for deep work and interactive work, e.g. meetings, conversations, etc. Work off-site or in a meeting room or coffee shop if you find it easier to focus there.

- Put up a sign on your office door or section when you are busy with deep work (e.g. deep work happening here, please do not disturb).

- Switch off your mail or social media notifications or turn your phone off for a period of deep work and then check in. Tim Ferris suggests you add an auto-responder to your mails stating when and how you will be responding (e.g. at 11am and 3pm), or how to get you urgently if absolutely necessary.

- Communicate to your team, boss or family how important deep work is to the overall success of the team or unit, so that they learn to respect your boundaries.

---

25 Lasoe, 2020.
26 Newport, 2018.

5.6 Habit #6: Conscious energy

When we are bombarded daily with so many demands on our minds and bodies to analyse, process, solve, be vigilant, stay calm, manage conflict, chase a deadline, sit for hours, stare at a computer screen… we can quickly run out of energy. Our bodies emit electromagnetic energy which fuels our ability to live in the world. This can be reduced significantly over time if we spend too much time in rapid brain wave states or uncomfortable physical positions and don't spend enough time recharging through movement, mindfulness and effective rest and sleep. We all know that feeling of being "drained" or our brains feeling "fried". We need to regularly tune into our brains and bodies and learn when to take a break and switch off for a while with some diffuse thinking where our brains can just freewheel. Some quick options can include going for a walk, doing some yoga, playing with your dog or a child, sitting in a garden, staring into space, having a power-nap, listening to some uplifting music, dancing, jogging or practicing some relaxation exercises. The brain requires both focused attention and diffused thinking to be effective and to learn and perform.

Tony Schwartz, in his book "The Power of Full Engagement"[27] suggests reflecting on your energy in four areas – mind, body, heart and spirit, and notice what is energising or de-energising you in each of these areas. Anthony Robbins suggests starting your day, right with early morning rituals and hacks to set you up for the day such as connecting with your breath, your body, with nature and with your inner self.[28] Arianna Huffington, in her book *Thrive accentuates* the importance of a good night's sleep for health, effectiveness and happiness in life.[29]

5.7 Habit #7: Conscious communication

Much of our lives and energy are consumed by managing email, messaging, meetings and conversations – the way we get stuff

---

27 Loehr & Schwartz, 2003.
28 Huddleston, 2019.
29 Huffington, 2015.

done. When effective and efficient, these channels enable us to achieve our business and personal goals. However, when these are vague, unstructured, unfocused and unproductive they can become a muncher of our time and energy. Control what you can by mastering your own time and your communication. Influence others to improve communication through raising positive suggestions in your team or with your family members. Here are some quick tips and tricks, which we often forget:

Emails	Meetings
• Start with something friendly and personal	• Assess best communication channel – not always a meeting
• Be clear on the purpose, process and pay-off	• Clear objectives, agenda, prep and reason for participation
• Focus on who needs to take action – use @Jane	• Clear, simple, short presentations and visuals
• Don't replying all or copy all – be selective	• Minutes and actions distributed – standard templates
• Autoresponder on for how or when you can respond	• Start and end on time
• Manage mail on your mobile device for quick responses	• Agree post meeting comms to speak with one voice
Documents	**Diaries**
• Short and sweet – only info needed, exec summary	• Block out deep work and recharge time
• Structure: headings, logical story, bullet points, visuals and "read more" for easy reading	• Calendar invites – clear subject, purpose and agenda
• Best format for audience e.g. mail, word, ppt, excel, infographic	• Use "Doodle" or similar to co-ordinate multiple parties
• Central repository for version control standards	• Manage responses, apologies, expectations and catch up assertively
Messaging and texts	**Conversations**
• Manage notifications to remove distraction	• Start with rapport building
• Create time to respond in between deep work	• Clarify purpose, timing and minimise distractions (mobile)
• Manage groups through rules and settings	• Deep listening and empathetic responses
• Manage boundaries with colleagues or friends	• Use communication skills to listen, reflect, interpret, summarise
	• End with appreciation and encouragement

5.8 Habit #8: Conscious consumption

You have heard the adage: "We are what we eat." We can expand that to: "We are what we consume." This includes what we consume in the form of nutrition but also what we are feeding our consciousness every day. Take some time to reflect how much of your daily input consists of positive or uplifting data vs. negative or draining data. You may find you spend a lot of time absorbing news (especially negative, sensationalist or even false news to gain attention), people complaining, economic or financial reports signalling impending disaster, team meetings to resolve problems or social media triviality that adds no real value to real friendships and quality of life. You could choose to shift your input to filling your mind and energy with beautiful music, uplifting audiobooks, videos, learning programmes, positive constructive conversations and value adding feeds and comments on social media. Start your day with energising or calming input before interacting with the outside world. Set your filters to ignore or avoid too many negative influences in your day and build your own internal self-talk to boost your confidence and emotional resilience. Eat for energy and health – most of the time.

In our world of 24/7 connectedness, it can very therapeutic to try a digital detox. This can be one day a week e.g. on a weekend or for a deeper detox for a week or two while on leave or a personal retreat. It is important to completely remove yourself from your current way of thinking and daily habits to allow your brain to fully rest and create space for new ideas and insights. You can also develop daily **digital discipline** by limiting access to digital devices for yourselves and your children. Spend precious morning time on creating the mind- and heart space for your day (focus on intentions and attention). Connect with your family, your body and your nutrition. Then and only then, allow the outside world in and deal with urgent or important messages. In the evening, ban cell phones at mealtimes or at certain times and put your phone away at least 60 minutes before going to sleep to prevent the blue light effect on your sleep patterns.

5.9 Habit #9: Conscious impact

Another aspect of consciousness that we don't often think about is our daily impact on others and the planet. How conscious are we of our interaction with colleagues, waitrons, call centre agents, other service agents, our spouses, partners or children? What is our body language, our level of respect and appreciation, our level of presence when we speak to others? Do you check your phone in meetings or when someone is talking to you? Are we conscious of doing the right thing or influencing others to do the right thing for the benefit of our communities and planet? Often we are just in automatic mode following the masses. Be the one who brings a bit of consciousness to your own family or community or workplace. Be brave and start influencing for positive contribution and action.

5.10 Habit #10: Conscious choice

We discovered earlier that many people make poor choices. Chip and Dan Heath, in their book *Decisive: How to Make Better Choices in Life and Work*[30], explain the Four Villains of Decision-making and strategies to overcome them. Take your time when faced with a difficult or complex problem or dilemma and check your thinking against these four villains:

Narrow Framing: "The tendency to define our choices too narrowly, to see them in binary terms". We ask, "Should I break up with my partner or not?" instead of "What are the ways I could make this relationship better?"

Confirmation Bias: "When people have the opportunity to collect information from the world, they are more likely to select information that supports their preexisting attitudes, beliefs, and actions." We pretend we want the truth, yet all we really want is reassurance.

---

30 Heath & Heath, 2013.

Short-term Emotion: "When we've got a difficult decision to make, our feelings churn. We replay the same arguments in our head. We agonize about our circumstances. We change our minds from day-to-day. If our decision was represented on a spreadsheet, none of the numbers would be changing – there's no new information being added – but it doesn't feel that way in our heads."

Overconfidence: "People think they know more than they do about how the future will unfold."

For strategies to counteract the villains see more in their book and video summaries below.

> *"Remember that your perception of the world is a reflection of your state of consciousness."* –Eckhart Tolle

6. TIPS, TOOLS AND RESOURCES

If you are interested in exploring and learning more, here are some of our favourite tips, tools and resources to accelerate your journey to becoming a Wise Discerner. (See https://catalystconsulting.co.za/power-up8-resources/).

Blogs

14 reasons to become more conscious by Steve Pavlina: https://www.stevepavlina.com/blog/2006/07/14-reasons-to-become-more-conscious/

Book summary: Focus – The Hidden Driver of Excellence by Daniel Goleman: https://www.slideshare.net/ramadd1951/focus-the-hidden-driver-of-excellence-summary

How to escape the 'hyperactive hivemind' of modern work: http://www.bbc.com/capital/story/20190715-how-to-escape-the-hyperactive-hivemind-of-modern-work

Is busy the new stupid? You can't buy time… ; Nunzio Presta, Thrive Global, 2019: https://thriveglobal.com/stories/is-busy-the-new-stupid/

Videos

Before You Waste Time – WATCH THIS | by Jay Shetty: https://www.youtube.com/watch?v=vPaS85IA6oY

"Deep Work: Rules for Focused Success in a Distracted World" by Cal Newport: https://www.youtube.com/watch?v=_RMtnDaxmPw

Video Review for Decisive by Chip and Dan Heath: https://www.youtube.com/watch?v=Rhs1rjLJqhw&t=25s

Are You Ready for The 13-Weeks to Unstoppable Challenge?: https://www.youtube.com/watch?v=Cpfoq0NkHxQ

Busy is the new Stupid: https://www.youtube.com/watch?v=35sp4S2w9ZI

"Procrastination" Tales Of Mere Existence: https://www.youtube.com/watch?v=4P785j15Tzk

Inside the mind of a master procrastinator | Tim Urban: https://www.youtube.com/watch?v=arj7oStGLkU

How I Tricked My Brain To Like Doing Hard Things (dopamine detox): https://www.youtube.com/watch?v=9QiE-M1LrZk

Mel Robbins | One of the Best Talks Ever on Self-Motivation: https://www.youtube.com/watch?v=_BNDdamTDak

The Marshmallow Experiment – Instant Gratification: https://www.youtube.com/watch?v=Yo4WF3cSd9Q

Books

The 4-Hour Work Week: Escape the 9-5, Live Anywhere and Join the New Rich, Timothy Ferriss, 2011

Getting Things Done: The Art of Stress-free Productivity, David Allen, 2015

The Power Of Full Engagement: Managing Energy, Not Time, Is The Key To High Performance And Personal Renewal, Jim Loehr & Tony Schwartz, 2017

Eat that Frog!: 21 Great Ways to Stop Procrastinating and Get More Done in Less Time; Brian Tracy, 2017

Chip Heath & Dan Heath; Decisive: How to Make Better Choices in Life and Work; 2013

First Things First, Stephen Covey, 1996

Thrive: The Third Metric to Redefining Success and Creating a Life of Well-Being, Wisdom, and Wonder, Arianna Huffington, 2015

Stillness Is the Key Hardcover – October 1, 2019 by Ryan Holiday (Author)

Tools

Vision Board — A Powerful Tool To Manifest Your Life Desires: https://blog.mindvalley.com/vision-board/

Mindmovie — digital vision board: https://www.mindmovies.com | https://www.subliminalvisionboards.com/

Covey Time Management — Busting Loose of Time Wasters! https://www.timecounselor.com/covey-time-management.html

Chapter 9: CRITICAL THINKER

"The quality of all our doing depends on the quality of the thinking we do first." –Nancy Kline

1. THE QUALITY OF OUR THINKING...

Have you ever made a bad decision? Some decisions have a small impact and help us learn and adapt our daily life strategies or choices. Others can cost us dearly in time, money, broken hearts, health or credibility.

I remember a time during a leadership development programme roll-out across Southern Africa where I was driving or flying weekly, or more, to a new destination. I arrived at the airport with my co-facilitator for a late afternoon flight to Kimberley only to find there was a problem with our tickets. Assuming a glitch I hauled out my credit card and paid for the two flights. I did the same in Kimberley for the hire car and the hotel. I was only able to get hold of my local contact much later that evening, only to be informed that we were a week early for our workshop. I could feel the blood draining from my face, as I imagined explaining this to my boss and how long it would take me to pay off the credit card! My amazing project co-ordinator was on leave and the temp hadn't updated any changes in my diary. I was hugely embarrassed and even won an award for the most embarrassing moment at our company year-end function. It was a costly lesson, but one I could have avoided with a bit of critical thinking and checking of assumptions. My speed over sense (and a tired brain from too many trips and workshops) had compromised my decision-making capability... something that still comes back to bite me today!

What makes us lose our capacity for critical thinking when it matters most?

Our consumption of information has been shifting from books and academic articles to blogs and posts; from the written word to visual pictures, video and audio; and from researched facts to popular beliefs and opinions. We now have "Tinglish" (texting English) for abbreviated instant messaging. We have become so busy rushing through our mails, meetings and deadlines, that we don't have time for deep thinking or debate about problems and solutions. We often take the quickest route or make a gut-feel decision based on the superficial information at hand. We now have Google and apps – for maps, instructions, searching and even deciding. Our education systems have also slid down a slippery slope from robust debate, comprehensive analysis and essays arguing for different perspectives to online content and multiple-choice questions. It is no wonder that we are slowly losing our natural ability to memorise details, think critically, analyse, discern facts from fiction, figure out which information is vital for decisions and consider many viewpoints or perspectives of a problem to make wise decisions.

How many of you know your spouse or best friend's phone number without looking it up on your phone?

We all know people who seem to be in a constant state of drama and surprise. We observe them missing deadlines, coming late for meetings, breaking promises, making avoidable mistakes and saying things they regret. Often the response is... "Well I just hadn't considered that!"

How many times have you sat back after a disaster and wished you had thought things through a bit more thoroughly?

If we don't practice critical thinking, our neural paths start to weaken and we get rusty. Critical thinking helps us look at situations from multiple angles and explore many possible solutions, thereby preventing time-consuming and costly mistakes or re-work. There are many leaders and decision makers in organisations that have the same challenge on a much larger scale. Many multi-million-dollar enterprise wide technology projects go horribly wrong through a lack of robust questioning, planning and alignment across functions. Many expensive partnerships and collaborations break up because of assumptions of how things will work in the future without doing sufficient exploration of values, scenarios, role clarity and financial allocation testing. I am sure that Blackberry, Kodak, BlockBuster Videos, Borders Bookstores etc. had wished they had invested more energy in analysing the market, trends, technology disruptors, customers and potential competitors before investing in old technology or infrastructure, leaving them high and dry as new industry disruptors offered more exciting and relevant products and services. I am sure that many engineering or construction teams have wished for greater critical thinking in their decision-making process after bridges or buildings collapsed. Reviews of airplane crashes or failed space rocket launches often indicated errors in thinking, communication and ultimately decisions made.

Yes, mistakes happen – particularly if we are experimenting and innovating. We need a tolerance for failure AND a healthy dose of critical thinking to reduce the severity of avoidable errors. Richard Paul defines the thinking challenge as follows:

"Everyone thinks; it is our nature to do so. But much of our thinking, left to itself, is biased, distorted, partial, uninformed or down-right prejudiced. Yet the quality of our life and that of what we produce, make, or build depends precisely on the quality of our thought.

Shoddy poor thinking is costly, both in money and in quality of life. Excellence in thought, however, must be systematically cultivated".[1]

Paul suggests that a well cultivated critical thinker:

- raises vital questions and problems, formulating them clearly and precisely;
- gathers and assesses relevant information, using abstract ideas to interpret it effectively;
- comes to well-reasoned conclusions and solutions, testing them against relevant criteria and standards;
- thinks open-mindedly within alternative systems of thought, recognising and assessing, as need be, their assumptions, implications, and practical consequences; and
- communicates effectively with others in figuring out solutions to complex problems.

Our **definition of critical thinking** is as follows:

> Critical thinking is proactively thinking things through from all perspectives, asking the right questions, filtering for relevant information and, objectively analysing and integrating data to make wise collaborative decisions and resolve complex dilemmas in an unpredictable world.

2. THE IMPACT OF OUR THINKING

There are many **benefits** to thinking critically and making wise decisions. Critical thinkers are better at preventing and **solving problems** by thinking ahead and "working smarter, not harder". They are less likely to fall for scams, tricks or manipulation because they approach everything with a healthy amount of scepticism (e.g. the latest fad diet, Ponzi investment scheme or treasure hunter). They

---

[1] Paul & Elder, 2019.

make more reasoned and **balanced decisions** and also consider the unintended impact of decisions. They are more **creative and agile** in high change environments and can engage others in change through clearly **articulated ideas** and benefits. Critical thinkers **get more done** by planning and prioritising their time and anticipating barriers, and **learn faster** than others by organising their thoughts and new knowledge. They perform better at analytical and verbal reasoning **tests** that are often used in entrance exams and in recruitment and talent reviews. They are also better at preventing or **resolving conflict** through understanding multiple perspectives and are less emotional or biased in their response to people who are different to them.

If we rush high speed through life with many default assumptions, we can have many **regrets**. We may **repeat mistakes** (e.g. choosing the same type of relationships that are not good for you); make **bad decisions** (e.g. investing your hard earned savings in a get rich quick scheme, or new business venture or system) and **procrastinate** when action is needed (e.g. only working on that long report at the last minute). We can also suffer from many **misunderstandings and unnecessary conflict** (e.g. not considering the negative impact of insensitive statements or excluding key people from decisions).

3. DEFAULT THINKER OR MEANING MAKER?

Whether you are a natural or cultivated critical thinker or not, the good news is that critical thinking can be developed. Just like a computer programme or app can be upgraded, so we can update and upgrade our minds – with understanding (learning how to), practice (making new neural pathways) and persistence (continuing and repeating it until is a new habit). Two characters that can assist us to identify and then develop our critical thinking are the **default thinker** and the **meaning maker.** These play on opposite sides of the critical thinking continuum and you can observe yourself or get feedback from others to see where you might be spending most of your time. Pay attention to the circumstances or areas of your life where you are more accomplished, but also where you seem to make the same mistakes over and over again. Remember no position is necessarily good or bad, as we all move along this continuum in various situations and stages of life. It is useful, however, to accept ourselves as we are today, AND then figure out how building the mindsets and skills to spend more time a bit higher up on the continuum and make better decisions in life and work might be beneficial.

Default thinker
Expedient
Linear
Complicator

Meaning maker
Anticipator
Systemic
Integrator

Meaning makers are Anticipators, Systemic, Integrators

Meaning makers are **anticipators** who think **strategically** about the long-term and the **big picture.** They take time to **reflect** on different scenarios and possibilities and the unintended consequences of decisions. They watch trends in the environment so they can **anticipate change** and adapt their approach accordingly. They are continuously **asking questions** to gain additional data or insight to improve their problem solving and decision-making. See our critical questions list in our habits section.

Meaning makers **think systemically** about cause and effect and how all the different parts of a system interact with each other. They **gather and analyse relevant data** from multiple sources and organise it with an aim to understand, compare and find answers. They are good at creating **mental models** to clarify ambiguous situations and **challenge assumptions**. They **test and pilot** the most promising (not only the most popular) ideas to gain buy-in and confidence. They understand and **navigate complexity** and seemingly unsolvable dilemmas and the risky trade-offs that are sometimes required to minimise loss and maximise gain. For example, launching a new product may impact another product or division, whilst a new leader may have wide-ranging impact on the organisation's culture. They understand that there is not always a single, linear solution and that the way forward may need to emerge over a period of time as more data becomes available.

Meaning makers connect the dots, connect ideas and people, and **integrate** these to **make sense** of the "noise" into a few **simple** pictures, themes, roadmaps, or benefits. Meaning makers work smart and do more with less. They can find the simplest, least resource intensive method of getting to an outcome. This can include getting messages across in less words, removing bottlenecks, automating mundane tasks or being more focused in meetings.

Meaning makers **believe** that there is always a bigger picture, more perspectives or alternative options that they may not be aware of. They believe in asking the right questions and challenging assumptions and opinions. They believe in seeking out simpler and more effective ways to work and communicate.

They generally **feel** patient, expansive, thoughtful, reflective, insightful.

They use **language** such as "Have we considered everything?" "What are we not seeing?" "How can we simplify or make sense of this?" "Let's summarise the key issues and benefits".

They have daily **habits** like asking questions, testing assumptions, drawing diagrams of problems, thinking about unintended consequences, asking lots of questions, and being curious about what different people think.

We can learn from some of the famous critical thinkers and Nobel Prize winners over the years who have significantly impacted industries and humanity as a whole. Look up the life and work of people like Albert Einstein, Leonardo Da Vinci, Marie Curie, Nicola Tesla, Steve Wozniak, Bill Gates, Frances Arnold and Daniel Kahneman. (See links in the resources below.)

> **Masters of messaging**
>
> I have a colleague, Angela, who is brilliant at taking my 50-page slide packs and reconfiguring it into a few visuals, steps and key messages to make them much easier to digest and remember. The richness can come through the learning experience and the details can always be found later when needed. Another collaboration partner, Graeme, is exceptional at taking mounds of information and presenting to an executive with a few key insights, simple visuals, challenging questions and options on the way forward. He is very conscious of playing to his strengths and bringing a few key people into complement him without hanging onto all the work in a client project.

Default thinkers are Expedient, Linear, Complicators

There may be times that we are in a hurry, impatient or feeling a bit tired or lazy, and we can fall into the trap of being a **default thinker**. We are **expedient** and look for the quickest and easiest route to get the job done, without engaging our strategic or systemic critical thinking. We can be too quick to act and jump to conclusions based on our assumptions, filters, biases or stereotypes without all the facts, options or consequences. We look back with remorse when we realise the unintended impact of our 'too quick in the moment decisions'.

We can also get stuck in a **linear** approach and struggle to expand our thinking or imagination beyond the frame we find ourselves in e.g. industry, function, level, gender, worldview. This can perpetuate insular or silo thinking and "us vs. them" attitudes. We think certain courses of action are "obvious" without considering the ripple effect of changes on other parts of a system. We sometimes don't think we have the time to tune into the "wisdom in the room". We can also be set in our ways and intolerant or closed to new ideas and possibilities.

Default thinkers can also **complicate** situations by running or talking too fast or superficially without a deeper and wider investigation of an issue or problem. This can exacerbate conflict and damage relationships unnecessarily. We can also keep sharing new information as we hear it, without testing validity or integrating the parts into the whole picture. People who work with or for default thinkers often feel overloaded, overwhelmed and confused, without clarity, integration and making sense of the "noise".

We **believe** in the moment that we are smart and know the answers. We believe that our time is valuable and that we can get away with brilliant short-cuts. We think that a lot of things are "obvious" and can be resolved with minimum fuss. We believe that most people "don't get it" and that our experience is sufficient to figure out most dilemmas.

We generally **feel** impatient, arrogant and clever (and then surprised when things go wrong).

We use **language** like "It's obvious, can we get this over with?" "Just do it", "Don't worry about them", "We'll fix it", "We've got enough to work with", "Why aren't you done yet?"

We have daily **habits** like making assumptions, jumping to conclusions, believing what we hear and see online or from "experts", ignoring other inputs, making rash decisions, and fixing mistakes.

Critical Thinking Disasters

Some examples of poor thinking include major disasters such as the sinking of the Titanic (1912), the Space Shuttle Challenger disaster (1986) and the Deepwater Horizon (BP) oil spill disaster (2010). More recent business mistakes include launching New Coke (1985) to a 20% market share drop, Kodak's inability to see digital photography as a disruptive technology (1991-2012) and the leadership errors of the now ex-CEO and founder of Uber (2019). There are so many people and organisations we can learn from – Samsung's Galaxy Note 7 blow up phone, many career ending tweets, walking out of a job prematurely, getting a tattoo of a lover, multiple air accidents with the Boeing 737 series, and many more.[2] You can view more bad business decisions in our resources section.

4. SEEING IS BELIEVING

From the descriptions above you may already have identified where you are on the continuum. Remember the way you naturally operate today is a result of past influences, experiences, learning and practice, which have resulted in you forming deep unconscious beliefs about yourself and the world. Have a look at the following list of beliefs with an open mind and a curiosity which might be programmed into your sub-conscious without you even being aware of it. It can be a bit unsettling to realise that you may have hidden beliefs that you consciously would not subscribe to but are driving your thinking and behaviour. Awareness is the first step toward change.

---

2   Gardner, 2018.

FROM believing...	TO believing...
• I know how this works. I've done it before • I can do it quicker and better than others • Let's get this over with so we can move on • It's obvious • People still don't get it – after all I've shared	• What are we not yet seeing – what's the bigger picture? • Other people can add valuable perspectives • Go slow to go fast – involve others for ideas and buy-in • It takes time and questions to understand an issue • Keep it simple (KISS) – how can we visualise this?

Challenging our paradigms: Professor Jansen

I heard Professor Jansen, ex Vice-Chancellor of University of the Free State (UFS), advisor and speaker talk at a learning conference. He told a story of meeting the parents of his son's fiancé for the first time. His son had met a Dutch girl (from the Netherlands) and had asked her to marry him and it was now time to introduce the parents. He recounted how he, as a black man, entered the house of these foreign white people with such narrow beliefs and baggage from the past which led to some tense moments and initial antagonism. Over time, he grew to know and love them as dear friends. He humbly acknowledged how many times he misinterpreted comments and body language, through his own racial biases and insecurities, and reacted in anger. It is very brave of him to tell this story in a country fraught with deep racial antagonism and stereotypes, borne out of very difficult or traumatic experiences and social conditioning. He is a shining example of someone who has actively challenged his own and other's limiting beliefs and paradigms to find a way to move forward as human beings not separated or prejudiced by the colour of our skin.

5. DAILY HACKS AND HABITS FOR CRITICAL THINKING

Meaning makers have daily habits that help them think things through and make wise decisions. Some of our favourites are outlined below with more links to resources in the tips and resources section.

5.1 Habit # 1: Time to think

Nancy Kline is one of the great modern writers on thinking and encourages us to create time to think (and listen) for ourselves and others. When you wish to create a conducive environment for building trust, solving problems, collaborating and innovating, she encourages us to do a quick check on the 10 components of a thinking environment to create space for original thinking. Make this a daily habit with yourself, your family and your team.[3] For more details see the links below.

Attention	Listen with palpable respect and interest without interruption	**Diversity**	Welcome divergent thinking and diverse group identities
Equality	Mutually treat each other as thinking peers and give equal turns and attention	**Encourage-ment**	Give courage to go to the current edge of ideas by moving beyond internal competition
Incisive questions	Remove assumptions that limit our ability to think for ourselves, clearly and creatively	**Feelings**	Allow sufficient emotional release to restore thinking
Information	Supply the facts and dismantle denialism	**Appreciation**	Offer acknowledgement of a person's qualities. Practice a 5:1 ratio of appreciation to criticism
Ease	Offer freedom from internal rush or urgency	**Place**	Create a physical environment that says, 'You matter'

---

3   Kline, 2010.

5.2 Habit # 2: Think fast AND slow

Daniel Kahneman, a Nobel prize winner for economics, explains in his book "Thinking Fast and Slow" how two systems in your brain are constantly fighting over control of your behaviour and actions and how this leads to errors in memory, judgment and decisions.

System 1 (our survival brain)	System 2 (our creative brain)
Automatic and impulsive and operates instinctively (automatically) without much conscious awareness, e.g. eat the entire bag of chips in front of the TV.	Very conscious, aware and considerate and helps you exert self-control and deliberately focus your attention, e.g. staying calm and constructive in a difficult meeting.

Build a daily habit of pausing, breathing deeply to bring back a calm awareness, and only then considering your options before rushing into automatic (and not always health) thoughts and actions. View the video: 10 BEST IDEAS | Thinking Fast And Slow | Daniel Kahnerman | Animated Book Summary[4] – links in the resources section.

5.3 Habit # 3: Critical questions

Build your natural questioning repertoire to understand situations more fully. Here is a checklist of questions from www.wabisabilearning.com[5] to ask, including who, what, where, when, why and how.

---

4   Kegley, 2016.
5   Wabisabi Learning. (n.d).

Who	... benefits from this? ... is this harmful to? ... makes decisions about this? ... is most directly affected?	... have you also heard discuss this? ... would be the best person to consult? ... will be the key people in this? ... deserves recognition?
What	... are the strengths/weaknesses? ... is another perspective? ... is another alternative? ... would be a counter argument?	... is the best/worst case scenario? ... is most/least important? ... can we do to make a positive change? ... is getting in the way of our action?
Where	... would we see this in the real world? ... are there similar concepts/situations? ... is there the most need for this? ... in the world would this be a problem?	... can we get more information? ... do we go for help with this? ... will this idea take us? ... are the areas for improvement?
When	... is this acceptable/unacceptable? ... would this benefit our society? ... would this cause a problem? ... is the best time to take action?	... will we know we've succeeded? ... is it relevant to me/others? ... would this cause a problem? ... should we ask for help with this?
Why	... is this a problem/challenge? ... is it relevant to me/others? ... is this the best/worst scenario? ... are people influenced by this?	... should people know about this? ... has it been this way for this long? ... have we allowed this to happen? ... is there a need for this today?
How	... is this similar to _____? ... does this disrupt things? ... do we know the truths about this? ... will we approach this safely?	... does this benefit us/others? ... does this harm us/others? ... do we see this in the future? ... can we change this for our good?

5.4 Habit #4: Paradigm Busting

We all build a set of paradigms and worldviews (way of looking at things, or map of the world) as we grow up, socialise and experience life from our own unique lens and through those around us. Some of our paradigms help us stay safe and achieve success (work hard, save money, minimise risk, avoid certain groups of people, etc). However, some of these paradigms can severely limit our ability to think clearly and creatively. They can also limit who we will listen to and respect, what we will consider, how we show up and the quality of our thinking and decisions. There are many studies of how the external paradigms of important influencers (parents, teachers, bosses) impact our view of ourselves and what we believe we are capable of.

Use the table below to make a list of all your key and well entrenched possibly limiting paradigms, biases, stereotypes, assumptions, judgements, beliefs and strong opinions (similar to the personal beliefs we are asking you to reflect on in this book) and consider alternative paradigms that could expand your thinking and options, e.g. from young people are lazy and have nothing of value to add to my current dilemma. To get a clearer idea of the impact of paradigms, have a look at Covey's *7 Habits Paradigms* Video[6] in the resource links below.

	Current Paradigm (limiting)	Alternative Paradigm (expansive)
People	For example, young people are lazy and have nothing of value to add to my current dilemma	For example, young people bring a different and fresh perspective to dilemmas
Money, investment		
Relationships		
Family, children		
Food		
Health		

5.5 Habit #5: Cognitive flexibility

Psychology Today[7] defines cognitive flexibility as "the ability to switch between different tasks simultaneously, and applying concepts from one context toward solving a problem in another unrelated or new situation". It is useful when needing to adapt to novel scenarios and information such as moving to a foreign country, unexpected demands in the workplace, and/or a last-minute change of plans. An analogy is having a remote for the TV

---

6   Covey, 2011.
7   Verdolin, 2019.

to change channels at will, rather than having to do this slowly and manually. Consider how flexible you are in the following three adaptability areas from a CCL article "Learn-to-adapt":[8] cognitive flexibility, emotional flexibility, and dispositional flexibility.

Cognitive Flexibility	Emotional Flexibility	Dispositional Flexibility
Able to incorporate different thinking strategies and mental frameworks into planning, decision-making and managing day-to-day work. Simultaneously hold multiple scenarios in mind and can see when to shift and inject a change. Readily learns from experience and recognises when old approaches don't work.	Able to vary approach to dealing with own and others' emotions. Comfort with transition, including grieving, complaining and resistance. Give and take between them and others (not dismissive or shutting down discussions), and moves the change or agenda forward.	Operate from a place of optimism grounded in realism and openness. Acknowledge bad situations but simultaneously visualise a better future. Ambiguity is well tolerated. See change as an opportunity rather than as a threat or danger.

Another way to build your cognitive flexibility is to practice thinking from different perspectives or brain dominance. Try the Six Thinking Hats approach below or read the Six Thinking Hats summary[9] in the links below.

White Hat (info): focus on the available data, analyse, learn.
Black Hat (caution): Look at potentially negative outcomes cautiously and defensively – why they might not work.
Green Hat (creativity): Brainstorm creative solutions – freewheeling with little criticism of ideas.
Red Hat (emotions): use intuition, gut reaction, and emotion. Think how others could react emotionally.
Yellow Hat (optimism): Use optimism and positive thinking to see all the benefits of the decision and the value in it.
Blue Hat (management): Use to manage processes and time, e.g. chairing meetings, achieving a deadline, meeting quality standards.

8   Center for Creative Leadership, 2020.
9   Goeke, 2016.

Tip: Take the Herrmann Brain Dominance test to see your preferred thinking style: Analytical (logic, facts), Sequential (structured, organised), Interpersonal (emotional, sensory) or Imaginative (intuitive, big picture).[10]

This will help you realise your default thinking style. It will also give you some areas to expand how you think about any problem.

5.6 Habit #6: Simplify & Make Sense

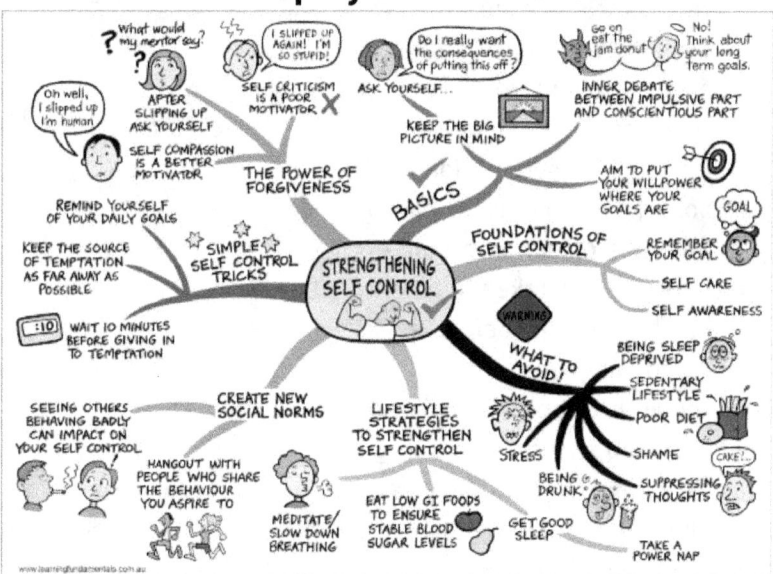

When it feels like there is an overwhelming amount of information and dilemmas that are difficult to solve, sometimes it helps to make sense of the problem through a picture to show the systemic nature of all the interacting elements. You can use mind maps, concept maps, decision trees, storyboards, infographics, matrices, picture boards and many other techniques. (See the example mind map.)[11] A picture forces you to summarise the key points and issues, simplify the elements, identify direction of inputs and outputs, and is worth a thousand words. The brain can remember a significantly higher portion of information through a picture than through words.

---
10 Smith, 2019.
11 Learning Fundamentals, 2020.

Simplify presentations and documents by creating executive summaries or additional notes pages or addendums. See the questions a critical thinker asks summarised in an infographic.[12] Use bullet points or illustrations where possible. Simplify the language to plain English. Be clear about the purpose and action required by the audience. When we were working with Heineken South Africa, one of the values was Keep It Simple. The MD at the time made a rule that all submissions for decisions had to come to him in presentations of no more than 20 slides. He used to take the time to sit with his leaders before a big leadership engagement session and coach them on the content of their slides to ensure the message was clear, simple, visual and meaningful. This can take a bit longer in the beginning, but as with most skills, the more you practice, the better you get.

5.7 Habit #7: Dissenting Voice

We often fall into the trap of confirmation bias, i.e. hunting for information that confirms our initial assumptions (which are often self-serving). We need to actively seek out the dissenting voice (the few who disagree with the majority) and ask disconfirming questions. If we can spark constructive disagreement in our teams, we are more likely to think critically about more options and challenge our assumptions and biases. Here are some examples of disconfirming questions:

---

12 Educational Technology and Mobile Learning, 2014.

- Imagine that the option you are leaning toward simply vanished as a feasible alternative. What else could you do?
- Imagine that the alternative you are currently considering actually turns out to be a terrible decision. Where could you go looking for the proof of that right now?
- What would you tell your best friend to do, if he/she was in the same situation?
- If you were replaced tomorrow, what would your successor do about your dilemma?

Another great tool is the **4 Steps of Deep Democracy**.

THE 4 STEPS			How to do it	Why to do it
1		GATHER ALL THE VIEWS	Go far and wide, and get the opinions of all stakeholder groups. Be patient and make time to do this.	This ensures all voices are heard and considered.
2		LOOK FOR THE NO	Actively seek out the view that is different to the one you hold/the popular view.	Doing this contains potential resistance and adds wisdom.
3		SPREAD THE NO	Stay open, interrogate the alternate view for the part of it that resonates with you.	This brings perspective and enables you to see the whole picture.
4		MAKE AN INCLUSIVE DECISION	Add the wisdom of the alternate view by asking what it needs to come along.	This mines the wisdom and incorporates it into the final call.

Step 1: Gather all the views, i.e. asking as many people as you can for their opinions, ensuring that they are representative of all stakeholder groups.

Step 2: Look for the No: actively elicit the alternative, counter, minority or unpopular view.

Step 3: Spread the No: actively encourage deliberate consideration of minority views by checking who else agrees or at least identifies with it – prevents scapegoating and losing the wisdom.

Step 4: Make an inclusive decision: after considering all the views, ensure you ask minorities, "What do you need to come along?" and then build that wisdom into the final decision.

For an insightful description of the four steps in COVID-19 decision times, read *Deeply democratic decision-making – the antidote for civil disobedience* by Candida DiGiandomenico.[13] (See the link in the resources section.)

5.8 Habit #8: Stop doing list

Most days we focus on our never-ending TO-DO LIST and seem to never experience a sense of achievement that we have completed it, as more and more demands and uncontrollable distractions flood in. Try a different approach with a STOP-DOING LIST. This allows you to focus on the highest value, most important tasks, and gives you the awareness of what to say no to… or least not now. Aspects to guide your stop doing list are shown below. Read the article: *Saying yes to no: the power of a stop-doing list for more ideas.* (See link in the resource section.)

Aspects to consider	Guiding principles for STOP DOING list
Core personal values	
Purpose and long-term plans	
Priority stakeholders you need to keep happy	
Pareto principle (80% results from 20% effort)	
Energy vampires to avoid (people & activities)	
Pay-offs of To Do's (benefits to completion)	

Keep in mind **The #ParetoPrinciple** or the 80/20 rule. It states that only 20% of the inputs are responsible for 80% of the results/outputs, e.g. you probably wear 20% of your clothes 80% of the

---

13 DiGiandomenico, 2020.

time. Potentially only 20% of a book has 80% of its most important info. Generally, 20% of your business clients are responsible for 80% of your revenue. Think of the inverse: 80% of your effort is only producing 20% of your results.[14] Are you busy or productive? How can you do less and focus on the 20% that matters? Read the *80/20 principle* book summary. (See link in the resource section.)

> "The quality of all our doing depends on the quality of the thinking we do first. The quality of a person's attention determines the quality of other people's thinking. The greatest gift you can give another is the framework in which to think for themselves."
> –Nancy Kline

6. TIPS, TOOLS AND RESOURCES

If you are interested in exploring and learning more, here are some of our favourite tips, tools and resources to accelerate your journey to becoming a Meaning Maker. (See https://catalystconsulting.co.za/power-up8-resources/).

Blogs

What is cognitive flexibility: https://mentalhealthdaily.com/2015/07/24/what-is-cognitive-flexibility/
Deeply democratic decision making: https://www.shine.global/post/deeply-democratic-decision making-the-antidote-for-civil-disobedience
Saying yes to no: the power of a stop doing-list https://www.forbes.com/sites/robertglazer/2018/09/12/saying-yes-to-no-the-power-of-a-stop-doing-list/#1494c2ba3b79
Six thinking hats summary: https://fourminutebooks.com/six-thinking-hats-summary/
The 80/20 principle book summary: https://fourminutebooks.com/the-80-20-principle-summary/

---

14 Goeke, 2016.

Videos

Nancy Kline's 10 Components of Thinking Environments: https://www.youtube.com/watch?v=wutIaSf37lI

Top 10 Worst Business Decisions in History in our resources section: https://www.finance-monthly.com/2018/04/top-10-worst-business-decisions-in-history/

Thinking Fast And Slow | Daniel Kahnerman | Animated Book Summary https://www.youtube.com/watch?v=tiyTYGY5X3Y

What is a Paradigm: https://www.youtube.com/watch?v=6o1le2GesiI

7 Habits Paradigms: https://www.youtube.com/watch?v=w5UQ1ZSIQ84

Books

Nancy Kline – Time to Think, More time to Think

Daniel Kahneman – Thinking Fast and Slow

Edward De Bono – 6 thinking hats, Lateral thinking, Think before its too late, How to have a beautiful mind

Tools

Critical thinking test: https://www.psychometrictest.org.uk/critical-thinking-test/

Brain Dominance test: https://www.herrmann.com.au/complete-your-hbdi-survey/

Chapter 10
COLLABORATOR

"As you navigate through the rest of your life, be open to collaboration. Other people and other people's ideas are often better than your own. Find a group of people who challenge and inspire you, spend a lot of time with them, and it will change your life". –Amy Poehler

1. UNLEASHING VALUE ACROSS BOUNDARIES

The term 'collaboration' is thrown around to get people to work together (within and across teams) more effectively to achieve common goals. Executive teams are pushed to collaborate more across their siloed functions. Customer facing units are being asked to find ways to collaborate in servicing clients in a consistent, co-ordinated way. Agile teams (squads) are required to collaborate with other squads or chapters to source and build overall technical expertise. Head office centres of excellence need to work collaboratively and share resources with divisions. Lean research and development teams are encouraged to engage with external start-ups or experts to accelerate innovation. Senior executives are encouraged to find ways of outsourcing or crowdsourcing parts, solutions, production or distribution. Small businesses, non-profits and community groups often need to collaborate out of necessity to deliver on bigger projects requiring skills, resources or technology outside of their own.

Collaboration is not just teamwork. It is about creating value across boundaries. Internal collaboration can cross divisional, functional, brand, team or regional boundaries. External collaboration can cross the boundaries of industries, businesses, expertise, communities and even competitors in a unique way or "co-opetition" (co-operative competition).[1] Anywhere there is an "Us and Them" perception (race, gender, politics, economics, etc.) there is an opportunity to challenge some paradigms through exploring collaborative opportunities, unleashing value for all.

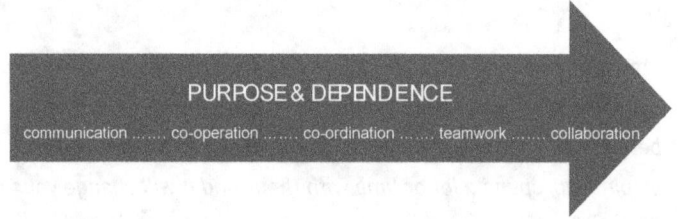

Collaboration requires going beyond the basics of communication, co-operation and co-ordination to find the spirit of teamwork within and across boundaries to unlock value. The higher the common purpose (think saving lives during COVID-19) and the dependency on each other for success (think core capabilities in a few specialist areas), the higher the chances that collaboration can work over the longer term.

Collaboration is not new. It has just had a resurgence of attention with the increasing speed of change and demand for "new" products, services, tech functionality or entertainment. Many inventors, movie producers, musicians, artists, fashion houses and sports stars have achieved great success through collaborations. Some well-known movie director-actor collaborations with many box-office hits have been Martin Scorsese/Leonardo DiCaprio, Quentin Tarantino/Samuel L. Jackson and Steven Spielberg/Tom Hanks.[2] Disney and Pixar have together earned eight Oscars and over $10 billion in revenue. Brothers Joel and Ethan Coen have

---

1   Brandenburger, & Nalebuff, 1996.
2   Morgan, 2020.

been nominated for 13 Academy Awards together. Some great music collaborators include Beyoncé, Rihanna, Lady Gaga, Jay-Z and Pitbull. Many sports stars have had multi-year success with coaches or as brand ambassadors, for example, Cristiano Ronaldo with Nike. Woolworths and musician Pharrell Williams joined forces in a 'mission to change the world'. (See the video in the resources section.)[3]

Over the COVID-19 pandemic period there have been many local and global examples of collaboration to save lives, as "doctors, researchers, engineers and scientists from all fields have worked together tirelessly to confront the outbreak with an unprecedented spirit of collaboration".[4] Many artists, schools and organisations have collaborated virtually to produce some amazing inspirational videos, music, learning, concerts and apps to keep connected with their communities during lockdown. One of my favourites was the Roedean School Choir singing *Hallelujah* virtually. (See the link below.)[5] With economic uncertainty and disruption around any corner, we need to be leaner and smarter with our resources and focus on our core capabilities that create true value, and then figure out how to outsource or collaborate the things we are less effective or efficient at.

In business, strategic partnerships can expand brand reach such as Starbucks/Spotify and Marriott Hotels/Netflix. Some previously "unthinkable" collaborations are happening in the automotive industry. Ford/Volkswagen and BMW/Daimler are collaborating to fast-track their technological capabilities in electric vehicles, autonomous technology, and mobility services.[6] Many well-known collaborations can be traced back to executives, specialists or entrepreneurs who demonstrated some unique mindsets and skills. These include many of the core capabilities mentioned so far in this book. Amy Wilkinson, in *The Creator's Code: The Six*

---
3   Kekae, 2015.
4   UN News, 2020.
5   Media Rodean School, 2020.
6   Curry, 2019.

Essential Skills of Extraordinary Entrepreneurs[7], says, "Even the best and brightest rely on networking minds. Nobel prizes awarded in recent years increasingly honour teams, not solo scientists …. To build a reusable rocket at SpaceX, Elon Musk draws on minds as varied as NASA engineers, thermodynamic physicists, navigational software programmers and business managers."

In life, we network and collaborate with friends and colleagues in playing computer games, sharing knowledge, creating online forums or TikTok videos. We take turns to do the "nasty" work, help each other complete tasks and cover for each other when the chips are down. Building and nurturing a network of people you can share with, learn from and ask for help in times of need is a powerful source of wisdom and wealth.

Our **definition of collaboration** is as follows:

> Collaboration is about effectively communicating, sharing and building trusted relationships and networks to achieve common goals across boundaries. It requires trust, empathy, vulnerability, and an abundance mindset to unleash joint value in often challenging circumstances or conflicting priorities.

2. DISASTERS AND DERAILERS

Despite many success stories, and the obvious need for collaboration, there is still an enormous amount of team dysfunction, cross-functional power dynamics, conflict and failed joint ventures. Partnerships dissolve and businesses fall, often with significant financial and personal loss. Even some of the most established companies can make basic collaborative mistakes, as the *New York Times* article headline indicate: "How McKinsey Lost Its Way in South Africa: When the godfather of management consulting landed its biggest contract ever in Africa, it made the

---

[7] Wilkinson, 2016.

worst mistake in its nine-decade history."[8] U2 and Apple thought that automatically downloading U2's latest album to all iPhones would be greatly appreciated. Not so much. Public apologies were necessary. Another partnership that felt the changing consumer mood was Shell and Lego when Greenpeace released a video on Shell's questionable environmental practices and suggesting it was not cool for kids to play with toys that supported this partnership. There are many more. (See more Brand Partnerships That Failed Miserably[9] in the resources below.)

I have actively cultivated a collaboration mindset for many years. Over the years, I have had many deeply satisfying collaborative relationships with business partners, co-authors, mentors, licence holders, consulting partners on projects and alliance partners that offer complementary expertise to mine. I am enjoying working collaboratively as a volunteer with a global workgroup to build support tools for 100 international NeuroChange trainers. There is something magical about getting onto a weekly Zoom call with people from multiple countries, sharing ideas and working together to create something valuable for others.

I have also had many collaboration disasters and disappointments where things fizzled out, ideas got hijacked, values conflicts got in the way or the trust was irrevocably broken. Some have been working with small consulting firms or associates, where the drive for short-term income is greater than the appetite for long-term sharing and value. I have also had many a conversation or workshop sharing our approaches and tools, only to find them offering it to their clients in slightly different packaging a little while later. A big lesson (that I had to learn a few times over) was helping a friend or family member in need by offering some temporary work opportunities, only to have it thrown in my face when expectations exceeded the offer. It has taken me a long time to recover from these failures, struggling to figure out my own and

---

8   Bogdanich & Forsythe, 2018.
9   Kosin, 2017.

others' part in them. High expectations (sometimes desperation), without unambiguous clarity of process, and an existing emotional dynamic, is a recipe for disaster. As the saying goes: Hindsight is a perfect science! I have become more discerning. I also believe that with the right values, beliefs, intent and careful communication, collaboration can be magical.

Collaboration by nature is an unnatural concept. We are born and raised to compete for resources and be the fittest to survive. We are schooled in setting goals and driving for results – fast. Collaboration often starts with some exciting ideas and exciting benefits, and then takes a huge amount of time, effort, give and take and patience to make it work. In a time -and energy-scarce world, how do we find the time to collaborate AND remain responsive to our own stakeholder needs (which pay the bills)? Collaboration by its very nature requires slowing down and many robust conversations to explore ways of working. Does the additional time and effort really justify a more aligned solution in the longer term? Whilst many groups or organisations start off with the right intent to work together and even set up the structures to do so, the reality is often frustrating, the results disappointing, and the waste of resources can be significant.

A few years ago, I was busy with an HR consulting project that required several brands within a group to collaborate on a group strategy, technology platform and ways of working to leverage economies of scale. I experienced the dilemmas that many HR executives and group forum teams face as they struggle to balance their local mandate with a vague group intent. I wrote an article outlining the "7 derailers of collaboration"[10], and why collaboration often goes wrong in practice and is perceived as a huge waste of time and resources. (See the summary in the box.)

---

10 Craig, (2018).

Derailers of collaboration

Purpose: no clear purpose or joint target or motivation (recognition or reward) for working together.

Process: no clear process for collaborating – meetings, members, mandates, reports to decision makers.

Power: no recognition of power dynamics and moving from "my turf, my team, my rewards" to sharing the risk, the costs and the limelight.

Priorities: conflicting priorities between their own boss/customers and their group forum role where there are less direct consequences for non-participation in meetings or non-delivery of agreed actions.

People: carefully selected forum member (experts and influencers) often replacing themselves in meetings with less skilled or experienced people. Also not always coming, with the right attitudes and behaviours required for collaboration with too many silos and egos competing for recognition or resources.

Principles: ways of working not discussed leading to assumptions, lack of communication and conflict.

Practices: new collaborative workflows often not fully understood by all parties and therefore people go back to the old way of doing things.

According to a *Harvard Business Review* article, "Collaborative Overload"[11], i.e. the time spent by managers and employees in collaborative activities has ballooned by 50% or more in the last two decades. Their data tells us, however, that up to a third of value-added collaborations come from only 3% to 5% of employees. It is often the smartest and most collaboratively minded that we want on our projects. Unfortunately, so does everyone else, which

---
11 Rebele, & Grant, 2016.

leads to overload and "institutional bottlenecks". It turns out that 60% of employees want to spend less time responding to ad hoc collaboration requests and just focus on their own deliverables.

What I have learnt is that collaboration is not the answer for all opportunities or resolving all challenges. Whilst a collaborative mindset opens up possibilities, it is also important to be discerning and ask critical questions (see Critical Thinking Chapter) to ascertain the probability of success in any joint venture. Questions to elicit collaboration potential can be useful:

- Is there a clear purpose, common goal and obvious benefits for both parties?
- Are there common values, a trust base and an abundance mindset from both parties?
- Are there complementary expertise or offerings that both are willing to share?
- Is there the appetite to invest time to establish feasibility and align on key roles and financials?
- Is there the maturity to have robust conversations to manage expectations and potential conflict?
- Are there competing priorities that will derail the intended collaboration efforts?

As the Centre for Creative Leadership in "Boundary Spanning in Action"[12] highlights: "When times are tough, our natural tendency is to hunker down. Battle lines are drawn. Organizational silos get taller. Worldviews shrink, attitudes narrow, and positions tighten. All too often, boundaries create borders that divide groups into Us and Them. The result can be fractured relationships, diminished resources, suboptimal results, and divisive conflict. Yet, boundaries are also frontiers. Wherever group boundaries collide and intersect, there is potential for different ways of working and new forms of

---

[12] Horth, 2014.

collaboration. Boundaries can reveal new frontiers for solving pressing problems, driving innovation, and leading breakthrough change."

> "If you want to go fast, go alone. If you want to go far, go together."
> –African Proverb

3. WHAT'S TRUST GOT TO DO WITH IT?

Trust is the most critical element to being an effective collaborator. According to the Edelman Trust Barometer[13], which has measured trust in more than 25 countries globally over two decades, trust in institutions is evaporating at an alarming rate. In 2019, trust in business is rated at just 56% and CEO credibility only 47%. Trust in social media is a dismal 43%. Overall trust in the political and social systems we live in is at an all-time low, with only one out of five people in the general population believing that the system is working for them.

It can be hard to see how trustworthy we appear to others. It is easier to criticise the actions of others. Francis Frei[14], a Harvard Business School Professor who

From: *Begin with Trust* by Francis Frei & Anne Morriss.

consulted at Uber at the height of their struggles, shares the three drivers of trust in her YouTube video: "How to build (and rebuild) trust".[15] They are authenticity, logic and empathy. Authenticity comes across as experiencing the real you (not telling me what I want to or need to hear). Empathy is present when I believe you care about me and my success (not just yours or the company). Logic is knowing that you can do it (confidence) and that your reasoning and judgement is sound (credibility in making decisions). She says that when trust is

---
13 Edelman, 2019.
14 Frei & Morriss, 2020.
15 Frei, 2018.

lost, it can almost always be traced back to a breakdown in one of these three and that most of us will have a "wobble" in at least one of them. How are you doing with trust (and maybe ask for outside perspectives)?

Empathy: often a struggle for impatient, smart, analytical, high achievers.

- Are you ever late for meetings or change them at the last minute because something more important has come up?
- Do you multi-task on your devices during meetings, thereby coming across as disengaged or that other work is more important?
- Do you put away your device in one-on-one interactions to be fully present?

Logic: often a struggle for those with fuzzy logic, assumptions and lack of clarity in communication:

- Do people trust your judgement, and therefore your opinion or guidance?
- Do you speak from verifiable data and first-hand information or hearsay and hunches?
- Are you willing to reveal that you don't have all the answers and can learn from others?
- Are you communicating your ideas effectively and with logic or a crisp narrative that makes sense?

Authenticity: often a struggle for those with fear of judgement or criticism for being different or not enough. How different is your professional persona from the one that shows up around family and friends?

- Are you willing to be real and vulnerable (and face potential critics) to allow your unique strengths to shine?

- Do you withhold your true self for fear of being judged as "different" or "not good enough"?
- Do you pay more attention to what you think people want to hear or more attention to what you need to say?
- Do you take exquisite care of people who are different from you, confident in the knowledge that their difference is the very thing that could unleash your potential and your organisation's?

Trust begins with you and most importantly when you start to trust yourself. It is about knowing yourself, being honest with yourself (about your ambitions and needs) and having an accurate self-concept of your strengths and potential "wobble" areas. It is also trusting your own clarity of purpose and direction so that you can articulate it. Self-trust is felt by others and encourages a sense of trustworthiness.

Trust is about trusting your team. Amy Edmondson reinforces this message in her research on team effectiveness and psychological safety which you can watch on YouTube: "Building a psychologically safe workplace."[16] Her data showed that higher performing teams are more willing to take risks and acknowledge their mistakes without fear of judgment or ridicule, i.e. be vulnerable and transparent.

Trust is about practicing all the mindsets and skills of a trusted collaborator. See the habits and hacks section to check in on yours.

> *"Collaboration is important not just because it's a better way to learn. The spirit of collaboration is penetrating every institution and all of our lives. So learning to collaborate is part of equipping yourself for effectiveness, problem solving, innovation and life-long learning in an ever-changing networked economy."*
> –Don Tapscott

---

16 Edmondson, 2014.

4. DOES IT COME NATURALLY?

Now it is time for you to identify how natural collaboration is for you. There are times to compete and there are times to build trust and collaborate when the potential gain from working together is greater than the individual gain. How flexible are you and how easily can you adapt your approach when the need arises? Have a look at the **independent competitor** and the **Trust Cultivator** identities below and check out which one you spend more time in. Our invitation to you is to expand your default behaviours and explore alternative ways of being, which will automatically increase your choices and opportunities in life.

Independent competitor
Independent
Sensitive
Protector

Trust cultivator
Inclusive
Trusted
Resolver

Trust cultivators are Inclusive, Trusting, Resolvers

Trust Cultivators are **inclusive.** They are naturally appreciative of the unique contributions and different ideas that diverse people can bring to a situation. Their acceptance of people and their nature to include rather than exclude, makes them natural networkers. They often think of people they have come into contact with and send them a quick message, an interesting resource link and connect and comment on social media activity. They are also exceptional at identifying strengths of others and finding synergies across boundaries.

Trust Cultivators are **trusting and trustworthy.** They build healthy, trusting relationships by being authentic and demonstrating empathy and appreciation of where other people are coming from or feeling. They are open-hearted and have an abundance mindset. They believe in trusting first and rather being proven wrong than being suspicious from the start. They deliver on their promises, have a sense of fairness and are honest about needs, expectations and feedback, which cultivates trust between people and groups.

Trust Cultivators are **resolvers.** They are often called upon to facilitate conflict by helping opposing parties seek common ground. They are able to help different people and groups explore win-win solutions, highlight the balance of losses and gains, and negotiate an acceptable way forward. In their own teams they notice underlying tension and bring it to light in a constructive way for resolution to release energy back into the team.

They believe in the power of group work and synergy (1+1 = 3). They believe in the exchange of energy through sharing and learning together. They believe in growing the pie, not fighting over it. They know the power of trust to speed things up and that conflict is normal and a necessary part of diversity that just needs to be managed right. Lastly, they know they don't have all the answers and love including others' ideas and solutions to a problem.

They generally **feel** positive, optimistic, appreciative, trusting and inclusive.

They use **language** like "Let's do this", "Imagine the possibilities", "What is the win-win here?", "Together we can do more".

They have daily **habits** like sharing knowledge freely, connecting across boundaries, smoothing the waters, taking time to have the important conversations, and clarifying ways of working to achieve a common goal.

> **A trusted collaborator, Charmaine Smith from Infundo**
>
> One of my collaborator heroes is my friend Charmaine, founder of Infundo Consulting, who has been enabling deep, systemic transformation in educational systems and communities for over 12 years. Charmaine and her team have been influential in the upliftment, education and empowerment of over 20,000 South African youths; facilitating development and earning opportunities for many. They have built a community across the country of staff; coaches; facilitators; psychologists; mentors; and digital learning and curriculum specialists who work together with business, communities, and government to achieve this vision. The Infundo team focuses on resolving unconscious dynamics to enable systems flow to return. Many projects bring together groups with seemingly disparate agendas which are transformed into a beneficial outcome for common growth. There are many uplifting stories of young people with little hope, getting through school or learnerships, mentoring others and getting into university or meaningful jobs. In my own personal collaborations with her, I have always found her refreshingly honest, open to ideas and options, generous with her appreciation, self-aware and focused on outcomes to ensure expectations are met with transparency and integrity. She now sits as a director on a number of Boards to advise on social impact and developmental strategies for lasting change.

Independent competitors are Independent, Sensitive, Protectors

On the opposite side of the continuum are the **independent competitors**. If you have grown up with strong role models with mindsets of "winner takes it all", "if you want it done properly do it yourself" or a strong protection of their reputation at all costs, then you may find yourself defaulting to this end of the continuum, especially under stress or highly competitive conditions. Also, if through life experience you may have had some negative experiences with trusted people, you may be less inclined to start with a trust first mindset.

Independent competitors can be fiercely **independent** and prefer to be in control of their own time and destiny. They may be part of a team and be willing to contribute, if they can craft their own piece of the work out for themselves to do in their own way. When feeling overwhelmed or irritated with people, they can withdraw and isolate themselves from their team. This independence can stem from a self-preservation instinct, a scarcity mindset or an over-developed ego that believes they know better (something that many smart people suffer from). They can sometimes come across as aloof, self-centred and arrogant if they haven't learnt the finer nuances of emotional intelligence and empathy.

Independent competitors can also be quite **sensitive**. Previous life experiences may have convinced them to avoid criticism, feedback or getting too close to others for fear of feeling those nasty, unwanted feelings again. They may be naturally cautious, suspicious, risk averse, hedge their bets and believe that trust takes time and needs to be earned. This can show up as closed and defensive when trying to engage them on ideas or work or behaviour that could do with some additional perspective and input.

Independent competitors are excellent **protectors.** They are great to have on your side, as a mentor or in your team, as they will protect you, cover for you and ensure you have what you need. They are protectors of boundaries, resources and their inner circle or team. They will want to compete and win and can often be sore losers. They will also protect what they have built up or created over time, sometimes resulting in them hanging onto the past a bit too tightly. Protection can work in the right circumstances or with external competitors, but an "us and them" or "win-lose" mindset can severely hamper collaboration and joint efforts and escalate unnecessary conflict.

They believe that teamwork is messy and that they should be in control of their own time and energy. They believe they must protect their legacy, keep their cards close to their chest and would rather not risk trusting anyone without evidence as most people are in it for themselves.

They can tend to feel superior, suspicious, defensive, nervous and isolated... especially when the going gets tough.

They use **language** like: "It's quicker and easier to do it myself", "It's not my problem", "I told them so, I'm not sure I trust them", "What is the hidden agenda here?"

They have daily **habits** like protecting their ideas, holding back information, waiting before committing, seeking recognition or a public "win", refusing requests for meetings, closing down and avoiding input from others.

There are many examples of political leaders in power today who could sit on both sides of this continuum. Instead of making any controversial comparisons, let's have some fun with some much loved (and hated) TV series characters.

> **Game of Thrones Character Examples**
>
> If you are a Game of Thrones fan you can have fun thinking through some of the characters that fall further to the independent competitor type. You might think of sweet Daenerys Targaryen, who started off with a warm hearted approach to free slaves and bring tribes and armies together, only to end up burning a city to the ground through her hate and hurt from too much suffering and loss. How about Tywin Lannister, the ruthless king who would stop at nothing to protect his power and his family name? You also might think of Cersei Lannister whose character regressed from having some warmth, into a selfish, spiteful, power hungry queen. In contrast there is Jon Snow, who was able to unite many previously conflicting regions and forces to fight for a common cause.

5. RECALIBRATE TO COLLABORATE

To cultivate an empowering identity of the Trust Cultivator, it is useful to examine the underlying beliefs that you have adopted from role models, experiences and the highs and lows of life. Notice the situations when you have a tendency to pull back into yourself and be fiercely independent. In my own experience, collaboration does not come easily and requires some very conscious re-programming of beliefs about others and the world, as well as a capacity for forgiveness and redemption. Many people entering collaborative spaces have great intentions to make it work but not yet the mindsets and skills to put it into practice, and so can make some unfortunate blunders. The good news is that collaboration can be learnt with intent and practice. Identify from the examples below some beliefs you could shift, adopt and practice.

FROM believing…	TO believing…
• I prefer being in control of my time and energy	• I love seeing what will emerge from the group
• I will share when I can and am ready	• Through sharing I gain energy and learn
• Everyone is in it for themselves	• 1+1 = 3 achieve synergy, grow the pie
• Trust is risky and must be earned	• Trust speeds things up – is the new currency
• Conflict is messy and should be avoided	• Conflict is a necessary part of diversity

It takes a village to raise a child

I met Khanyisile Simelane when I needed someone to help me take care of a large property and conference centre just out of town. Khanyi was an exceptional human being, with an incredible resilience and hope for her family's future, a wide smile, a generous heart and always went the extra mile with effort and care. She crept into our hearts, as did her two young daughters who grew up with us and years later her son, who was born on our property.

After 10 years together we had to say goodbye during my divorce but remained friends and I continued supporting the family in whichever way I could, eventually helping her to buy a house for her family. A few years into this new phase she passed away suddenly from undiagnosed cervical cancer, leaving three children aged 23, 18 and 11. In shock and sadness from deep loss of a very special friend, I didn't know what to do. Her sister arrived for the funeral and then disappeared never to be heard from again. The eldest child had major health challenges, the middle child was trying to navigate matric and the youngest was struggling to fit in at a new primary school. I was running a consulting business which required a lot of travel and I was in a new marriage (requiring a lot of attention)!

So, I did my best to figure out how to make this work. I was driven by an underlying drive to prevent suffering – from hunger, loneliness or lack. I was working by day in-between juggling school runs and dealing with the emotional fall-out of this tragic situation. I was also trying to figure out whether to sell the house or somehow keep their only "home" and memory of their mother intact in a way that was financially viable. I was also trying to be sensitive and help them deal with death in an African culturally acceptable way, which included sessions with Sangomas (traditional spiritual healers) and visits to their homeland. This was all stretching my budget and my energy thin.

And then close to burnout, one day I gave up when the eldest needed to get rushed to hospital while I was facilitating an Exec session, and I just said **I cant!** It was the worst feeling in the world, not knowing the risk of this call, but also knowing that I just didn't have it in me. What transpired was one of my greatest gifts in this life. Their neighbours, hearing of their plight, came over, stepped in and became an important part of their support system (and mine). It ultimately allowed them to stay in their home or move freely between our homes, knowing they had a safe haven here too. It enabled me to continue earning in my business to support them and do our best to balance cultural integration in a diverse but unequal society.

Eight years, and many moments of laughter and tears later, I am so proud of what they have each become to find their niche in life, despite their difficult early years and circumstances. This could all not have happened without their neighbours and community, my husband's support and an amazing bunch of primary school rugby parents and scouts leading to a rugby scholarship for the youngest at a private school. His journey into a young man has been guided by incredible teachers, sports coaches and support staff. I have been supported emotionally and spiritually by many through this time. This has been true heartfelt collaboration in action – and only happened when I let go of control and let others in to help me hold the weight of this new responsibility and allow it to evolve in its own unique messy way.

> *"Ubuntu speaks of the very essence of being human – of being generous, hospitable, friendly, caring and compassionate. You share what you have. It is to say, 'My humanity is caught up, is inextricably bound up, in yours'. We belong in a bundle of life. We say, 'A person is a person through other persons'."*
> –Desmond Tutu

6. DAILY HACKS AND HABITS FOR COLLABORATION

Trust Cultivators have daily habits that build trust in self, and trust with and through others for a greater collaborative outcome. Some of our favourites are outlined below with more links to resources in the tips and resources section.

6.1 Trust starts with you

Trust starts with you. Often those who don't trust themselves due to insecurity, fear of failure, procrastination, previous disappointments or betrayals or even self-interest, struggle to take the first step in trusting others. Self-trust means tuning in to your inner voice, listening to your intuition, trusting your gut and ultimately having a healthy trust in life itself – and that there is meaning in both the highs and lows in life. It is also the belief that I will be able to handle anything that comes my way.

Tip: Take the Martha Beck Trust-o-meter test[17] for how well you have learnt to listen to and trust yourself.

6.2 Cross boundaries

There are many ways to cross boundaries inside and outside of your organisation.

- Set up or request to join a cross-functional team to work on a significant problem or opportunity that can bust silos and bring breakthrough innovation.

---
17 Beck, 2020.

- Invite people from other areas, departments or companies to a collaboration meeting – include clients, suppliers, competitors, collaborators, consultants or even different sectors, e.g. non-profits, to get different perspectives.

- Set up discussion forums with people from all levels to gain insight into certain issues.

- Create an agenda item to step into the shoes of another department or customer and imagine what they might experience or say.

- Attend events, workshops, conferences or meetings outside your industry, function or area of expertise.

Tip: List all the imaginary boundaries that are avoided or not crossed, e.g. competitor conversations, multi-level dialogue, listening to the youth or new hires... and break through them.

6.3 Forge common ground

One of the best ways to motivate and sustain collaboration over the longer-term is to establish a common purpose, goal or way of working. Key questions to encourage this are:

- What is the bigger win if we work together – goal, customer?
- What strengths or voice are we missing?
- How do we share and celebrate the wins?
- How do integrate distinctive capabilities or resources to achieve greater success?
- How can we reconcile conflict between groups to uncover new solutions?

Tip: It can really help to meet in a neutral zone (safe space) and temporarily suspend the identity and any power symbols of either party. Arrange activities to break the ice and set aside natural tendencies to think with identity to create a collaborative mindset. Watch the video *Letting go of our EGO*[18] to assist with you to get into a neutral zone.

6.4 Collaborative Attitude

Collaboration doesn't work without collaborative mindsets and skills. Review the following brief descriptions and identify your focus areas using the acronym C.O.L.L.A.B.O.R.A.T.E.

Mindset & Skill	Description	Strength (S) Focus area (F)
Commmunicate	Clear, unambiguous, authentic communication. Gives updates and feedback. Keeps everyone in the loop.	
Outline	Outlines the vision, the benefits and roadmap to joint success. Articulates with passion and clarity to influence.	
Learn	Is open to ideas from others. Is willing to learn and ask for help. Has humility, manages ego and is willing to apologise for mistakes.	
Let go	Is willing to... let go own ideas or status... share resources, credit or power... compromise... forgive unintentional mistakes or omissions.	
Abundance	Has an abundance mindset, i.e. grow the pie, not fight over a piece. Trusts that short-term sacrifice can be for long-term gain.	

---

18 Pick Up Limes, 2019.

Mindset & Skill	Description	Strength (S) Focus area (F)
Brave	Is willing to... have honest conversations... share feelings or reservations... ask for and give feedback.	
Ownership	Is aware of and shares own abilities, ideas and possible contributions to the team. Encourages others to do the same.	
Relationships	Nurtures networks and contacts through regular contact, caring and value add. Is able to facilitate conflicting views to gain compromise or consensus.	
Accountable	Is consistent, reliable and delivers on promises. Manages expectations and communicates proactively when things change.	
Transparency	Openness on personal reasons and benefits for collaborating. Transparency of joint goals, income splits, risks and rewards.	
Embrace	Respect and embrace difference and diversity including values, culture, perspectives, ways of work, communication preferences and ways of handling conflict and stress.	

Tip: Ask some colleagues or family members to help you choose your top strengths and focus areas.

6.5 Collaborative learning

You can significantly accelerate your own learning through cross-boundary or collaborative learning and networking. Here are some ideas:

- **Learning circle:** Initiate a learning circle or community of practice to share learning on a specific topic. This can be a virtual group where you post ideas and share information.

- **Learning buddy:** Connect with someone who can be your learning or accountability partner to keep you honest and focused on your intentions. This can be a friend, colleague, coach or mentor.

- **Network learning:** Write up a networking list of people you have met or could meet through meetings, conferences, online forums, LinkedIn etc. and reach out to them, share info or have a virtual or physical chat.

- **Design thinking:** Host a design thinking session to imagine an alternative future. Use visuals, colours, story-telling or drawing to create an ideal future and work out what it might take to get there.

- **Go walk about:** Walk about your organisation, eating or social areas, or other organisations. Observe to learn, ask questions, listen attentively, share generously.

- **Swap shoes:** Try rotating or swapping jobs or locations, trading team members or shadowing someone else for a day.

Tip: Start with people you know well and expand from there. Trust your intuition and reach out to people who seem like-minded and link up for a short conversation with them. You could end up with a global network of people you can learn with.

6.6 Set up collaborative meeting principles

When we sit in or run meetings, there are many opportunities for collaboration in the team or across groups when we set up the meeting right and facilitate the meetings along some collaboration principles. Consider some of these:

- **Divergence:** Take a few mins to move away from task focused work and allow some free flow of ideas without constraint. In this way we tap into our creative aspects of ourselves and may surprise ourselves with what we come up with.

- **Foolish Fun:** Step into the archetype of The Fool, or the Court Jester. Be open, curious, unafraid to look silly or have a beginner's mind. The Fool can bring fresh eyes and potentially some very fresh, different ideas.

- **Freedom to Fail:** Start a meeting with an open permission to fail or there is no right and wrong. This can help overcome some conditioned needs to "get it right", "look good" and "never fail".

- **Spirit of Yes And:** This automatically gives acceptance to another's ideas AND at the same time an opportunity to build on them. It also avoids the need to agree with or disagree with, but rather allows the space just to BE with.

- **Credit to the Room:** If we separate ideas from the initiators of the ideas and ensure each idea becomes a team idea, we remove the need to compete for attention or "wins".

- **Robust Debate, External Unity**: Allow team members to challenge ideas, and have robust debates or disagreements in the room and then decide on a unified decision or communication to the outside world.

- **Tip:** Set up an agenda item at the start and end of every meeting to go through some principles and then summarise the key messages for communication.

6.7 Set up collaboration tools

In our ever expanding and evolving digital world, leverage the many collaboration tools available and emerging. Some current options include:

- **Social media:** Create a group on your favourite social media platform to connect and collaborate with others.

- **WhatsApp groups:** Create a group for before, during or after a conference, workshop or on a new project to make it easy to connect and share.

- **Tech options:** Play with different options to see what works for you, e.g. MS Teams, Slack, Mural, Miro, Trello, Monday, Google Docs, Yammer, Asana. Many reviews are available online and most options are free.

Tip: Set up the clear purpose of each group or platform and guidelines for everyone to avoid irritation, overload or clutter. Take time to on-board members to ensure it is user-friendly and effortless to join.

"Individual commitment to a group effort – that is what makes a team work, a company work, a society work, a civilisation work."
–Vince Lombardi

7. TIPS, TOOLS AND RESOURCES

If you are interested in exploring and learning more, here are some of our favourite tips, tools and resources to accelerate your journey to becoming a Trust Cultivator. (See https://catalystconsulting.co.za/power-up8-resources/).

Articles/Blogs

The World Economic Forum. How collaboration is the modern company's secret weapon: https://www.weforum.org/agenda/2019/01/how-collaboration-is-the-modern-company-s-secret-weapon

Dilemma flipping and 7 factors derailing collaboration by Debbie Craig: https://catalystconsulting.co.za/blogs/

Harvard Business Review, Collaborative Overload, by Cross, Rebele, Grant, Jan-Feb 2016: https://hbr.org/2016/01/collaborative-overload

Begin with Trust, by Frances X. Frei and Anne Morriss, May–June 2020 Issue: https://hbr.org/2020/05/begin-with-trust

Understanding the trust equation: https://trustedadvisor.com/why-trust-matters/understanding-trust/understanding-the-trust-equation

Books

The SPEED of Trust: The One Thing that Changes Everything, Stephen M.R. Covey; Free Press, 2006, 2018

Trust, Iyanla Vanzant, Smiley Books, 2015

Videos

How to build (and rebuild) trust | Frances Frei: https://www.youtube.com/watch?v=pVeq-0dIqpk&t=20s

Building a psychologically safe workplace | Amy Edmondson | TEDxHGSE: https://www.youtube.com/watch?v=LhoLuui9gX8&t=261s

3 Steps to Accelerate the Speed of Trust... in 3 Minutes – Stephen M.R. Covey: https://www.youtube.com/watch?v=IriCJ3z5tVs

10 ways to have a better conversation, Celeste Headlee: https://www.youtube.com/watch?v=R1vskiVDwI4

Letting go of our EGO: https://www.youtube.com/watch?v=nbAwOS1FZIw

Tools

Speed of trust assessment: https://www.speedoftrust.com/speed-of-trust-measurement-tools

Free trustworthiness assessment: https://executiveexcellence.com/can-pass-trust-test-2/

Free trust in self-assessment: http://www.oprah.com/omagazine/the-trust-test_1

> *"Collaboration is important not just because it's a better way to learn. The spirit of collaboration is penetrating every institution and all of our lives. So learning to collaborate is part of equipping yourself for effectiveness, problem solving, innovation and life-long learning in an ever-changing networked economy". –Don Tapscott*

Chapter 11

CONTRIBUTOR

"Only those who have learned the power of sincere and selfless contribution, experience life's deepest joy, true fulfilment."
–Tony Robbins

1. "ME FIRST" VS. "UBUNTU"

As the race for consumption increases and the pressure from social media to prove our latest purchase, party, experience or achievement mounts, it is tempting to jump onto the consumer train leading to FOMO and a state of "never enough".

Many of us have grown up in societies with a competitive, scarcity mindset that encouraged us to work hard for our goals. We were taught to do more to get ahead, fight to survive, save for a rainy day, be faster and fitter than your rivals, and grab opportunities before they got gobbled up by others. This has created a world view of separation, 'us vs. them', the haves and have-nots, the winners and the losers. This has promoted a primary focus on self and our inner circle to the exclusion of others. The result? A culture of excess and risk avoidance, and a deep divide of inequality.

Some of us have been lucky enough to grow up in a society or community where sharing is caring and you never go to sleep on an empty stomach. Resources are shared and our own identity and worth is a reflection of the community we serve.

The COVID-19 pandemic has shocked everyone into a different way of seeing the world. We have been forced to recognise our fragility and interdependence with other countries and people. We have seen both selfish acts of "me first" and also many wonderful examples of selfless contribution to those in need, both in our own communities and on a global scale with multi-million dollar donations, initiatives and acts of kindness. There is an increasing call for a global reset in the way that we value people and planet versus profit at any cost.

> **Ubuntu**
>
> Ubuntu is an African term that mean "humanity towards others" or "I am because we are". It is "the belief in a universal bond of sharing that connects all humanity". It is a recognition that other people make up the whole of who we are, in an inter-dependent society and that we only sustain through a sense of community. This shows up as a sincere warmth with which people treat both strangers and members of the community and enables the formation of spontaneous friendships and communities.[1]

We may have noticed thousands of people with the spirit of "ubuntu" – initiatives to bring relief to the old, frail, poverty stricken and to create a sense of community through contact groups, donation drives, virtual house parties, shared online learning and support offers, shared playlists, community mask making and shopping runs. We cheered for front-line health workers who went above and beyond their call of duty. We smiled when we saw news feeds of "closed" restaurants making, donating, or delivering meals to hospitals to keep the spirits and important nourishment up. We were uplifted with virtual fund-raising concerts.

We unfortunately also observed much fear and panic and witnessed the ugly under-belly of the "me first" consumer stockpiling food, masks, toilet paper and other essentials with little thought for those around them. We fumed in anger at politicians with hidden

---

[1] Wikipedia, 2020.

agendas and nonsensical strategies. We also cried at the sight of aggressive and deadly responses to those resisting unnecessary controls or protesting for change.

As many traditional family values break down and we spend less time learning from our busy parents and distant grandparents, the quality and integrity of public and corporate leadership seems lacking. It is no wonder that many people decide, often out of necessity, that I am in this alone, it is up to me and I'm going to take what I can get. Many popular celebrities of the selfie generation dominate our screens with a superficial quest for likes or shares for choreographed poses, sensationalist tweets, enhanced body parts, fabulous party pics or celebrity gossip. In our circles closer to home, the addiction to gain attention, popularity and belonging through social media followers, groups or connections causes wide-spread insecurity, self-doubt, anxiety, depression and other mental health issues.

It is time to pause and ask ourselves a few key questions: **Who am I? Where am I going? How do I want to feel? What am I doing about it?**

Do you want to be a superficial entitled status consumer, or do you want to be an accountable community builder, mentor and contributor? We may feel that we have limited time or means to contribute, but it is often those with little who make the most difference, even if it is just a few minutes a day or week or the time to share some encouraging words.

Joseph Munyambanza

This is powerfully demonstrated by Joseph Munyambanza, who lived in a refugee camp in Uganda from the age of six. At 14 he was sponsored to attend a decent school outside the camp. He was so grateful for the experience that he founded a non-profit organisation that empowers young leaders to tackle the greatest challenges facing their communities – at just 14 years

> old. At the age of 17, he ran a tutoring programme for 52 students and opened two hostels for 100 students that allowed students to attend better schools at a lower cost. Whilst attending the African Leadership Academy as a sponsored young leader, he raised funds to build the first secondary school in his refugee camp. At a young age he enabled the education of 300 children per year in his refugee camp and has sent over 12 graduates to colleges in Africa and in the USA. He has become an advisor on international education to the UN Secretary General and is currently working with the Minister of Education of the DRC to enable one million children to enroll in school for the first time.[2]
>
> You can view the story on Youtube: *The ripple effect of training young leaders* by Fred Swaniker.[3]

Our **definition of contributor** is as follows:

> Contributors figure out how to apply their strengths and talents to make a difference to people, communities and planet... and not just chase short-term status and personal gain.

2. DOING GOOD IS ACTUALLY GOOD FOR YOU

It is a well-researched fact that people who have a sense of meaning and contribution to something bigger than themselves feel more engaged and empowered in their lives. They attract a great deal of support and have more meaningful relationships. It feels good to help people. The feeling of achievement and personal pride lasts long after the event, unlike the short-term hit of dopamine when we feel socially accepted for a short while as we entertain, surprise or educate our friends with our snippet of the day or week. Once the dopamine wears off, and we settle back into the insecurity or doubt about ourselves, we then spend precious time finding a way

---

2 Swaniker, 2014.
3 African Leadership Academy, 2019.

to get that "feel good" feeling back, often resorting to unhealthy habits of snacking, smoking, drugs, internet shopping, watching mindless videos or worse.

Acts of kindness can release hormones that contribute to your mood, overall well-being, as well as lead to a longer and healthier life. High levels of the "bonding" hormone oxytocin are typically found in people who are very generous toward others. Oxytocin stimulates the 'tend-mend' response, as opposed to the 'fight-flight' response to stress, and can lead to a greater sense of calm and well-being. It can also encourage more trust in relationships. It has been found that altruistic behaviour may also trigger 'feel-good' chemicals like dopamine and endorphins, and perhaps even a morphine-like chemical the body naturally produces to reduce pain. Being kind can also increase serotonin, a neurotransmitter that helps regulate mood. Levels of oxytocin can be influenced by our upbringing and what we are exposed to and experience with our mirror neurons early on in life. This may mean just working a bit harder initially to rebuild the neural path to instinctive kindness.[4]

Givers thrive in interdependent roles where collaboration matters

"A study of more than 600 medical students, found that the selfish ones – people who focused on their own progress, and cared little for others – performed very well in their first year. These "takers" were good at extracting information, and by offering little in return they were able to focus on their own progress. Those who were more generous with their time and were willing to offer insights to their fellow students, the "givers", got left behind. But here is the curious thing. By the second year, the kinder cohort had caught up, and by the third year had overtaken their peers. Indeed, by the final year, the givers had gained significantly higher grades. Indeed, a kinder attitude was a more powerful predictor of school grades than the effect of smoking on lung cancer rates. What was going on? The givers hadn't changed, but the structure of the programme had shifted. As students progress through

---

4   Davis, 2020.

> medical school, they move from independent classes into clinical rotations and patient care. The further they advance, the more their success depends on teamwork and service. Whereas takers sometimes win in independent roles where performance is only about individual results, givers thrive in interdependent roles where collaboration matters".[5]

We have seen many acts of heroism and altruism, from the firefighters on 9/11 to the frontline health workers during COVID-19. In the UK, more than 700,000 volunteers stepped forward to help the NHS. In South Africa, an owner of a grocery store franchise, SPAR, decided to close down its stationery section and remove all frozen burgers to help neighbouring stores (a family owned stationery store and a burger joint) survive the COVID-19 pandemic. He stated in a post, "As owner-run businesses, we now more than ever, need to support each other".[6] Internet service providers doubled internet speeds, training companies offered free training, digital providers (of books, yoga, etc.) opened up their subscriptions for all.

It certainly felt good to run a series of webinars for my network on this book's topic and facilitate many group mediations to help people find a sense of calm in the craziness. It was also heart-warming to see how much my Catalyst team were contributing in both their personal and role capacities. Many of our associates helped us and our networks with free sessions and coaching on a variety of relevant topics. Despite actively contributing and supporting my team and family and donating to surrounding communities, it often felt that it wasn't quite enough! Many did what they could and are still contributing. Others chose to ignore advice, rebel against restrictions or take a holiday. Many people don't wait for disasters but volunteer regularly to help others by making food, caring for the vulnerable or cleaning up a local beach or park.

---

5   Syed, 2020.
6   Lindeque, 2020.

What is your story of this time? What would you have liked it to be? What will you do differently next time or as part of your life? What if a big positive that can emerge from this crisis is a surge in kindness. Not just short-lived kindness, but kindness as a core value and sustainable part of our societies?[5]

3. CONSUMING OR CONTRIBUTING – WHAT'S YOUR BALANCE?

For us to shift our perspective and world view and work towards sustainable feelings of positive pride and satisfaction, we need to identify where we might be spending most of our time. What is keeping us hooked in the ego state of consuming, claiming status or showing up as entitled? What could we believe about ourselves, others and the world to spend more time being accountable and contributing to others, our team and communities around us? I encourage you to explore what these two extreme identities look like and start setting a course to that identity that will bring the most life satisfaction in the longer-term.

Status consumer

Entitled
Consumer
Status builder

Community builder

Accountable
Contributor
Mentor

Community builders are Accountable, Contributors and Mentors

Community builders are **accountable.** They take responsibility for the roles they sign up for in life – as a spouse, friend, sister, parent, employee or employer, project team member, neighbour, online forum member – and they give of their best. When they make commitments, they follow-through with them. When they see bad things happening to others or in their organisation, they speak up and do something about it. They take responsibility for their actions and behaviour and are willing to admit when they are wrong or made a mistake. They do the right thing, even (especially) when no-one else is watching.

They are **contributors** who get satisfaction from adding value. They give ideas, time, effort and energy (and financial or other resources when they have them) to solve problems or improve ways of work. When interacting virtually or in the real world, they actively share their knowledge, ideas and skills, not just using and adapting what others have created or built. They have a spirit of generosity and share first without expecting anything in return.

They are **mentors** who see their role as developing the next generation of leaders and the community as a whole. They reach out and get to know people in their neighbourhood or the communities they care about. They naturally share knowledge, advice or connections to help people grow and achieve their dreams. They also encourage and recognise potential and share a sense of hope for the future. They fulfil their promises and get stuff done. They never forget the people who helped them become who they are, and keep their memories and stories alive.

They believe in being part of the solution rather than complain about the problem. They believe in citizenship, making a difference and leaving a legacy for future generations. They believe in doing the right thing even when no-one is watching. They believe in being grateful for the opportunities and people that helped them get to where they are today. They believe that every day is a day to make a difference, no matter how small.

They generally **feel** generous, loving, kind and compassionate

They use language like: "It's up to us". "How can we help?", "Let's get involved ... pitch in ... share what we can", "Let's stay true to who we are", Sorry, I was wrong, let's fix it", "Let's be thankful."

They have daily **habits** like sharing, mentoring, checking-in, gratitude journals, being an active citizen, writing or texting thank you notes, telling stories of hope and possibility, and apologising when they are wrong.

> ### Fred Swaniker – a contributor in action
>
> Fred is a shining example of someone who translates his vision for change into action. He realised many years ago that Africa was facing some serious socio-economic challenges with over 200 million youths (forecasted to double by 2045), over 60% of them unemployed and over 70% of them living on less than $2 per day. Fred feels passionately that the only way to harness the youth of tomorrow is to build the next generation of ethical, entrepreneurial African leaders to lead Africa toward an economically viable and sustainable continent. He has launched four organizations to this end – The African Leadership Academy, The African Leadership Network, The Global Leadership Adventures, and The African Leadership University with many famous projects and alumni under their belt. Together these organisations are aiming to educate and groom over 3 million leaders by 2060 and create a powerful network of over 6,000 leaders who work together to address the continent's greatest challenges. Fred has been recognized by the World Economic Forum as a Young Global Leader and was listed by Forbes magazine among the top 10 young power men in Africa 2011.[7]

If we spend time exploring an alternative identity, we may be able to see how we can sometimes show up when we feel hard done by or when life is getting us down. There is a purpose, a time and a place for all identities. Figure out what works for you and get some extra input from people who will be honest with you.

---

7   Rise Africa Rise, 2020.

Status consumers are Entitles, Consumers and Status Builders

Status consumers can feel **entitled**… they feel that life owes them something. They might believe they have been deprived of certain opportunities or access to resources. A sense of entitlement appears across the spectrum. Rich kids can feel deprived of their parents' love. Middle-class youngsters constantly compare themselves to those who seem to have better clothes, friends, cars, schools etc. It appears in those who see another life on TV or social media that they can never live up to. It can also appear in those who took initiative and found themselves moving from the breadline to the boardroom. Entitlement is an attitude more than economics. It is about immediate gratification and "me" and the "more" and the "now" generation.

Status consumers can also **consume** more than they contribute. They are happy to consume the ideas, goods and attention of others, with no qualms to use what others create without adding their bit in return. This extends to downloading or sharing other people's creations without permission and with little appreciation of the time and effort of the originator. Why add value when no-one will really notice? Why work hard, when I get what I need by doing the minimum? Why write a blog, made a video or share my knowledge when there is so much already out there?

Status consumers are excellent **status builders** that create an external persona and manage what other people see. They seek recognition through likes, wows, laughs, shares or retweets, and love winning the followers game. They experience events through the lenses of their mobiles. They chat rather than talk, comment rather than converse, and voice note rather than dialogue. They tend to overinvest in the coolest clothes or latest fads to show off but under-invest in real relationships, character building experiences and life lessons.

They believe that life is short, and life is cheap, so take what you can. They believe they deserve better and why not just follow the crowd. They believe that status = success. Or they might believe that don't have something of value to share.

They generally **feel** hard done by, envious, troubled and not enough as they are.

They use **language** like "It's not fair", "Have you seen the latest...", "I wonder how I can get more ..." or "why bother, I'll just do the minimum."

They have daily **habits** like spending hours on social media and comparing their lives to others, dreaming up ways to get likes and shares, sleeping in, living off others, and figuring out what they can get for minimum effort.

Who comes to mind? Do you have friends or colleagues like this? Do you notice some celebrities, politicians or business leaders who spend a lot of time polishing their egos in the press or on social media? Who are some positive role models that use some of these characteristics in a healthy way to raise their online profile for income opportunities? Who leaves an uncomfortable feeling when you listen to them talk about themselves and what they do?

We love to hate or hate to love them

Often it is the most popular people who we love to hate or hate to love, and who give us some lovely evidence (and some ammunition) to place them on the continuum. Some of the most followed celebrities on Twitter this year, with 50 to over 100 million followers, are artists and entertainers such as Justin Bieber, Katy Perry, Rihanna, Taylor Swift, Lady Gaga, Kim Kardashian, Cristiano Ronaldo and Ellen DeGeneres.[8] There are also some global leaders and commentators such as Barack Obama and Donald Trump. Many of them have self-confessed high egos that have got them

---
8   Pope, 2019.

to where they are today. Some, however, such as Kayne West and Drake, create controversy or polarisation through their tweets and actions and are losing respect due to their self-obsessed narcissism. Many fans live for their celebrities and social media communities. Many others identify themselves with their online personas. People feel good about making a difference through personal commentary and sharing tweets and posts on local and global tragedies such as the terrorist attacks in Paris or the #metoo or #blacklives matter campaigns. But, do they ever actually get off their couches to make a difference in the real world, to really change national policy, care for the survivors or save lives? Who are your social media lovers? Who are your social media haters? Does it matter?

Use this opportunity to find your own balance between consuming and contributing. Are you creating something original for people to enjoy? Are you leaving the world a better place for you being here? What do you truly believe?

4. BE INSPIRED AND BELIEVE

How can we become inspired to believe? Some days, when we are a bit tired or down, we may not have the energy or motivation or feel like contributing, and that's ok. Being a community builder does not mean giving something of yourself 24/7. It means finding that sweet spot between giving and receiving with gratitude and noticing when the balance is out and when you could do a little more or allow others to support you in some way too. Take a good look at some of your own beliefs that you are proud of and help you feel energised and good about yourself. Notice some of the beliefs that might be limiting how you could contribute to the world and make just a small difference. Sometimes the act of a quick note or call of appreciation can go a long way in contributing and building. Notice that it is not about the time, the money, the experience or the energy needed. It is mostly about an attitude that make the contributing part of your day or something you inspire others who have the time and money to do something with.

STATUS CONSUMER	COMMUNITY BUILDER
FROM believing...	TO believing...
<ul><li>It's not my problem or my job</li><li>Other people do it, so why shouldn't I?</li><li>Life is short, take what you can</li><li>I deserve to be treated like...</li><li>I am too young, poor, inexperienced to add value</li></ul>	<ul><li>I am accountable and a citizen</li><li>It is better to do the right thing even when no-one's watching</li><li>What can I do today to make a difference?</li><li>What or who can I be grateful for today?</li><li>How can I leave a legacy for future generations?</li></ul>

Here is an amazing story of Michele Sohn, someone with a community builder mindset who chose early on in the pandemic, before lockdown even hit, to make a difference.

#10millionmasks

Michele was sitting at home just before lockdown was announced and wanted to find a way to help. She thought, what if she could find a way for the people to make cloth masks for everyday use AND help the makers earn a little extra money for much needed food? She did her research, consulted with medical professionals found designs, spoke to some friends and co-founded a social movement called #10millionmasks. As she says on her radio interview in the link below, it started with an idea on Sunday, a campaign by Wednesday and a movement with sewing and distribution networks across South Africa and in eight countries within two weeks. Not only are they providing an incredible idea and something for people to do to feel useful and empowered, but they are helping to reduce the demand for medical masks that front-line medical staff need the most. She has managed to combine her strategic intellect, ideas, love for sewing... mini-businesses, her creative agency background and her network to build the media channels to get the message out there. All of this cost her mainly time, social capital (her network) and only a very little money for initial examples and communication efforts.[9]

---

9   10 Million Masks, 2020.

"It is in your hands to create a better world for all who live in it."
—Nelson Mandela

5. DAILY HACKS AND HABITS FOR CONTRIBUTORS

In this last "C" of contribution we will explore how we are doing with a few check points: the legacy test, the ego test, the accountability test, the citizen test and the gratitude test. These will give you some ideas of what great contributors do (or don't do) in their daily habits. Select a few of the ideas from each "test" to integrate into your daily thinking and routines.

5.1 Legacy check-point

Ben Angel, author of "Unstoppable", found in his research that people with a strong sense of purpose achieved their goals 70% of the time, as opposed to those who didn't have a sense of purpose. Furthermore, people with purpose were 31% less likely to be afraid of failing, 35% less likely to doubt themselves, 23% less likely to procrastinate and 34% more likely to have the stamina required to reach their goals.[10] When I entered my first summit with Singularity University, I was struck by their big purpose question on a banner outside: "How can you impact a billion lives?" This inspired me to pay a different level of attention to the programme and search for even bigger ways to make a difference with the skills, resources and networks I had or could still build. What kind of legacy do you want to leave behind? What do you want people to remember about you? Maybe some of these attitudes and habits can help.

#	Statement	Opportunity √
1	I have a clear life purpose (vision, mission, legacy) written down, visible in my home or workspace, and read and review it regularly.	

---

10 Ben Angel, 2019.

#	Statement	Opportunity √
2	I understand why I do what I do which helps me prioritise my time and generates energy for action.	
3	I know what I care about and am most passionate about and ensure I make time for these activities to fulfil my soul.	
4	I have a clear idea about who is important and how I want to impact them in my work or home life every day (individuals or groups).	
5	I ask myself at the end of every day – did I have a good day, what did I do in support of my purpose, what can I do better or differently tomorrow?	
6	I regularly imagine myself standing in the shoes of future generations and think about my contribution to the world they will live in.	
7	I often ask myself – how can I be of greatest service today?	
8	I regularly make charitable contributions (money, skills, time) to families, organisations or NGOs to help those less fortunate than me.	
9	I spend time mentoring people who can benefit from my experience, wisdom, contacts or skills.	
10	I pay attention to role models who make a significant difference to inspire me to take action in my own way.	

Tip: On waking each morning, spend a few moments looking at your vision board, goals, diary or mind movie, and remind yourself who you want to be and what is most important for you to live your purpose and leave a legacy. If you can do this in alpha brain state, this is so much more powerful for priming the brain to remind you of this regularly throughout the day. Check in again with yourself at the end of the day and ask yourself, "How did I do and what could I do differently tomorrow?"

For more on living a purposeful life, view books, blogs and videos by Stephen Covey, Simon Sinek, Jay Chetty and Ben Angel in our resources list below.

5.2 Ego check-point

The ego is the "I". Your ego is that part of you with specific traits, beliefs, and habits that protect you from harm as you grow up and get socialised in the world. Your ego develops an identity to protect you from confusion, disconnection, and loss of love that you might experience. It starts off as a very rigid identity or "personality" with clear black and white opinions and responses. We start off with everything being about us (ego-centric) and then develop over time with a healthy balance of self-confidence, humility, and community. Ego development happens at different paces for people depending on their exposure to life, trauma, learning and honest feedback. In your younger years, it is very defensive and protective and hates to be judged or rejected. Many people have not evolved past the ego-centric state, leading to a lot of ego-boosting, defensive behaviour to hide the fragile ego and insecurity inside. Once we develop beyond our ego identity, we see the ego as something separate from ourselves and watch how it plays out under stress. We can then hopefully stop, and think and choose, rather than let our egos run our lives. We can acknowledge the intent of protection but soften the ego to allow for a more appropriate response as we learn and grow. Have a look at the statements below for opportunities to evolve your ego personality.[11]

---

11 Power of Positivity, 2020.

#	Statement	Opportunity √
1	I often feel like I never have enough (money, time, goods, power, etc.) and have an insatiable desire to attain more to look and feel good enough.	
2	I sometimes feel envious when others I know publicly succeed and secretly wish it were me.	
3	I like being the centre of attention in meetings, parties, conversations and will often redirect the attention back to me.	
4	I am constantly comparing myself to others who seem "more" talented, attractive, smarter or successful, and that upsets me.	
5	I crave respect, recognition and external validation and complain, sulk or use sarcasm when it's not forthcoming in the way that I need it.	
6	I am often defensive and perceive disagreements as personal "attacks". I often attack back to make me feel better and end up in many conflicts.	
7	I tend to focus more on what I need to stay safe (less on others) unless something directly affects me and I will benefit too.	
8	I can be over-confident and set unattainable goals out of pride or ego and then get frustrated and make excuses or blame others when I can't achieve them.	
9	I can easily get my way if I tell people what they want to hear or use what I know motivates them, i.e. am good at manipulating or controlling others.	

#	Statement	Opportunity √
10	I often over-analyse and have obsessive thoughts about what did or could go wrong and how embarrassing that was or could be.	

Tip: Give your ego a name and identity and start a conversation with it to encourage the idea that you are separate from your ego and are in charge of your thoughts, feelings and actions, and not caught in an automatic loop of defensive reaction to life. For more on how to identify, acknowledge, name, work with and integrate the ego in a healthy way, read "How to do ego work" or take the Ego Test in the links below.

5.3 Accountability check-point

People who take accountability have a core value of integrity and believe that their word is their bond. When they make promises and commitments, they take them seriously. Accountability can be hard work and requires an enormous amount of awareness and communication with others to manage expectations. Often what we say and what other people hear are very different. We need to work at creating clarity, especially with big commitments that impact us significantly. If we practice being clear and accountable with the little things, like "I'll send you that document or call you tomorrow", then the bigger stuff comes more naturally, e.g. contracts, agreements, team roles, parenting and relationship commitments. You won't always get it right, so when you do mess up or choose on the odd occasion to just walk by, let it go and not make the effort... notice it with compassion and start again tomorrow. Accountability is an amazing tool in your toolbox for building self-esteem and confidence with yourself over time... and being seen as trustworthy by others.

Have a look at some statements of accountability and see where there may be room for improvement.

#	Statement	Opportunity ✓
1	I take commitments and promises seriously and think carefully before agreeing to something (including deliverables and deadlines).	
2	I don't avoid making commitments or keep my options open through vague statements (e.g. "Let's get together sometime soon.").	
3	I stick to commitments and promises made and always let people know if and why I can't deliver on these without making it a habit to re-contract.	
4	I honour the promises I make to myself including mental and personal health i.e. diet or exercise programme, positive self-talk.	
5	I don't justify or make excuses when I haven't followed-through on a commitment i.e. Something else came up or I just didn't have the time.	
6	I take responsibility without blaming others for mistakes or non-delivery of agreed actions.	
7	I have no problem saying no when I am unable or unwilling to keep a promise – even to those in authority.	
8	I take ownership of team outcomes and go the extra mile to deliver i.e. not clocking out at 4pm if things are not finished.	
9	I am honest about not knowing the answers to questions.	
10	I get back to people if I say I will.	

Tip: Journal daily to notice the little promises you make (to yourself and others) and how many of these you live up to or don't. Notice how you feel when you do or don't. Notice if you feel bad or a bit guilty. We often don't realise the impact of these feelings on our energy and self-trust, and therefore on our important relationships. Also take some time to notice how many people around you are strong on integrity of their word. Do you let them off the hook or do you help them see their impact in a compassionate way? Our relationships are often a mirror for our inner world. For more on how to identify, acknowledge, name, work with and integrate the ego in a healthy way, read "Extreme Ownership: How U.S. Navy SEALs Lead and Win" listed in the resources below.

5.4 Citizenship check-point

The concept of citizenship was born in Ancient Greece. Greek education at the time was designed to instruct citizens in the values, intellectual frameworks, and habits-of-mind required to be "free men" (in the time before gender equality!). That is, to actively participate in the political system that shaped their lives and guaranteed their freedoms. Today, being a citizen means that you're part of a group (country), and that you have legal and political rights within that group. It brings with it both privileges and obligations. How many of us are enjoying privileges equally to our obligations? How many of us are less active and hoping and trusting that others will take the lead in creating a better life for all? Is there something more you could be doing to help build the nation now and for the future. A nation is, after all, only as healthy as its individual citizens, as we have seen with such stark reality through the COVID-19 pandemic.[12]

"Before you are a leader, success is growing yourself. When you become a leader, success is about growing others." –Jack Welch

#	Statement	Opportunity √
1	I know the political and governance landscape of my country and how I can make my voice and vote count.	

---

12 Fabrega, 2020.

#	Statement	Opportunity √
2	I follow the rules and guidelines that have been set out for the safety and quality of life of all, e.g. acting and driving safely, disposing of rubbish responsibly, recycling, conserving water and electricity, paying taxes, etc.	
3	I speak positively about my country and support my country's heroes who excel in sport, the arts, business, innovation, etc.	
4	I show respect and dignity to all in my community, e.g. shop keepers, petrol attendants, traffic officers, old people, homeless people, other people's children.	
5	I embrace diversity and am tolerant of other races, economic classes, lifestyle choices and religions.	
6	I am productive and earn an income or contribute in kind without expecting handouts or others to look after me.	
7	I actively support my local community forums, events and businesses, e.g. local shops, markets, festivals, theatres, art exhibitions, charity drives, sports, etc.	
8	I contribute to charities, projects or do pro-bono work to pay it forward, e.g. clean-ups, community gardening, fund raising, helping out neighbours, lift clubs, etc.	
9	I share my knowledge, skills and sharable resources generously to help others, e.g. pass on links to articles, tools, tips and contacts to.	
10	I post, write blogs or poems, send quotes, make videos, comment and share on social media with an intent to add value.	

Tip: Life is all about finding that unique balance of giving and receiving, contributing, enjoying, supporting others and allowing others to support you when you need it. Being a citizen is less about agreeing with what our leaders are saying or doing, but showing up in a way that makes you part of the solution rather than just criticising, rationalising your choices or being part of the problem. It also feels really good to be of service to others without a hidden motive or agenda. Start small with something that comes naturally to you and develop from there. Read "Community: The Structure of Belonging" by Peter Block.

5.5 Gratitude check-point

Gratitude is one of the highest frequency emotions that can shift your mood, your mental state and your immune system immediately. It is powerful in quickly shifting us out of victim or survival emotions and back into seeing the bigger picture of what is important. I remember a colleague in my early team building years who was a great example of someone who went the extra mile in appreciating my contribution. I would regularly receive a personal, hand-written note and a small but thoughtful gift of appreciation for sometimes I felt just doing my job. Because of that, she will always be special in my memories. Another mentee of mine who interned with us for about eight months still calls and texts to this day to say thank you for the opportunity we gave her and how it has shaped her thinking and life. Because of this, I think of her often and am motivated to do more of the same for others, knowing sometimes the little things make the biggest difference.

#	Statement	Opportunity √
1	I am thankful every day for being alive and having a life to live.	
2	I reflect every day on what I am grateful for.	

#	Statement	Opportunity √
3	I keep a gratitude diary where I write down my gratitudes regularly.	
4	I write thank-you notes or texts to others who I appreciate.	
5	I love what I do and who I do it with.	
6	I publicly recognise other's contributions to my success in work or life.	
7	I am grateful for all I have to live a fulfilling life – health, family, income, etc.	
8	I am grateful for all the lessons I receive, which can be very uncomfortable at times.	
9	I am grateful for all the special relationships I have in my life which teach me about myself and help me grow.	
10	I am grateful for and show thanks to all the people who contribute to my daily life through their input, e.g. food preparers, shopkeepers, government workers, traffic officers, car mechanics, refuse removers, gardeners, security guard, receptionists, etc.	

Tip: Develop a gratitude practice through writing in a gratitude journal, creating a gratitude scrapbook, posting daily or weekly gratitude moments on social media, or sharing what you are grateful for with your family over a special meal. You can also join a Gratitude Practice Facebook Group. See link below.

The key to life is not accumulation, it is contribution."
–Stephen Covey

6. TIPS, TOOLS AND RESOURCES

If you are interested in exploring and learning more, here are some of our favourite tips, tools and resources to accelerate your journey to becoming a Community Builder. (See https://catalystconsulting.co.za/power-up8-resources/).

Blogs

How to do Ego work: https://yourholisticpsychologist.com/how-to-do-ego-work/

Videos

The ripple effect of training young leaders | Fred Swaniker | TEDxEuston: https://www.youtube.com/watch?v=nqIVuGkE99k
Start with why -- how great leaders inspire action | Simon Sinek | TEDxPugetSound:https://www.youtube.com/watch?v=u4ZoJKF_VuA
How to Find Your Purpose | Jay Shetty on Impact Theory: https://www.youtube.com/watch?v=GXoErccq0vw
What is The Meaning of Life? Ben Angel, Unstoppable: https://www.youtube.com/watch?v=hUDbiRK4pps

Books

Extreme Ownership: How U.S. Navy SEALs Lead and Win Hardcover, 2015, Jocko Willink
Community: The Structure of Belonging, by Peter Block

Tools

Ego assessment: https://www.3smartcubes.com/pages/tests/ego-problem/ego-problem_questions/
Accountability assessment: https://www.davidirvine.com/how-accountable-are-you/
Gratitude Practice Facebook Group: https://www.facebook.com/thegratitudepractice/

Chapter 12
CALL TO ACTION

"Vision without action is merely a dream. Action without vision just passes the time. Vision with action can change the world."
−Joel Barker

Congratulations for adventuring with me to get this far. I trust that by now you have some ideas, intentions, questions and some renewed curiosity for your own path to building resilience potential. It is now time to turn your intentions into ACTION. Here are some suggested steps:

STEP 1: Reflect a bit deeper on where you might be on the continuum of the eight capabilities.

STEP 2: Seek feedback from others to calibrate your view of self vs. how others perceive you.

STEP 3: Identify two to three capabilities to prioritise that will impact the most important areas of your life.

STEP 4: Set some goals and action plans for yourself in each of these priority areas. Write them down or put them up on a vision board or screen saver.

STEP 5: Set up some quiet time daily to visualise your future self in alpha brain wave and coherent heart state (see techniques in Chapter 3).

STEP 6: Practice the beliefs, feelings and habits daily that will rewire your brain toward who you want to show up as more often.

STEP 7: Start to notice how you create more opportunities, connections and enhanced results in life and work.

STEP 8: Spend as much time in a state of appreciation and gratitude for what you have in your life AND for what you are creating through shifting your mindsets and habits.

To help you with Step 1 to figure out where you are and where you would like to spend more time, we have two options. You can do a quick self-review here in the book or you can take our FREE RESILIENCE POTENTIAL ASSESSMENT by clicking on the link[1] below to complete the assessment and receive a free report.

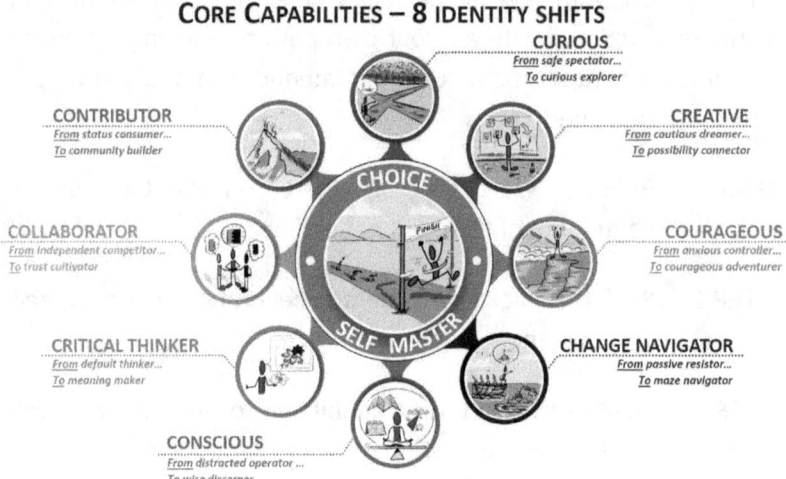

---

1   Catalyst Consulting, https://catalystconsulting.co.za/survey/

1. RESILIENCE POTENTIAL SELF-ASSESSMENT

Remember when you do any self-assessment that everyone has been exposed to different life experiences and learning opportunities and therefore have different strengths and weaknesses or less developed aspects of themselves. Aim to be very self-aware and discerning as to who you compare to and what your strengths and weaknesses might be in relation to the average. Are you a little, a lot above or below average? Would others agree or disagree with your self-assessment?

Some warning signs that you may need some more input or feedback from others to calibrate your view of self can be the following:

- When you have too many strengths – you might be over-estimating your brilliance.
- When you have too few strengths – you might be under-estimating your capability.
- When your answers are all in the middle – you might not be able to differentiate your strengths from your areas of development.
- When your assessment[2] is inconsistent across capabilities – you may need to look a little deeper for real strengths and development areas, and not just the superficial view.

Rate yourself on the continuum using the summary descriptors and beliefs below.

---

[2] Catalyst Consulting, https://catalystconsulting.co.za/survey/

Almost Never	Sometimes	Often	Almost Always
Almost never show up in this way. Tend toward the far left of the continuum.	Sometimes show up in this way. Tend more toward the left of the continuum.	Often show up in this way. Tend more toward the right of the continuum.	Almost always show up in this way. Tend toward the far right of the continuum.

To help you reflect honestly and avoid the tendency toward picking the middle, we have created four options based on frequency. If you honestly show up more of the time on the left of the continuum, select "almost never" or "sometimes". If you know (and others will confirm this) that you show up more of the time on the right of the continuum, select "often" or "almost always". You can go back the chapters to get a more detailed description of each capability. Even if you may not identify with ALL of the descriptors and may sit on both sides on some of them, take a good estimate and choose the most accurate in terms of frequency. You can always circle the ones that you are unsure of for later consideration and development. Once you have finished selecting your frequency of showing up in this way across all the capabilities, complete the action plan below.

	Definitions and characteristics	Almost Never	Some-times	Often	Almost Always
1	**CHOICE**: I am aware and conscious of my thoughts, feelings, behaviour and my impact on others. I am able to stay calm and choose appropriate action toward my goals. i.e. How often am I more the **RESPONSIVE CREATOR** (aware, disciplined responsive) vs. the reactive victim (in the moment, spontaneous, reactive)?				

	Definitions and characteristics	Almost Never	Some-times	Often	Almost Always
2	**CURIOUS:** I go beyond the obvious and actively seek new information and ideas – about the world, people, relationships and my own potential. I question, experiment and take risks for rapid learning. i.e. How often am I more the **CURIOUS EXPLORER** (seeker, engager, experimenter) vs. the safe spectator (cautious, opiniated, spectator)?				
3	**CREATIVE:** I harness my own and others unique ideas to create innovative solutions to problems and evolving circumstances. i.e. How often am I more the **POSSIBILITY CONNECTOR** (authentic, ideator, connector) vs. the cautious dreamer (follower, pretender, dreamer)?				
4	**COURAGEOUS:** I believe in myself and am willing to grow and move through fear despite ambiguity and uncertainty. I am willing to fail fast, be vulnerable and have honest conversations for meaningful growth focused relationships. i.e. How often am I more the **COURAGEOUS ADVENTURER** (resilient, optimistic, adventurer) vs. the anxious controller (anxious, vigilant, controller)?				
5	**CHANGE NAVIGATOR:** I hold onto a worthwhile vision through rapid change and disruption, with determination and resilience. I bounce back from disappointments or criticism and try again. I engage the hearts and minds of others and help them navigate the scary journey of change. I commit and follow through to get results. i.e. How often am I more the **MAZE NAVIGATOR** (embracer, navigator, influencer) vs. the passive resistor (resistor, passenger, dramatizer)?				

	Definitions and characteristics	Almost Never	Some-times	Often	Almost Always
6	**CONSCIOUS:** I am aware of my intentions, my thoughts and where my attention is. I focus my mind and my time to get important work done and relationships built. I make conscious choices about what I allow into my mind and body. i.e. How often am I more the **WISE DISCERNER** (discerner, decisive, focussed) vs. the distracted operator (drifter, deflector, distracted)?				
7	**CRITICAL THINKER:** I think things through from all perspectives, ask the right questions, and analyse and integrate relevant data to resolve complex dilemmas in an unpredictable world. i.e. How often am I more the **MEANING MAKER** (anticipator, systemic, integrator) vs. the default thinker (expedient, linear, complicator)?				
8	**COLLABORATOR:** I communicate and build trusted relationships and networks to achieve common goals across boundaries. I demonstrate trust, empathy, vulnerability, and an abundance mindset to resolve conflict and unleash joint value. i.e. How often am I more the **TRUST CULTIVATOR** (inclusive, trusting, resolver) vs. the independent competitor (independent, sensitive, protector)?				
9	**CONTRIBUTOR:** I apply my strengths and talents to make a difference to people, communities and the planet, with long-term community success in mind i.e. How often am I more **COMMUNITY BUILDER** (accountable, contributor, mentor) vs. the status consumer (entitled, consumer, status builder)?				

2. RESILIENCE POTENTIAL ACTION PLAN

CAPABILITY	INTENTION	BELIEVE & FEEL	HABIT & HOW OFTEN	SUPPORT
Which of the eight capabilities plus CHOICE are the most important to focus on now, e.g. courage?	What is the end result that you wish to achieve, e.g. health, wealth, career, relationship, confidence, etc.	What do you need to believe and feel to realise your intention, e.g. I can do it, change is opportunity, fail fast = learn fast, confident, excited, grateful.	What are the habits you need to practice consistently (how often) to rewire your brain, e.g. exercise, visualise, save, speak up.	What support do you need to practice beliefs or habits toward your intention, e.g. accountability partner, coach, business partner, funding, etc.
1				
2				
3				

3. RESILIENCE POTENTIAL COMMUNITY

Let us know how you are doing via our Facebook page (https://www.facebook.com/Catalyst-Consulting-Pty-Ltd-282594455087547/) so that you can share your progress and struggles with others and join in our community of life-long learners and innovators. You can also request a coach from our community of fabulous coaches. Good luck on your journey and we look forward to hearing from you.

Contact us through our website www.catalystconsulting.co.za.

Chapter 13
BUILDING THE 8Cs IN ORGANISATIONS

1. THE IMPERATIVE FOR BUILDING META-CAPABILITIES

Never before has the need for foundational meta-capabilities been so important and so urgent, as we are faced with yet another series of dramatic changes in the world of work. As you have seen throughout this book, there is a significant increase in the requirement for talent and leaders who can rapidly adjust to changing business and customer circumstances. Organisations need people who can innovate, influence and implement with speed, while keeping people engaged AND keeping customers or stakeholders aligned and committed.

In recent times, we have experienced first-hand the impact of disruptive global change on our productivity, energy, mental health AND on our overall business risks and sustainability. To stay in the game and on the playing field (never mind, winning the game), organisations need people who are:

- intensely **curious** (about themselves, others and the world);
- uniquely **creative** (experimenting, learning and willing to fail);
- **courageously** committed (to their vision for self, team or cause);
- **consciously** choosing (where to focus attention and how to show up);

- **critical thinkers** (who can resolve dilemmas and make meaning out of noise);
- trusted **collaborators** (who combine perspectives and strengths into lasting relationships and value);
- **change** navigators (who navigate the maze of change for positive impact); and
- generous **contributors** (who build lasting healthy communities).

Building these capabilities takes dedicated intention and focus. If we don't invest in developing these in our organisations, we may find ourselves spending a lot of energy on managing and recovering from crisis to crisis. We see the direct impact of "firefighting" stress on our leaders, who are in the line of fire between shareholders, key customers and staff. Proactive, customer-focused thinking and planning requires people who can embrace change, manage stress and make optimal decisions. This takes self-mastery to be aware of impact, habits and choices in every moment.

Imagine a team, a unit or a company aligning on a purpose and a vision, adapting responsively to change, and being energised and engaged to do their very best every day. Imagine an organisation armed with the critical thinking, emotional maturity and courage to collaborate and make great decisions for all stakeholders, both now and in the future. Imagine a place with a culture that strives toward people being the best versions of themselves, where they help each other and the organisation to grow and evolve. We cannot leave this to chance. We need to make some conscious and intentional choices and investments for reaping the future benefits.

2. SHIFTING TALENT STRATEGIES

Every few years there are new talent trends or priorities based on economic, political, social or technological pressures. In recent years, the focus has been to attract and retain top talent, manage succession planning, identify and shift core strategic capability and build sustainable talent pipelines. A lot of the work that we are busy with now is reshaping organisations in response to current and expected disruption and change. This includes designing future operating models, structures, capability and culture to deliver to shifting global and local customer demand. It is important to consider leadership capabilities, technical capabilities AND core capabilities that will ensure success and adaptation to change, no matter the strategy.

With such sudden and dramatic change in our working lives, and in how talent is being sourced, managed and rewarded, new fit-for purpose mental models are needed. Talent is going to be much more informed, globally connected, discerning, mobile, digitally savvy and thus more demanding. They are likely to focus their attention on organisations that can customise their talent offering, allowing for flexibility, learning, challenge and purpose. Other workforce segments will require a culture of continuous learning and adapting to new technologies, tasks, timeframes and teams. The "new normal" will be about balancing the needs of stable, low change functions; dynamic, fast changing units; AND a growing pool of gig economy flexi-workers. Rapid skills matching, on-boarding, teaming, upskilling, delivering and off-boarding will be largely digitised. This new style of psychologically contracting with full, part-time and flexi-workers will need to be supported by a new breed of agile HR and business leaders to enable a fulfilling employee experience journey. We have been re-imagining the future of people management using the 6Ms for ease of reference:

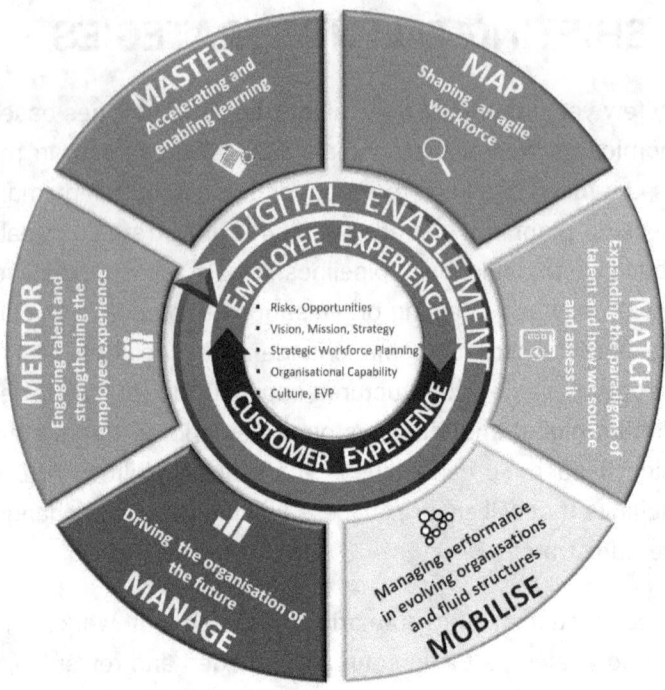

- **Mapping** is shaping an agile future-fit workforce within shifting operating models and structures. It includes agile roles, smart teams and understanding the capabilities required.

- **Matching** is sourcing both internal and external talent to match shifting roles, teams and skills. It includes differentiated EVP for unique talent segments using digitised and gamified talent profiling.

- **Mobilising** is optimising performance and potential within agile, smart teams. It includes agile, growth-focused, multi-source performance and culture fit coaching, rapid on-boarding, teaming, upskilling, off-boarding and optimising talent across teams.

- **Managing** is ensuring that all touch points of the employee experience is digitised, user-friendly and guided optimally to enhance engagement and manage risks. It includes systems, data analysis, decision-making and risk response capability.

- **Mentoring** involves leaders engaging, developing and retaining talent throughout their life cycle in the company, regardless of which teams they move through. It includes self-service and validated profiling and design thinking to customise talent offerings for specific segments and effective succession management.

- **Mastery** is creating the learning culture and leader readiness for enabling accelerated, self-driven, whole person, collaborative learning for growth and impact. It includes future-fit learning options and support.

Being effective, productive, relevant and resilient in this highly fluid and evolving way of working requires the meta-capabilities mentioned above. It also requires leaders who can both role model and develop these in others.

3. BUILDING FOUNDATIONAL CAPABILITIES – WHAT NOT TO DO

Before we get into how best to build these, it is sometimes useful to know what not to do. From our many years of experience in the field, we see lots of what goes right and what goes wrong – often unintentionally. A lot of valuable time, energy and money can be wasted on learning that is not relevant, customised, practical or measured. So here is our not to do list:

- **DO NOT…** do nothing and leave learning to chance or book groups of people on training to hit the numbers, hoping they will learn something. Most people find only 10 – 15% of non-customised, large group training relevant, and forget most of it afterwards if it is not reinforced and integrated into their day-to-day roles.

- **DO NOT…** leave learning up to the individual with access to online modules hoping they will be motivated and ready for self-driven learning. Without a learning culture, encouragement and recognition, adoption rates of online learning platforms are a tiny fraction of the employee population.

- **DO NOT...** expect mindset shifts and transformational experiences to happen with self-directed online learning only, without some robust conversations and opportunities for insight. The ah-ha moment and learning impact is often attained through a combination of activities and input from others.

- **DO NOT...** prioritise leadership or technical skills above core or foundational skills. An integrated approach to build a solid foundation or platform upon which to build should be the focus.

- **DO NOT...** only focus on leaders to build foundational skills. Front line and support staff play a key role in your day-to-day culture and decisions. Pick your change champions at all levels and have a cross-cutting approach.

- **DO NOT...** see learning new skills in isolation of culture and employee experience. It is critical that the culture is ripe for learning and encourages space to experiment and fail fast.

4. BUILDING FOUNDATIONAL CAPABILITIES – WHAT TO DO

We have had to rapidly develop capability and implement new systems, processes and cultures in many turnkey projects. Our recommended principles for ensuring future-fit learning are not surprisingly also categorised into 8Cs:

1. **Clarify audience:** Understand that your target audience requires foundational skills and identify the leadership, technical and foundational capabilities required.

2. **Cost vs. impact:** Assess the impact of budget invested in people that will have the biggest impact on the culture and learning of others at different levels (your change influencers).

3. **Critical mass:** Choose a sufficient percentage of your target audience to embark on learning journeys to build a common language, culture and tools around the foundational skills, which then can then spread to others. A few people attending programmes as individuals will struggle to make a big organisational impact by themselves.

4. **Customised journeys:** Spread the learning over 6-12 months with a combination of self-driven digital learning, facilitated sessions, collaborative team-based learning projects and coaching to ensure learning is embedded and impactful.

5. **Strategy alignment:** Closely align your learning journeys to strategy, culture and role. Master classes can be utilised to build onto existing learning journeys but must be integrated into the overall outcomes and expectations.

6. **Collaborative action learning:** Build social and team skills and feedback-rich environments by designing relevant team-based action learning projects with tracking and accountability.

7. **Coaching:** Provide access to group coaching for common tricky aspects to create opportunities for individual and group insight and transformation, and accelerated learning for key individuals where speed is necessary.

8. **Change management:** Ensure learner readiness for a new way of learning through effective communication, system on-boarding, expectation management, leader engagement, and group launch sessions to build important connections and energy for the journey.

9. **Calculate:** Track and measure the impact of the learning – on individual performance, skills, engagement and self-confidence, as well as team and organisational impact.

5. LEARNING JOURNEY EXAMPLES, OPTIONS AND TIPS

The Quantum Shift learning journey can be customised in many different ways depending on the audience, speed and outcomes required. The impact is best when the learning journey is over a number of months, a blend of digital, self-driven and facilitated learning and team-based projects for workplace application. Shorter webinars or master-classes can also be utilised to enhance other learning or work activities. The modules include the 8Cs as follows:

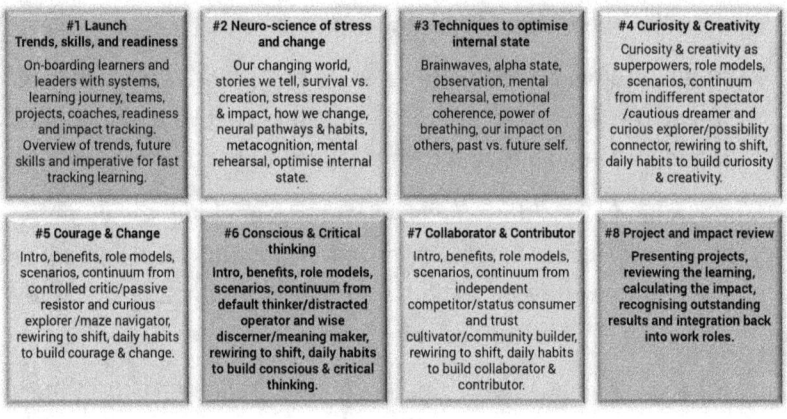

#1 Launch Trends, skills, and readiness	#2 Neuro-science of stress and change	#3 Techniques to optimise internal state	#4 Curiosity & Creativity
On-boarding learners and leaders with systems, learning journey, teams, projects, coaches, readiness and impact tracking. Overview of trends, future skills and imperative for fast tracking learning.	Our changing world, stories we tell, survival vs. creation, stress response & impact, how we change, neural pathways & habits, metacognition, mental rehearsal, optimise internal state.	Brainwaves, alpha state, observation, mental rehearsal, emotional coherence, power of breathing, our impact on others, past vs. future self.	Curiosity & creativity as superpowers, role models, scenarios, continuum from indifferent spectator /cautious dreamer and curious explorer/possibility connector, rewiring to shift, daily habits to build curiosity & creativity.
#5 Courage & Change	#6 Conscious & Critical thinking	#7 Collaborator & Contributor	#8 Project and impact review
Intro, benefits, role models, scenarios, continuum from controlled critic/passive resistor and curious explorer /maze navigator, rewiring to shift, daily habits to build courage & change.	Intro, benefits, role models, scenarios, continuum from default thinker/distracted operator and wise discerner/meaning maker, rewiring to shift, daily habits to build conscious & critical thinking.	Intro, benefits, role models, scenarios, continuum from independent competitor/status consumer and trust cultivator/community builder, rewiring to shift, daily habits to build collaborator & contributor.	Presenting projects, reviewing the learning, calculating the impact, recognising outstanding results and integration back into work roles.

For more information on our training, consulting and coaching experience, case studies, frameworks and examples, go to www.catalystconsulting.co.za.

LIST OF REFERENCES

Prologue: Invitation to an Adventure References

1. Campbell, J. (2014). *The Hero's Journey: Joseph Campbell on His Life and Work (The Collected Works of Joseph Campbell)*. Novato, CA: New World Library.
2. *The Matrix*. (1999). [DVD]. Jana Wachowski & Lilly Wachowski. Sydney: Warner Bros, Silver Pictures & Village Roadshow Pictures.
3. *Alice in Wonderland*. (2010). [DVD]. Timothy Walter Burton. London: The Walt Disney Pictures, Roth Films & The Zanuck Company.
4. *The Hunger Games*. (2012). [DVD]. Gary Ross. Los Angeles: Lionsgate, Color Force & Lionsgate Films.
5. Computing and Commerce Association (CCA). (2017). *Jack Ma: A Story of Success Through Failure*. [Online]. Available from: https://www.ccamonash.com.au/articles/2018/1/2/jack-ma-a-story-of-success-through-failure#:~:text=Jack%20Ma's%20life%20is%20perhaps,police%20force%20and%20even%20KFC [Accessed: 5 May 2020].
6. Astrum People. (2020). *J.K. Rowling Biography: Success Story of the 'Harry Potter' Author*. Available from: https://astrumpeople.com/jk-rowling/ [Accessed: 5 May 2020].

Chapter 1 References

1. Schwab, K. (2015). *The Fourth Industrial Revolution What It Means and How to Respond.* Available at: https://www.foreignaffairs.com/articles/2015-12-12/fourth-industrial-revolution [Accessed: 13 July 2020].
2. CNBC. (2015). *Google's Eric Schmidt: 'The Internet Will Disappear'.* Available at: https://www.youtube.com/watch?v=Tf49T45GNd0 [Accessed: 13 July 2020].
3. Prensky, M. (2001). *Digital Natives, Digital Immigrants.* Available at: https://www.marcprensky.com/writing/Prensky%20-%20Digital%20Natives,%20Digital%20Immigrants%20-%20Part1.pdf [Accessed: 24 April 2020].
4. Wikipedia. (2020). *AlphaGo versus Lee Sedol.* Available at: https://en.wikipedia.org/wiki/AlphaGo_versus_Lee_Sedol [Accessed: 13 July 2020].
5. Ashton, K. (2009). *That 'Internet of Things' thing.* Available at: http://www.itrco.jp/libraries/RFIDjournal-That%20Internet%20of%20Things%20Thing.pdf [Accessed: 13 July 2020].

6. UPS. (2016). *ORION: The algorithm proving that left isn't right*. Available at: https://www.ups.com/us/en/services/knowledge-center/article.page?kid=aa3710c2 [Accessed: 24 April 2020]
7. Eastwood, B. (2016). *Patients key to making sense of medical data*. Available at: https://mitsloan.mit.edu/ideas-made-to-matter/patients-key-to-making-sense-medical-data [Accessed: 24 April 2020].

Chapter 2 References

1. Goodreads. (n.d.). *Alvin Toffler Quotes*. Available at: https://www.goodreads.com/quotes/8800-the-illiterate-of-the-21st-century-will-not-be-those [Accessed: 13 July 2020].
2. McKinsey Global Institute. (2018). *Skill shift: Automation and the future of the workforce*. Available at: https://www.mckinsey.com/featured-insights/future-of-work/skill-shift-automation-and-the-future-of-the-workforce#:~:text=Demand%20for%20all%20physical%20and,see%20a%20surge%20in%20demand [Accessed: 13 July 2020].
3. World Economic Forum. (2020). *The 3 key skill sets for the workers of 2030*. Available at: https://www.weforum.org/agenda/2018/06/the-3-skill-sets-workers-need-to-develop-between-now-and-2030/ [Accessed: 9 April 2020].
4. Strauss, V. (20 December 2017). The surprising thing Google learned about its employees – and what it means for today's students. *The Washington Post*. Available at: https://www.washingtonpost.com/news/answer-sheet/wp/2017/12/20/the-surprising-thing-google-learned-about-its-employees-and-what-it-means-for-todays-students/?utm_term=.e0d3941bdf9b [Accessed: 9 April 2020].
5. Harrel, M. & Barbato, L. (2018). *Great managers still matter: the evolution of Google's Project Oxygen*. Available at: https://rework.withgoogle.com/blog/the-evolution-of-project-oxygen/ [Accessed at: [Accessed: 9 April 2020].
6. Korn Ferry. (2019). *The Self-Disruptive Leader. Korn Ferry*. Available at: https://infokf.kornferry.com/rs/494-VUC-482/images/KF-Disruptive%20Leader%20Final-Digital.pdf [Accessed: 9 April 2020].
7. Korn Ferry. (2020). *Accelerating through the turn. Preparing for a future beyond the crisis*. Available at: https://www.kornferry.com/challenges/recovery [Accessed: 10 June 2020].
8. Singularity University Summits. (2017). *The Future of Education | Sizwe Nxasana | SingularityU South Africa*. Available at: https://www.youtube.com/watch?v=obsZvO3YjHA [Accessed: 9 April 2020].

9. The Book Brigade. (2016). *Becoming Brilliant*. Available at: https://www.psychologytoday.com/us/blog/the-author-speaks/201608/becoming-brilliant [Accessed: 9 April 2020].

Chapter 3 References

1. Lally, P., van Jaarsveld, C.H.M., Potts, H.W.W. & Wardle, J. (2009). How are habits formed: Modelling habit formation in the real world. *European Journal of Social Psychology, 40*(6): 998–1009.
2. Lexico. (2020). *Neuroplasticity*. Available at https://www.lexico.com/definition/neuroplasticity [Accessed: 27 July 2020].
3. Team Tony. (2020). *Where focus goes, energy flows: Create a vision for your business and your life*. Available at: https://www.tonyrobbins.com/career-business/where-focus-goes-energy-flows/ [Accessed: 27 July 2020].
4. Wikipedia. (2020). *Hebbian Theory*. Available at: https://en.wikipedia.org/wiki/Hebbian_theory. [Accessed: 27 July 2020].
5. Hamilton, D.R. (2014). *Does your brain distinguish real from imaginary?* Available at https://drdavidhamilton.com/does-your-brain-distinguish-real-from-imaginary/ [Accessed: 27 July 2020].
6. Dispenza, J. (2019). *Evolve Your Brain*. Available at: https://blog.drjoedispenza.com/evolve-your-brain [Accessed: 27 July 2020].
7. Neurohealth. (2020). *Definitions*. Available at: https://nhahealth.com/brainwaves-the-language/ [Accessed: 27 July 2020].
8. Brian Tracy International. (2020). *Subconscious Mind Power Explained*. Available at: https://www.briantracy.com/blog/personal-success/understanding-your-subconscious-mind/ [Accessed: 27 July 2020].
9. Harvard Health Publishing. (2020). *Understanding the stress response*. Available at https://www.health.harvard.edu/staying-healthy/understanding-the-stress-response [Accessed: 27 July 2020].
10. Dispenza, J. (2013). *Breaking the habit of being yourself: How to Lose Your Mind and Create a New One*. Carlsbad, CA: Hay House, Inc.
11. HeartMath. (2020). *Heart-Brain Communication*. Available at: https://www.heartmath.org/research/science-of-the-heart/heart-brain-communication/ [Accessed: 27 July 2020].
12. Brain Facts. (2012). *Metacognition – I know (or Don't Know) that I Know'*. Available at: https://www.brainfacts.org/archives/2012/metacognition [Accessed: 27 July 2020].
13. Mayo Clinic. (2020). *How your brain works*. Available at: https://www.mayoclinic.org/brain/sls-20077047?s=1 [Accessed: 27 July 2020].
14. Dispenza, J. (2008). *Evolve your Brain: The Science of Changing Your Mind*. Deerfield Beach, FL: Health Communications, Inc.

15. Church, D. (2018). *Mind to Matter: The astonishing science of how your brain creates material reality.* Carlsbad, CA: Hay House Inc.
16. Ibid.
17. Dispenza, J. (2012). *Dr Joe Dispenza – Official News & Fan page.* Available at: https://www.facebook.com/DrJoeDispenzaOfficialNewsFanPage/posts/95-of-who-you-are-by-the-time-you-are-35-years-old-is-a-set-of-memorized-behavio/489097081115691/ [Accessed: 27 July 2020].
18. Goodreads. (2020). *Grit Quotes.* Available at: https://www.goodreads.com/work/quotes/45670634-grit-passion-perseverance-and-the-science-of-success [Accessed: 27 July 2020].
19. Lally, P., van Jaarsveld, C.H.M., Potts, H.W.W. & Wardle, J. (2009). How are habits formed: Modelling habit formation in the real world. *European Journal of Social Psychology, 40*(6): 998–1009.
20. Davis, D. & Hayes, J. (2012). What are the benefits of Mindfulness. *American Psychology Association, 43*(7) July/August. Available at https://www.apa.org/monitor/2012/07-08/ce-corner [Accessed: 27 July 2020].
21. Ibid.
22. Neuroclinic. (2020). *What are the Brain Waves Frequencies.* Available at: http://neuroclinicbarrie.com/neurofeedback/links-resources/brain-waves-frequencies/ [Accessed: 27 July 2020].
23. HeartMath. (2020). *The Science of HeartMath.* Available at: https://www.heartmath.com/science/ [Accessed 27 July 2020].
24. Duhigg, C. (2013). *The power of habit: Why we do what we do and how to change.* New York, NY: Random House.

Chapter 4 References

1. Grazer, B. & Fishman, C. (2015). *Six Kinds of Curiosity: And How You Can Use Them to Change Your Life.* Available at: https://www.porchlightbooks.com/blog/changethis/2015/six-kinds-of-curiosity-and-how-you-can-use-them-to-change-your-life [Accessed: 12 October 2019].
2. Gino, F. (2018). *The Business Case for Curiosity.* Available at: https://hbr.org/2018/09/curiosity [Accessed: 12 October 2019].
3. Dweck, C.S. (2016). *Mindset: The New Psychology of Success.* New York, NY: Ballantine Books.
4. Grazer, B. & Fishman, C. (2015). *A Curious Mind: The Secret to a Bigger Life.* New York, NY: Simon & Schuster.
5. *The Boy Who Harnessed the Wind.* (2019). [Online]. Chiwetel Ejiofor. Malawi: Participant Media, BBC Films, British Film Institute and Potboiler Productions.

6. *Space in Africa.* (2019). *SANSA @8; Meet 28 year old Lumka Msibi who sits on SANSA Board.* Available at: https://africanews.space/sansa-8-meet-28-year-old-lumka-msibi-who-sits-on-sansa-board/ [Accessed: 12 October 2019].

Chapter 5 References

1. Gary, A. (2016). *The 10 Skills You Need to Thrive in The Fourth Industrial Revolution.* Available at: https://www.weforum.org/agenda/2016/01/the-10-skills-you-need-to-thrive-in-the-fourth-industrial-revolution/ [Accessed: 24 August 2019].
2. World Economic Forum. (2018). *The Future of Jobs Report.* Available at: http://www3.weforum.org/docs/WEF_Future_of_Jobs_2018.pdf [Accessed: 24 August 2019].
3. Hobcraft, P. (2018). *The Innovation World is Changing Due to the 4th Industrial Revolution.* Available at: https://blog.hypeinnovation.com/innovation-fourth-industrial-revolution [Accessed: 24 August 2019].
4. Basinski, M. (n.d.). Vector illustration of think outside the box flat line design concept. Available from: www.123rf.com [Accessed: 24 August 2019].
5. Lets Techknow. (2019). *10 Great Examples of Crowdsourcing | World's Best Campaigns.* Available at: https://www.letstechknow.com/10-great-examples-of-crowdsourcing-worlds-best-campaigns/ [Accessed: 24 August 2019].
6. Land. G. (2015). *The Waste of Creative Talents. Learning Is Fun Everyday.* Available at: https://esinakay.wordpress.com/tag/george-lands-creativity-test/. [Accessed: 24 August 2019].
7. Robinson, K. (2007). *Do schools kill creativity?* Available at: https://www.youtube.com/watch?v=iG9CE55wbtY [Accessed: 24 August 2019].
8. OSHO International Meditation Resort. (2013). *Disappear into the Painting.* Available at: https://www.facebook.com/osho.international.meditation.resort/photos/disappear-into-the-painting-3-days-course-starting-on-23-decacrylics-a-wall-size/10152050026354000/
9. https://www.facebook.com/osho.international.meditation.resort/photos/a.381788418999/10152050026354000/?type=1&theatre [Accessed: 24 August 2019].
10. Strauss, V. (21 April, 2015). Sir Ken Robinson has a lot to say about U.S. school reform (it isn't good). *The Washington Post.* Available at: https://www.washingtonpost.com/news/answer-sheet/wp/2015/04/21/sir-ken-robinson-has-a-lot-to-say-about-u-s-school-reform-it-isnt-good/ [Accessed: 24 August 2019].

11. Gilbert, E. (2009). *Your elusive creative genius.* Available at: https://www.youtube.com/watch?v=86x-u-tz0MA [Accessed: 24 August 2019].
12. Gilbert, B. (11 April, 2019). Amazon CEO Jeff Bezos says multibillion-dollar failures are actually a good thing: 'If the size of your failures isn't growing, you're not going to be inventing at a size that can actually move the needle'. *Business Insider.* Available at: https://www.businessinsider.com/jeff-bezos-says-multi-billion-dollar-failures-necessary-for-amazon-growth-success-2019-4?IR=T [Accessed: 24 August 2019].
13. Vullings, R. (2013). *Idea Killers poster large – from the book: Creativity Today.* [Powerpoint Presentation]. Available at: https://www.slideshare.net/ramonvullings/idea-killers-poster-large [Accessed: 24 August 2019].
14. Baer, D. (2013). *How Dali, Einstein, And Aristotle Perfected the Power Nap.* Available at: https://www.fastcompany.com/90527155/peacock-struts-into-the-streaming-wars-touting-what-makes-it-different. [Accessed: 24 August 2019].

Chapter 6 References

1. Jeffers, S. (2006). *Feel the Fear ... and Do It Anyway.* New York, NY: Ballantine Books.
2. Quotespedia. (2020). *Franklin D. Roosevelt quotes.* Available at: https://www.quotespedia.org/authors/f/franklin-d-roosevelt/courage-is-not-the-absence-of-fear-but-rather-the-assessment-that-something-else-is-more-important-than-fear-franklin-d-roosevelt/ [Accessed: 10 January 2020].
3. Brown, B. (2011). *The power of vulnerability.* Available at: https://www.youtube.com/watch?v=iCvmsMzlF7o [Accessed: 10 January 2020].
4. Whyte, D. (2020). *David Whyte Essentials.* Langley, WA: Many Rivers Press.
5. South African College of Applied Psychology (SACAP). (2019). *The shocking state of mental health in South Africa in 2019.* Available at: https://www.sacap.edu.za/blog/counselling/mental-health-south-africa/ [Accessed: 10 January 2020].
6. Bourbeau, L. (2002). *Heal Your Wounds and Find Your True Self: Finally A Book That Explains Why It's So Hard Being Yourself.* Detroit, MI: Lotus Press.
7. Wikipedia. (2019). *Saray Khumalo.* Available at: https://en.wikipedia.org/wiki/Saray_Khumalo [Accessed: 10 January 2020].
8. Jeffers, S. (2006). *Feel the Fear ... and Do It Anyway.* New York, NY: Ballantine Books.

9. RethinkandFocus. (2019). *Comfort and Fear going together....* Available at: https://www.rethinkandfocus.com/429718297/6724247/posting/ [Accessed: 10 January 2020].
10. Jeffers, S. (2020). *The Five Truths About Fear.* Available at: http://www.susanjeffers.com/home/5truths.cfm. [Accessed: 10 January 2020].

Chapter 7 References

1. Wikipedia. (2020). *Caster Semenya.* Available at: https://en.wikipedia.org/wiki/Caster_Semenya [Accessed: 3 April 2020].
2. Discovery. (2018). *Caster Semenya, A new kind of hero.* Available at: https://www.discovery.co.za/corporate/news-caster-semenya-a-new-kind-of-hero [Accessed: 3 April 2020].
3. Greater Good Magazine. (2020). *Empathy – Defined: What is Empathy?.* Available at: https://greatergood.berkeley.edu/topic/empathy/definition [Accessed: 3 April 2020].
4. Change Cycle @ CCMC Inc. (2020). *The Change Cycle Series: The Change Cycle Overview.* Available at: https://changecycle.com/change-cycle/ [Accessed: 3 April 2020].
5. Rock, D. (2009). *Managing with the Brain in mind.* Available at: https://www.psychologytoday.com/sites/default/files/attachments/31881/managingwbraininmind.pdf [Accessed: 3 April 2020].
6. Lencioni, P. (2002). *The Five Dysfunctions of a Team: A Leadership Fable.* (1st ed.). San Francisco, CA: Jossey-Bass.
7. Ibid.
8. Korn Ferry. (2020). *Accelerating through the turn. Preparing for a future beyond the crisis.* Available at: https://www.kornferry.com/challenges/recovery [Accessed 3 April 2020].
9. Ries. E. (2012). *Eric Ries Explains the Pivot.* Available at: https://www.youtube.com/watch?v=1hTl4z2ijc4 [Accessed: 3 April 2020].
10. Abrahami, A. (2014). *3 Rules for Making a Successful Pivot.* Available at: https://www.entrepreneur.com/article/235168 [Accessed: 3 April 2020].
11. HFM Talent Index. (2020). *Learning Agility: Are your employees ready for the future?.* Available at: https://www.hfmtalentindex.co.za/product/learning-agility/ [Accessed: 3 April 2020].
12. Chibana, N. (2020). *7 Storytelling Techniques Used by the Most Inspiring TED Presenters.* Available at: https://visme.co/blog/7-storytelling-techniques-used-by-the-most-inspiring-ted-presenters [Accessed: 3 April 2020].

13. Booker, C. (2004). *The Seven Basic Plots: Why We Tell Stories.* London: Continuum Books.
14. *The best Exotic Marigold Hotel.* (2011). [DVD]. John Madden. India: Participant Media, Imagination Abu Dhabi FZ, Blueprint Pictures and Fox Searchlight Pictures.
15. Brainy Quote. (2020). *Thomas Edison.* Available at: https://www.brainyquote.com/quotes/thomas_a_edison_132683 [Accessed: 3 April 2020].
16. Duckworth, A.L. (2013). *Grit: the power of passion and perseverance.* Available at: https://www.youtube.com/watch?v=H14bBuluwB8 [Accessed: 3 April 2020].

Chapter 8 References

1. Kehoe, J. (2011). *Quantum Warrior: The Future of the Mind.* Montreal: Zoetic Inc.
2. Goleman, D. (2013). *Focus: The Hidden Driver of Excellence.* New York, NY: Harper Collins.
3. Brandon, J. (2019). *These Updated Stats About How Often You Use Your Phone Will Humble You.* Available at: https://www.inc.com/john-brandon/these-updated-stats-about-how-often-we-use-our-phones-will-humble-you.html [Accessed: 3 April 2020].
4. PsycheGuides. (2020). *Signs and Symptoms of Cell Phone Addiction.* Available at: https://www.psychguides.com/behavioral-disorders/cell-phone-addiction/signs-and-symptoms/ [Accessed: 3 April 2020].
5. Brandon, J. (2019). *These Updated Stats About How Often You Use Your Phone Will Humble You.* Available at https://www.inc.com/john-brandon/these-updated-stats-about-how-often-we-use-our-phones-will-humble-you.html [Accessed: 3 April 2020].
6. Dahl, M. (2014). *Are Our Phones Making Us Less Empathetic?.* Available at: https://www.thecut.com/2014/08/are-our-phones-making-us-less-empathetic.html [Accessed: 3 April 2020].
7. D'Auria, G. & De Smit, A. (2020). *Leadership in a crisis: Responding to the coronavirus outbreak and future challenges.* Available at: https://www.mckinsey.com/business-functions/organization/our-insights/leadership-in-a-crisis-responding-to-the-coronavirus-outbreak-and-future-challenges?cid=other-eml-alt-mip-mck&hlkid=37fc9d2ecd944a61a227b410ffa855ee&hctky=10140929&hdpid=16a43b5b-480b-4b3b-b8cf-bc20fcc11b08 [Accessed at: 3 April 2020].
8. Elmore, T. (2014). *Nomophobia: A Rising Trend in Students.* Available at: https://www.psychologytoday.com/za/blog/artificial-maturity/201409/nomophobia-rising-trend-in-students [Accessed: 3 April 2020].

9. Amatenstein, S. (2019). *Not So Social Media: How Social Media Increases Loneliness.* Available at: https://www.psycom.net/how-social-media-increases-loneliness/ [Accessed: 3 April 2020].
10. Goleman, D. (2013). *Focus: The Hidden Driver of Excellence.* New York, NY: Harper Collins.
11. Dawn, M. (2020). *Conscious Leadership Frequently Asked Questions.* Available at: https://ceoofyour.life/conscious-leadership-faq/ [Accessed: 3 April 2020].
12. Wikipedia. (2020). *Stanford marshmallow experiment.* Available at: https://en.wikipedia.org/wiki/Stanford_marshmallow_experiment [Accessed: 3 April 2020]
13. FloodSanDiego. (2010). *The Marshmallow Experiment – Instant Gratification.* Available at: https://www.youtube.com/watch?v=Yo4WF3cSd9Q [Accessed: 3 April 2020].
14. Robbins, M. (2018). *One of the Best Talks Ever on Self-Motivation.* Available at: https://www.youtube.com/watch?v=_BNDdamTDak [Accessed: 3 April 2020].
15. Presta, N. (2019). *Is busy the new stupid?.* Available at: https://thriveglobal.com/stories/is-busy-the-new-stupid/ [Accessed: 3 April 2020].
16. Better Than Yesterday. (2020). *How I Tricked My Brain To Like Doing Hard Things (dopamine detox).* Available at: https://www.youtube.com/watch?v=9QiE-M1LrZk [Accessed: 3 April 2020].
17. Connley, C. (2017). *Ashton Kutcher reveals the simple strategy that helps him avoid email overload.* Available at: https://www.cnbc.com/2017/12/12/ashton-kutcher-reveals-the-simple-strategy-that-helps-him-avoid-email-overload.html [Accessed: 3 April 2020].
18. AgentXPQ. (2006). *Procrastination Tales Of Mere Existence.* Available at: https://www.youtube.com/watch?v=4P785j15Tzk [Accessed: 3 April 2020].
19. Urban, T. (2016). *Inside the mind of a master procrastinator.* Available at: https://www.youtube.com/watch?v=arj7oStGLkU [Accessed: 3 April 2020].
20. The Time Counselor. (2020). *Covey Time Management – Busting Loose of Time Wasters!.* Available at: https://www.timecounselor.com/covey-time-management.html [Accessed: 3 April 2020].
21. Shetty, J. (2018). *Before You Waste Time – WATCH THIS.* Available at: https://www.youtube.com/watch?v=CtPYmcD8wpg [Accessed: 3 April 2020].
22. Ferriss, T. (2009). *The 4-Hour Work Week: Escape the 9-5, Live Anywhere and Join the New Rich.* New York, NY: Harmony.

23. Allen, D. (2015). *Getting Things Done: The Art of Stress-free Productivity.* New York, NY: Penguin Books.
24. Tracy, B. (2017). *Eat that Frog!: 21 Great Ways to Stop Procrastinating and Get More Done in Less Time.* Oakland, CA: Berrett-Koehler Publishers.
25. Lasoe, S. (2020). *This Is Nuts: It Takes Nearly 30 Minutes to Refocus After You Get Distracted.* Available at: https://www.themuse.com/advice/this-is-nuts-it-takes-nearly-30-minutes-to-refocus-after-you-get-distracted [Accessed: 3 April 2020].
26. Newport, C. (2018). *Deep Work: Rules for Focused Success in a Distracted World.* Available at: https://www.youtube.com/watch?v=_RMtnDaxmPw [Accessed: 3 April 2020].
27. Loehr, J.E. & Schwartz, T. (2003). *The Power of Full Engagement: Managing Energy, Not Time, is the Key to High Performance and Personal Renewal.* New York, NY: Free Press.
28. Huddleston Jr, T. (2019). This is Tony Robbins' 10-minute morning routine to 'change your day for the better'. *CNBC.* Available at: https://www.cnbc.com/2019/04/09/tony-robbins-10-minute-morning-routine-to-get-in-a-peak-state.html [Accessed: 3 April 2020].
29. Huffington, A. (2015). *Thrive: The Third Metric to Redefining Success and Creating a Life of Well-Being, Wisdom, and Wonder.* New York, NY: Harmony.
30. Heath, C. & Heath, D. (2013). *Decisive: How to make better choices in life and work.* New York, NY: Cornerstone Digital.

Chapter 9 References

1. Paul, R. & Elder, L. (2019). *The Miniature Guide to Critical Thinking Concepts and Tools (Thinker's Guide Library).* (8th ed.). Tomales, CA: Rowman & Littlefield Publishers/The Foundation for Critical Thinking.
2. Gardner, J. (2018). Top 10 Worst Business Decisions in History in our resources section. *Finance Monthly.* Available at: https://www.finance-monthly.com/2018/04/top-10-worst-business-decisions-in-history/ [Accessed: 20 June 2020].
3. Kline, N. (2010). *Time to Think: Listening to Ignite the Human Mind.* [Kindle Edition]. London: Cassell Illustrated.
4. Kegley, C. (2016). *10 BEST IDEAS, Thinking Fast And Slow, Daniel Kahnerman, Animated Book Summary.* Available at https://www.youtube.com/watch?v=tiyTYGY5X3Y [Accessed: 20 June 2020].
5. Wabisabi Learning. (n.d.). *The Critical Thinking Skills Cheatsheet.* Available at: https://wabisabilearning.com/blogs/critical-thinking/critical-thinking-skills-cheatsheet-infographic [Accessed: 20 June 2020].

6. Covey, S. (2011). *7 Habits Paradigms.* Available at: https://www.youtube.com/watch?v=w5UQ1ZSIQ84 [Accessed: 20 June 2020].
7. Verdolin, J. (2019). *3 Ways to Improve Your Cognitive Flexibility.* Available at: https://www.psychologytoday.com/za/blog/wild-connections/201912/3-ways-improve-your-cognitive-flexibility [Accessed: 20 June 2020].
8. Center for Creative Leadership. (2020). *Adapting to Change Requires Flexibility.* Available at: https://www.ccl.org/articles/leading-effectively-articles/learn-to-adapt/ [Accessed: 20 June 2020].
9. Goeke, N. (2016). *Six Thinking Hats Summary.* Available at: https://fourminutebooks.com/six-thinking-hats-summary/ [Accessed: 20 June 2020].
10. Smith, D. (2019). *Making Business matter. Ultimate Guide.* Available at: https://www.makingbusinessmatter.co.uk/hbdi-ultimate-guide/ [Accessed: 20 June 2020].
11. Learning Fundamentals. (2020). *Mind Maps.* Available at: https://learningfundamentals.com.au/resources/ [Accessed: 20 June 2020].
12. Educational Technology and Mobile Learning. (2014). *Questions a Critical Thinker Asks.* Available at: https://www.educatorstechnology.com/2014/11/6-questions-every-critical-thinker.html [Accessed: 20 June 2020].
13. DiGiandomenico, C. (2020). *Deeply democratic decision making – the antidote for civil disobedience.* Available at: https://www.shine.global/post/deeply-democratic-decision-making-the-antidote-for-civil-disobedience [Accessed: 20 June 2020].
14. Goeke, N. (2016). *The 80/20 Principle Summary.* Available at: https://fourminutebooks.com/the-80-20-principle-summary/ [Accessed: 20 June 2020].

Chapter 10 References

1. Brandenburger, A.M. & Nalebuff, B.J. (1996). *Co-opetition: A Revolution Mindset that Combines Competition and Cooperation.* New York, NY: Crown Business.
2. Morgan, C. (2020). *The most notable director/actor collaborations.* Available at: https://www.yardbarker.com/entertainment/articles/the_most_notable_directoractor_collaborations/s1__31359218#slide_1 [Accessed:12 June 2020].
3. Kekae, L. (2015). *The "Are you with us" campaign Pharrell Williams and Woolworths SA YouTube.* Available at: https://www.youtube.com/watch?v=7ns4NLcvBq8 [Accessed: 12 June 2020].

4. UN News. (2020). *Landmark collaboration to make COVID-19 testing and treatment available to all.* Available at: https://news.un.org/en/story/2020/04/1062512 [Accessed: 12 June 2020].
5. Roedean School. (2020). *Roedean School – Hallelujah – Virtual Choir.* Available at: https://www.youtube.com/watch?v=3y51WWrYodI [Accessed: 12 June 2020].
6. Curry, P. (2019). *Why automotive industry collaboration is important – and essential.* Available at: https://autovistagroup.com/news-and-insights/why-automotive-industry-collaboration-important-and-essential [Accessed: 12 June 2020].
7. Wilkinson, A. (2016). *The Creator's Code: The Six Essential Skills of Extraordinary Entrepreneurs.* New York, NY: Simon & Schuster.
8. Bogdanich, W. & Forsythe, M. (2018). How McKinsey Lost Its Way in South Africa: When the godfather of management consulting landed its biggest contract ever in Africa, it made the worst mistake in its storied nine-decade history. *The New York Times.* Available at: https://www.nytimes.com/?_ga=2.187927982.722721659.1593600951-1506895177.1593600951 [Accessed: 12 June 2020].
9. Kosin, M. (2017). *Brand Partnerships That Failed Miserably (And A Few That Worked).* Available at: https://www.urbo.com/content/brand-partnerships-that-failed-miserably-and-a-few-that-worked/ [Accessed: 12 June 2020].
10. Craig, D. (2018). *Dilemma Flipping and 7 Factors Derailing Collaboration.* Available at: https://catalystconsulting.co.za/wp-content/uploads/2019/06/Blog-Dilemma-Flipping-7-Factors-Derailing-Collaboration.pdf [Accessed: 12 June 2020].
11. Rebele, R. & Grant, A. (2016). *Collaborative Overload.* Available at: https://hbr.org/2016/01/collaborative-overload [Accessed: 12 June 2020].
12. Horth, D.M. (2014). *Boundary Spanning in Action: Tactics for Transforming Today's Borders into Tomorrow's Frontiers.* Available at https://www.ccl.org/articles/white-papers/boundary-spanning-in-action-tactics-for-transforming-todays-borders-into-tomorrows-frontiers/ [Accessed: 12 June 2020].
13. Frei, F.X. & Morriss, A. (2020). *Begin with Trust.* Available at: https://hbr.org/2020/05/begin-with-trust [Accessed: 12 June 2020].
14. Edelman. (2019). *Edelman Trust Barometer Executive Summary.* Available at: https://www.edelman.com/sites/g/files/aatuss191/files/2019-02/2019_Edelman_Trust_Barometer_Executive_Summary.pdf [Accessed: 12 June 2020].

15. Frei, F. (2018). *How to build (and rebuild) trust*. Available at: https://www.youtube.com/watch?v=pVeq-0dIqpk&t=20s [Accessed: 12 June 2020].
16. Edmondson, A. (2014). *Building a psychologically safe workplace*. https://www.youtube.com/watch?v=LhoLuui9gX8&t=261s [Accessed: 12 June 2020].
17. Beck, M. (2020). *The Trust Test*. Available at: http://www.oprah.com/omagazine/the-trust-test_1 [Accessed: 12 June 2020].
18. Pick Up Limes. (2019). *Letting go of our EGO*. https://www.youtube.com/watch?v=nbAwOS1FZIw [Accessed: 12 June 2020].

Chapter 11 References

1. Wikipedia. (2020). *Ubuntu*. Available at: https://en.wikipedia.org/wiki/Ubuntu [Accessed 4 April 2020].
2. Swaniker, F. (2014). *The ripple effect of training young leaders*. Available at: https://www.youtube.com/watch?v=nqIVuGkE99k [Accessed 4 April 2020].
3. African Leadership Academy. (2019). *Joseph Munyambanza*. Available at: https://www.africanleadershipacademy.org/staffuly/young-leaders/joseph-munyambanza-drc [Accessed 4 April 2020].
4. Davis, J.L. (2020). *The science of good deeds*. Available at: https://www.webmd.com/balance/features/science-good-deeds#1 [Accessed 4 April 2020].
5. Syed, M. (2020). *Coronavirus: The good that can come out of an upside-down world*. Available at: https://www.bbc.com/news/world-us-canada-52094332 [Accessed 4 April 2020].
6. Lindeque, B. (2020). *SPAR in Western Cape closes down stationery section and removes all frozen burgers*. Available at: https://www.goodthingsguy.com/business/spar-palm-grove/ [Accessed 4 April 2020].
7. Rise Africa Rise. (2020). *Meet 4 inspirational African social innovators*. Available at: https://riseafricarise.com/inspirational-african-social-innovators/ [Accessed 4 April 2020].
8. Pope, L. (2019). *Most followed Instagram Accounts in 2020*. Available at: https://learn.g2.com/most-followed-instagram-accounts [Accessed 4 April 2020].
9. 10 Million Masks. (2020). *Fair made, fairtrade products that support local communities*. Available at: https://www.10millionmasks.africa/ [Accessed 4 April 2020].

10. Angel, B. (2019). *What is the meaning of life?* Available at: https://www.youtube.com/watch?v=hUDbiRK4pps [Accessed 4 April 2020].
11. Power of Positivity. (2020). *9 Signs You're Letting Your Ego Run Your Life.* Available at: https://www.powerofpositivity.com/9-signs-youre-letting-ego-run-life/ [Accessed 4 April 2020].
12. Fabrega, M. (2020). *How to Be a Good Citizen – 10 Ways to Show Good Citizenship.* Available at: https://daringtolivefully.com/good-citizen [Accessed 4 April 2020].

Chapter 12 References

1. Catalyst Consulting. 2020. *Resilience Potential Self-Assessment.* Available at: https://catalystconsulting.co.za/survey/
2. Ibid.

INDEX

#10millionmasks, 227
Fourth Industrial Revolution, 1, 92

A

accountability check-point, 232
action plan, 242, 245
adults have only 2% creativity left, 73
adventure, 53, 96, 105, 109, 118, 123, 125, 128, 139
agile pivot, 134
anticipators, systemic, integrators, 172
anxious, vigilant, controllers, 107
anxious controllers, 107–108
Artificial Intelligence (A.I.), 5
attitude of creativity, 78
authentic connectors, 79
autonomous tech and robotics, 6

B

baseline or comfort zone, 36
be inspired and believe, 226
being conscious, 37, 47, 148
boy who harnessed the wind, 60, 69
building foundational capabilities, 251–252
building meta-capabilities, 247

C

cautious, 23, 57–58, 60–62, 65, 78–82, 203, 243, 254
cautious dreamers, 81–82
challenging our paradigms, 177
change navigator, 23, 73, 117, 119–122, 124, 127, 138, 243
change our brains, 28
changing focus of skills, 19
changing our behaviour, 27
character examples, 204
choosing in the moment, 122
citizenship check-point, 234
cognitive flexibility, 181–182, 187
collaboration tools, 213
collaborative attitude, 209
collaborative learning, 67, 211, 251
collaborative meeting principles, 212
collaborator, 23, 189, 197, 199, 202, 244, 254
connectivity, 2, 8
conscious attention, 47, 157
conscious being, 146, 157
conscious choice, 122, 153, 156, 163
conscious communication, 160
conscious consumption, 146, 162
conscious energy, 160
conscious impact, 146, 163
conscious intent, 154, 156
conscious space, 158–159
conscious time, 158
consciousness, 143, 146, 148, 156, 162–164
consuming or contributing, 221
contributor in action, 223
courage, 24, 39, 53, 92, 95–102, 105–106, 108–115, 122, 245, 248, 254
courage heroes, 106
courage to be vulnerable, 95, 98

courageous adventurers, 104–105, 107
creating new habits, 40, 47
creative brain documentary, 92
creative learning, 81
creativity, 20–21, 42, 49, 53, 60, 71, 73–78, 83–85, 87–88, 90, 92–93, 254
creativity can be learnt, 75
critical questions, 110, 172, 179, 196
critical thinker, 23, 167, 170–171, 184, 244
critical thinking disasters, 176
cross-boundaries, 207
cultivating identities, 40, 43
curiosity, 53–57, 59–62, 64–66, 68–70, 75, 111, 122–123, 134, 176, 239, 254
curious explorers, 57–59

D

data and data science, 9–10
default thinkers, 174–175
derailers of collaboration, 194–195
digital trends driving change, 1, 17
digitisation of money, 11
dinosaurs, 3–4
disasters and derailers, 192
dissenting voice, 184
distracted operators, 153–154
diversify perspectives & paradigms, 87
do it differently, 68
down the rabbit hole, 65
drifters, distracted, deflectors, 153

E

ego check-point, 230
embracer, navigators, Influencers, 123
emotional coherence, 40, 46, 254
emotions and addiction, 35
empathetic perspective, 129
empowered perseverance, 137
energy in motion, 85
entitled consumers and status builders, 224
expedient, linear, complicators, 174

F

fail fast, 66, 99, 106, 120, 243, 245, 252
fear, 24, 61, 81–82, 84–85, 95–97, 99–106, 108–114, 118, 121, 131, 139, 150, 153, 198–199
fintech, 2, 11
focused, decisive, discerners, 149
followers, pretenders and dreamers, 81
forge common ground, 208
forums and subscriptions, 15
future fit, 17, 28

G

gratitude check-point, 236

H

hacks and habits for collaboration, 207
hacks and habits for consciousness, 156

hacks and habits for contributors, 228
hacks and habits for courage, 109
hacks and habits for creativity, 84
hacks and habits for critical thinking, 178
hacks and habits for curiosity, 64
hero's journey, 140

I

ideators, 79
immigrants, 3–4
impact of our thinking, 170
inclusive, trusting, resolvers, 200
interdependent roles, 219–220
internet of things, 2, 7, 12

J

Joseph Munyambanza, 217

L

learning journey, 66, 254
legacy check-point, 228
let's get physical, 86
listen beyond the obvious, 66
Lumka Msibi, 63, 69

M

make time to learn, 67
master procrastinator, 155, 165
masters of messaging, 174
maze navigators, 123–124, 128
meaning makers, 172–173, 178
murky space, 124

N

natives, 3–4
navigating change, 128
new thought patterns, 40

O

opiniated, 60–61, 243
overwhelmed or focused, 147

P

paradigm busting, 180
passive resistors, 125–126, 139
playful imagining, 84
possibility connectors, 79, 84
power of 8, 22
power of choice, 27
practicing mindfulness, 41
Purpose, structure and hardwiring, 31
purposeful stories, 135

Q

quality of our thinking, 167, 180
quantum computing, 2, 9–10, 12
quick questions, 64

R

recalibrate to collaborate, 204
resilience potential, 239–241, 245
resilience potential community, 245
resilient, optimistic adventurers, 104
resist or to navigate, 121
resistors, passengers,

dramatizers, 125
risks of courage, 100
robust vulnerability, 99

S

safe spectators, 60–61
seekers, engagers and experimenters, 58
self-assessment, 115, 214, 241
shifting beliefs, 40, 44
shifting talent strategies, 249
simplify & make sense, 183
skill building, 15
South African rocket scientist, 63
space to flow, 90
status consumers, 224
stop doing list, 186
stress vs. restore response, 32
super-power, 53, 55

T

talent strategies, 249
team or key stakeholders, 129–130
technology trends, 4
test the tools, 88
think fast and slow, 179
thinker or meaning maker, 171
thoughts and habits, 37
time optimizers, 153
time to think, 44, 178, 188
tips, tools and resources, 14, 25, 50, 69, 92, 114, 140, 164, 187, 213, 238
trends driving change, 1, 4, 17
trust, 23, 59, 82–83, 105, 108–109, 118, 121, 131–132, 192–193, 196–205, 207, 211, 213–214, 244
trust cultivators, 200–201, 207
trust starts with you, 207
truths about fear, 109, 114

U

ubuntu, 207, 215–216
unleashing value across boundaries, 189

V

videos, 14, 50, 162, 165, 169, 188, 191–192, 214, 219, 230, 235, 238

W

websites & blogs, 14
William Kamkwamba, 60, 69
wise discerners, 149–152, 154, 156
worthwhile vision, 117, 119–120, 243

www.ingramcontent.com/pod-product-compliance
Lightning Source LLC
Chambersburg PA
CBHW071958220426
43662CB00009B/1185